Bronwen Calvert is an associate lecturer with the Open University in the North of England. Her research looks at embodiment in fantasy and science fiction narratives, with particular focus on cyberpunk fiction and the 'cult' female action hero of television.

'Bronwen Calvert's *Being Bionic: The World of TV Cyborgs* is an important exploration of an important subject. From *Doctor Who* to *Dollhouse*, from *Battlestar Galactica* to *Bionic Woman*, Calvert's scholarly erudition and probing interpretations illuminate the nature of our cyborgs, ourselves.

– Rhonda Wilcox, Gordon State College, USA; author of *Why Buffy Matters*

'Bronwen Calvert's *Being Bionic* is an insightful and comprehensive exploration of a fascinating subject: a treatise that is both instructive and accessible to the general reader. Highly recommended.'

– Eric Brown, author of *Helix* and science fiction reviewer for the *Guardian*

INVESTIGATING CULT TV

Series Editor: Stacey Abbott

The **Investigating Cult TV** series is a fresh forum for discussion and debate about the changing nature of cult television. It sets out to reconsider cult television and its intricate networks of fandom by inviting authors to rethink how cult TV is conceived, produced, programmed and consumed. It will also challenge traditional distinctions between cult and quality television.

Offering an accessible path through the intricacies and pleasures of cult TV, the books in this series will interest scholars, students and fans alike. They will include close studies of individual contemporary television shows. They will also reconsider genres at the heart of cult programming, such as science fiction, horror and fantasy, as well as genres like teen TV, animation and reality TV when these have strong claims to cult status. Books will also examine themes or trends that are key to the past, present and future of cult television.

Published and forthcoming titles:

Battlestar Galactica: Investigating Flesh, Spirit and Steel, edited by Roz Kaveney and Jennifer Stoy

Being Bionic: The World of TV Cyborgs, by Bronwen Calvert

The Cult TV Book, edited by Stacey Abbott

Dancing with the Doctor: Dimensions of Gender in the New Doctor Who Universe, by Lorna Jowett

Dexter: Investigating Cutting Edge Television, edited by Douglas L. Howard

I'm Buffy and You're History: Buffy the Vampire Slayer and Contemporary Feminism, by Patricia Pender

Investigating Alias: Secrets and Spies, edited by Stacey Abbott and Simon Brown

Investigating Charmed: The Magic Power of TV, edited by Karin Beeler and Stan Beeler

Investigating Farscape: Uncharted Territories of Sex and Science Fiction, by Jes Battis

Investigating Firefly and Serenity: Science Fiction on the Frontier, edited by Rhonda V. Wilcox and Tanya R. Cochran

Love and Monsters: The Doctor Who Experience, 1979 to the Present, by Miles Booy

Sounds of Fear and Wonder: Music in Cult TV, by Janet K. Halfyard

Time on TV: Narrative Time, Time Travel and Time Travellers in Popular Television Culture, edited by Lorna Jowett, Kevin Lee Robinson and David Simmons

Torchwood Declassified: Investigating Mainstream Cult Television, edited by Rebecca Williams

True Blood: Investigating Vampires and Southern Gothic, by Brigid Cherry

TV Horror: Investigating the Dark Side of the Small Screen, by Lorna Jowett and Stacey Abbott

Ideas and submissions for Investigating Cult TV to:
s.abbott@roehampton.ac.uk
pbrewster@ibtauris.com

BEING BIONIC
THE WORLD OF TV CYBORGS

BRONWEN CALVERT

I.B.TAURIS
LONDON·NEW YORK

Published in 2017 by
I.B.Tauris & Co. Ltd
London • New York
www.ibtauris.com

Copyright © 2017 Bronwen Calvert

The right of Bronwen Calvert to be identified as the author of this work has been asserted by the author in accordance with the Copyright, Designs and Patents Act 1988.

All rights reserved. Except for brief quotations in a review, this book, or any part thereof, may not be reproduced, stored in or introduced into a retrieval system, or transmitted, in any form or by any means, electronic, mechanical, photocopying, recording or otherwise, without the prior written permission of the publisher.

Every attempt has been made to gain permission for the use of the images in this book. Any omissions will be rectified in future editions.

References to websites were correct at the time of writing.

ISBN: 978 1 78453 648 0
eISBN: 978 1 78672 102 0
ePDF: 978 1 78673 102 9

A full CIP record for this book is available from the British Library
A full CIP record is available from the Library of Congress

Library of Congress Catalog Card Number: available

Contents

List of Illustrations		viii
Acknowledgements		x
	Introduction: Troubled Boundaries and Transformative Cyborgs	1
1	Exterminate, Upgrade: *Doctor Who*	20
2	Resistance, Assimilation and the Collective: *Star Trek: The Next Generation* and *Voyager*	45
3	Toasters and Replicas: *Battlestar Galactica*	68
4	'Between Life and Death': Embodiment and Virtuality in *Caprica*	91
5	The Cyborg as Action Hero: *Bionic Woman*	114
6	Us and Them: *Terminator: The Sarah Connor Chronicles*	136
7	Hacking the System: *Dollhouse*	158
8	Complete Control: *Fringe*	182
	Conclusion: Cyborg Futures	206
Notes		215
Filmography and TV		222
Bibliography		224
Index		237

List of Illustrations

1. The Borg invade the *Enterprise*: 'Q Who?', *Star Trek: The Next Generation* (2.16, Paramount Television 1987–1994) — 2
2. Oswin Oswald, 'Asylum of the Daleks', *Doctor Who* (7.1, BBC Wales/British Broadcasting Corporation/Canadian Broadcasting Corporation 2005–) — 34
3. The TARDIS takes embodied form as Idris, 'The Doctor's Wife', *Doctor Who* (6.4, BBC Wales/British Broadcasting Corporation/Canadian Broadcasting Corporation 2005–) — 40
4. Captain Janeway allows herself to become Borg to carry out her mission, 'Unimatrix Zero II', *Voyager* (7.1, Paramount Television/United Paramount Network 1995–2001) — 53
5. Seven of Nine first appears as Borg, 'Scorpion Parts I and II', *Voyager* (3.26/4.1, Paramount Television/United Paramount Network 1995–2001) — 54
6. Boomer with the Cylon Raider, 'Six Degrees of Separation', *Battlestar Galactica* (1.7, British Sky Broadcasting (BSkyB)/David Eick Productions/NBC Universal Television/R&D TV/Stanford Pictures (II)/Universal Media Studios 2004–2009) — 77
7. Sam as Cylon Hybrid, 'Islanded in a Stream of Stars', *Battlestar Galactica* (4.18, British Sky Broadcasting (BSkyB)/David Eick Productions/NBC Universal Television/R&D TV/Stanford Pictures (II)/Universal Media Studios 2004–2009) — 89
8. The U-87 Cylon prototype represented as Zoe-A (Alessandra Torresani), *Caprica* (David Eick Productions/Universal Media Studios 2009–2010) — 99
9. Jaime's bionic legs with 'anthrocytes', 'Pilot', *Bionic Woman* (1.1, NBC Universal Television/Universal Media Studios 2007) — 133

List of Illustrations

10 Catherine Weaver as the threatening liquid-metal cyborg, 'Samson and Delilah', *Terminator: The Sarah Connor Chronicles* (2.1, Bartleby Company/C-2 Pictures/Warner Bros. Television/Halcyon Company/Sarah Connor Pictures/Syfy 2008–2009)   149

11 Wendy imprinted as Caroline in Alpha's makeshift chair, 'Omega', *Dollhouse* (1.12, 20th Century Fox Television/Boston Diva Productions 2009–2010)   176

12 Priya's 'authentic' tattoo, 'Epitaph One', *Dollhouse* (1.13, 20th Century Fox Television/Boston Diva Productions 2009–2010)   179

13 Observer tech burrows into Peter's neck, 'An Origin Story', *Fringe* (5.5, Bad Robot/Warner Bros. Television/FB2 Films/Fringe Element Films 2010–2013)   201

14 Peter experiences Observer vision, 'Through the Looking Glass and What Walter Found There', *Fringe* (5.6, Bad Robot/Warner Bros. Television/FB2 Films/Fringe Element Films 2010–2013)   202

15 Three clones, 'Variation Under Nature', *Orphan Black* (1.3, Temple Street Productions 2013–)   212

Acknowledgements

When I began this project, little did I know what a fascinating, challenging and rewarding one it would be. Stacey Abbott and Lorna Jowett have been my tireless supporters through all the peaks and troughs that writing brings. I look forward to much more television shenanigans – Go Trio!

Thanks to Madeleine Hamey-Thomas and everyone at I.B.Tauris for help and feedback. My thanks to the libraries of the Open University, Newcastle and Northumbria Universities, and the University of British Columbia, Vancouver. The ever-helpful staff at Gateshead Central Library's Sound Gallery proved over and over again why public libraries are an essential part of life.

I owe many thanks to all the members of the Summer and Autumn Writing Groups, especially to Simon Brown, Helen Wheatley, Catherine Spooner, Rachel Moseley, and Faye Woods, for all your fantastic solidarity and advice. Thank you to Gosia Drewniok, Cynthea Masson, Anne Liddon and Julie Hawk who understand the importance of post-it notes and a good pen, and to Sarah Law and Neil Smith who know about writing deadlines as well as Daleks. Thank you to my North East academic friends Rachel Lister, Elayne Chaplin, Colm O'Brien and Martin Wheeler, and to my Norwich gang, especially Kirsty Savory and Ali Calvert, who helped with all forms of decompression. To my parents Steve and Helene, who never fail to believe in me, and to Stephen Calvert and all my family, thank you. Thanks and happy memories to Greer Gibson, who was as obsessed as I was by the original *Bionic Woman*. And last and most importantly, to Greg Walker, who cannot get away from cyborgs: thank you for always being there.

Introduction: Troubled Boundaries and Transformative Cyborgs

It is Stardate 42761.3 and Captain Jean-Luc Picard is in command of the USS *Enterprise*. The ship and its crew are engaged on a 'continuing mission to seek out new life and new civilizations', and they have encountered a troublesome new alien in the form of an omnipotent being known as 'Q'. They have met Q before; on that occasion he put the *Enterprise* crew on trial for humanity's crimes (*Star Trek: The Next Generation*, 'Encounter at Farpoint' 1.1); on this second meeting, he begs to be allowed to join the crew ('Q Who?' 2.16). Picard rejects the possibility that the *Enterprise* might need any help, even from an omnipotent being, in their explorations, and he rashly states, 'I do know that we are ready to encounter [anything] – that's why we're out here.' Q's retort is to transport the *Enterprise* seven thousand light years away from the nearest star base, for 'a taste of your future', which soon appears. It is a cube-shaped spacecraft filled with humanoid beings that do not register as individual life forms, that are augmented with machine and technological components, and speak with one collective voice to announce, 'We are the Borg'. Within a short time, a series of Borg 'drones', humanoids with technological attachments as shown in Figure 1, appear on the *Enterprise* and begin to take control of the ship.

The Borg turn out to be so fearsome and relentless that eventually Picard has to beg for Q's help, and they only narrowly escape the encounter.

1

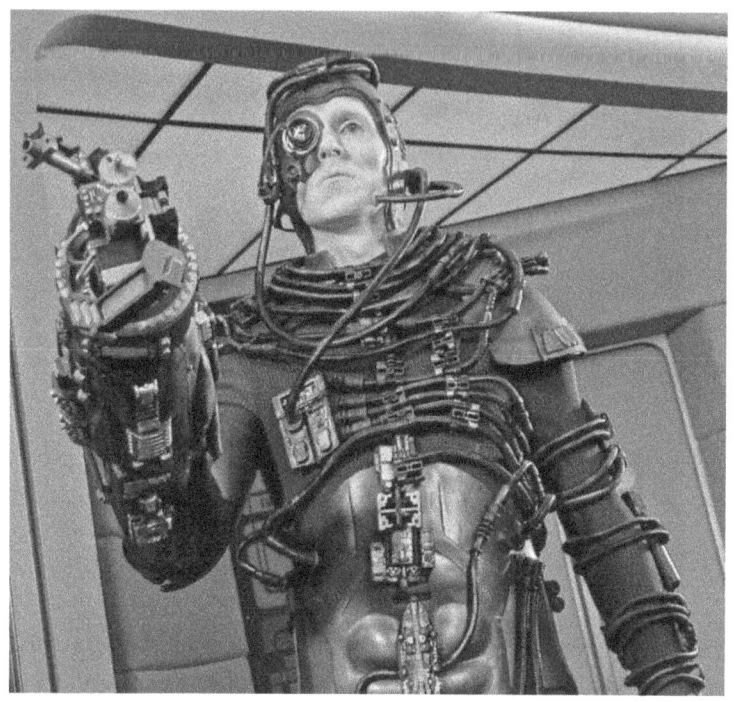

Figure 1: The Borg invade the *Enterprise*: 'Q Who?', *Star Trek: The Next Generation* (2.16)

Q's intention is to show Picard and the rest of the crew their lack of 'readiness' when faced with the unknown beings of the mysterious universe. And the most frightening thing Q can show them is a genderless, identity-less cyborg that is bent on destroying everything in its path. While the Borg proved to be a highly popular addition to the *Star Trek* universe, appearing throughout the *Next Generation* and *Voyager* series and in *Star Trek* feature films, 'Q Who?' demonstrates some of the reactions associated with the television cyborg, especially the combination of fear and fascination that this image attracts.

The cyborg, a mostly theoretical being that incorporates organic and machine/technological parts, has a long history through Western philosophical thought and explorations in fiction. In the twentieth and twenty-first centuries, as actual technological developments continue to focus our attention on the interactions between human beings and machines, the cyborg continues to reflect our own unease about such interactions, as well as our fascination with them. As Scott Bukatman argues, '[t]echnological spaces and objects prevail in the public imagination and serve as loci for the anxieties that arise in response to rapid change' (1993: 4), and we might see the cyborg both as an object and as a kind of (embodied) space that attracts such feelings. Science fiction, which – to paraphrase Darko Suvin – can be viewed as 'the [narrative] of cognitive estrangement' (1972: 132) maintains a focus on 'the interface of technology with the human subject' (Bukatman 1993: 8), and creates images through which we can explore our own engagements with technology. Whether it is analysed as a real-world possibility, as a fictional image, or as a theoretical model, the cyborg encourages us to think about how technology interacts with the body and with society, how artificial embodiment can reveal human qualities that are generally taken for granted, and how the presence of a cyborg can provoke us to reassess aspects of corporeal existence that are thought of as 'natural' and unchanging. Television provides another fictional space for us to explore this image and its associations.

Popular science fiction television series bring the image of the cyborg into our own homes. Other imaginary science fiction beings do not have the duality of the cyborg, and this gives the cyborg a particular status. The varied cyborgs of television are like us, and at the same time they are completely different. They can act as mirrors, or as monsters. Cyborg images feed into explorations of self, such as the means we use to construct identity, or the ways we deal with those we consider to be different from ourselves (as we can see from the *Star Trek* example, Picard and Q deal with the Borg by running away). The image of the cyborg enables science fiction television narratives to explore versions of embodiment, especially to think through ideas of gender and race, and aspects of identity that may be constructed or performed. The cyborg encourages links to real-world events, such as the prevalence (and potential threat) of technology that is constantly developing and changing (and that may not be altogether under control), surveillance societies, and terrorism.

In Rosi Braidotti's terms, the cyborg is one manifestation of the 'teratological imaginary' where 'the monstrous, the grotesque, the mutant and the downright freakish' are represented in the form of 'borderline figures' that also include the vampire and the zombie (2000: 156). Donna Haraway offers a more positive reading in which the cyborg encourages the breakdown and deconstruction of binary oppositions (nature/culture, male/female and so on). Elizabeth Grosz suggests possibilities for a 'cyborg' identity that is created through various transformations of the human body. These transformations produce bodies that can be seen as 'text, a system of signs to be deciphered, read, and read into', in other words, as 'marked' bodies; and/or as 'sites of struggle and resistance' which trouble and confuse boundaries that have been thought of as permanent and fixed (Grosz 1995: 34, 36). Equally relevant to examinations of the image of the cyborg is Judith Butler's work on performativity and masquerade, which is particularly relevant in narratives in which cyborgs attempt to 'pass' as human. Cyborg 'passing' frequently reveals or emphasizes aspects of performance that are inherent in human corporeality, especially those connected with the presentation of gender. Such performances can underline the potential for hybridity in the cyborg body, not only the hybridity that involves the interweaving of the organic and the technological, but ways in which the cyborg can adopt hybrid or multiple roles as part of its embodiment.

In television narratives, the cyborg takes on all these identities: the monstrous other, the 'boundary-crossing' entity, and the hybrid, 'performing' body. All of these allow for the exploration of cultural anxieties about the body in relation to technology; for example, fears of the ways technology may act upon the body, terror of loss of identity, or difficulties in defining 'the other'. But additionally, cyborg identities offer positive possibilities for embodiment, as in the image of the cyborg as action hero.

In this book, I examine different versions and ways of representing the cyborg, in television series that date from the 1960s to the present day. Because of the wealth of critical and theoretical perspectives in relation to cyborgs and cyborg theory, I begin with an overview of some key historical and theoretical perspectives that are particularly relevant for examinations of the cyborg. I consider some of the ways analysis of the cyborg can illuminate ideas around corporeality and virtuality, especially in relation to gender, before turning to consider the specific connections between the cyborg and science fiction television.

Cyborg History

The cyborg is a thoroughly contemporary image that brings together aspects of the machine and the organic, and dramatizes new technological developments. The idea of the artificial body itself, however, is not a new one. Anxieties about embodiment have found expression in the images of statues, dolls, mannequins, automata and androids – things that are nearly, but not quite, like us. The image of the cyborg is 'a new manifestation' of a long historical Western preoccupation with artificial embodiment and of 'the simultaneous revulsion and fascination with the human body' as Claudia Springer notes (1991: 304). There are fictional versions of such bodies in the living statue Galatea from Greek myth via Ovid's *Metamorphoses*, the doll-woman Olympia in E.T.A. Hoffmann's 'The Sandman' (*Nachtstücke* 1816–17), the ideal android woman of Villiers de l'Isle-Adam's *L'Eve Future* (1886) or the cinematic android Maria in Fritz Lang's *Metropolis* (1927).

Similarly, ideas relating to cyborg embodiment reach through Western philosophical history, from the concept of the separation of soul and body expounded by Aristotle and Plato, to the Enlightenment ideas of body-as-machine and disembodied mind as described by Descartes and La Mettrie, and on into contemporary preoccupations with technology and the future of the human body. In particular, Cartesian dualism, which constructs mind and body as oppositional pairings, resonates through critical thinking on the cyborg and cyborg embodiment. In his *Meditations* (1641), Descartes suggests that the thinking self is 'entirely and absolutely distinct from [the] body, and can exist without it' (1993: 90) and that it is 'the mind alone [...] that is requisite to a knowledge of the truth' (1993: 95). La Mettrie's *L'Homme Machine* (1747) sets out the theory that the body is a machine or automaton. La Mettrie follows Descartes' notion of a separated body and mind, but sees the body as a series of reflexes or 'innate force' (1996: 28) as 'an animal or a construction made from springs' like a clock mechanism (1996: 31). The binary of mind–body and the idea of the body as construction follow the cyborg into twentieth- and twenty-first-century fictions and criticism.

Cyborg Manifesto

The starting point for any study of the cyborg, in whatever context, must be Donna Haraway's germinal essay 'A Manifesto for Cyborgs'. Since its original version appeared in 1985 (revised version 1991), this work has served as foundation, launch pad and 'de rigueur reading' Soufoulis, 2003: 91) for critical studies of technology, virtual reality, and forms of artificial and augmented embodiment, whether actual or fictional; any study of the broad field of 'cyberculture' starts with the 'Manifesto'. For me, Haraway's work offers a way to analyse technology and embodiment in ways that do not privilege one over the other, or reject one in favour of the other. Haraway's imaginary cyborg is a body interwoven with technology, a body that serves as a focal point through which to connect things that are thought to be impossibly oppositional. So, dichotomies, boundaries like 'mind and body, animal and human, organism and machine, public and private, nature and culture, men and women, primitive and civilized' (1991a: 163) can be broken down, transgressed and confused through the figure of the cyborg. The cyborg even holds the power to deconstruct these boundaries, rendering them obsolete. What Haraway attempts in her 'Manifesto' is an erosion of the certainty of any term that is commonly thought of as universal. These breakdowns and erosions are extremely helpful for any analysis of cyborg representations.

As Elaine Graham points out, cyborgs 'challenge the givenness of categories of racial identity and gender difference by which humanity has so often been stratified. Cyborgs thus transcend the processes of dualism upon which western modernity, patriarchy and colonialism have been founded' (2001: 309). Perhaps surprisingly, the image of the cyborg can provide a means to deal with both technology and embodiment in a way that cuts across binaries/boundaries. The cyborg can be viewed productively, as neither posthuman nor technophilic but as a body that exists in itself, and is at the same time interwoven with technology. The cyborg's reconstructed and challenging body is a useful reminder that 'bodies are never nonmaterial'; it 'rebukes the disappearance of the body' (Balsamo 1995: 39, 33) and demonstrates that, as Sandy Stone says, 'life is lived through bodies' (1991: 113).

Cyborg Corporeality

Elizabeth Grosz's work on 'corporeal feminism' is a particularly useful approach to theories of embodiment, and one that meshes well with analyses of the cyborg image. Grosz's work redefines corporeality and challenges the idea of the body as object. In this she rejects Cartesian dualism which 'identifies subjectivity and personhood with the conceptual side of the

Introduction: Troubled Boundaries and Transformative Cyborgs

opposition while relegating the body to the status of an object, outside of and distinct from consciousness' (1987: 4). This kind of viewpoint makes the body into 'an "objective", observable entity', and, in particular, emphasizes the female body through the 'presumption that women, more than men, are tied to their fixed corporeality' (Grosz 1987: 5). Such enforced parallels of the female with the body, with nature, biology, and consequently, identification as object work to separate women from gender-neutrality, disembodiment, culture and subjectivity. Grosz's rethinking of the body focuses on body as subject rather than object, and stresses that the idea that any body can exist in a neutral or 'objective' state is false. Embodiment, according to Grosz's analysis, includes both male and female bodies, and these bodies are particular, not universal: 'there is no monolithic category, 'the' body. There are only *particular kinds of bodies*' (1987: 5, emphasis in original).

By redefining the body as subject, it is possible to find new ways of approaching embodiment: from the inside, the 'body can be approached [...] from the point of view of its being lived or experienced by the subject' and from the outside, there is the 'recognition of how [the body] forms a surface for inscription' (Grosz 1987: 9–10). Grosz stresses that these two ways of thinking about the body should not be seen as a new binary opposition, but as a connection (1987: 14). Thinking through connection means that bodies can be seen as boundaries, borderlines, spaces in which the exterior and the interior do not represent a mutually exclusive dualism. Grosz declares that the body, seen in this new way, 'can be regarded as a kind of *hinge* or threshold; it is placed between a psychic or lived interiority and a more sociopolitical exteriority' (1995: 33, emphasis in original). And so the body becomes an experience of embodiment, as well as a surface for cultural and social inscription.

We can connect the textualized or inscribed body as defined by Grosz (1995: 35) with Judith Butler's notion of the body as a performative space, especially as regards gender and sexuality. Grosz envisions gender as 'an open materiality, a set of (possibly infinite) tendencies and potentialities which may be developed' within or upon bodies that are 'neither "blank" nor programmed' (1994: 191, 190). Butler describes gender in similar terms as 'an identity tenuously constituted in time, instituted in an exterior space through a *stylized repetition of acts*' (1990: 140, emphasis in original). When Butler calls gender a 'persistent impersonation' and asks whether (for example) 'being female constitute[s] a "natural fact" or a cultural performance' (1990: x) she, like Grosz and others, calls into question notions of 'natural' or inherent femininity and complicates the connection between the body and the female.

The strategy of reclaiming embodiment that we see in Butler's and Grosz's work connects in turn to ways of thinking about bodies that are particular, not universal. If 'the body' is not a fixed, universal category, but is endlessly open, performed, and particular, then we can allow for *plurality* in the way we think about bodies. Critics working with the terms of difference/plurality invoke the body as a boundary or threshold. In Braidotti's terms, '[t]he "body" in question is the threshold of subjectivity […] the body is […] to be thought of as the point of intersection, as the interface between the biological and the social' (1989: 90). This idea can also be seen in Butler's description of the 'variable boundary' of the body (1990: 139) and in Grosz's vision of the body as a 'hinge' (1995: 33). With this description, the body becomes the point at the centre which experiences plurality; the insistence on difference in turn becomes a way to 'confound, disrupt, and render ambiguous the meaning of any fixed binary opposition' (Scott 1988: 48). A process of thinking that involves 'both-and' rather than 'either-or' has the potential to dismantle binary oppositions, so that body *and* mind, nature *and* culture, and other binary oppositions become areas of difference/plurality. This brings us back to Haraway's 'Manifesto' and the ability of the cyborg to act with 'transgressed boundaries, potent fusions, and dangerous possibilities' (Haraway 1985: 71). The ideas around plurality and particular bodies help with analyses of male and female cyborg bodies – or to be more accurate, cyborg bodies that may be gendered male or female. The body as 'variable boundary', 'threshold' or 'hinge' connects with the body of the cyborg, which is hybrid and liminal. The imaginary cyborg takes up a position that is plural, located, different and partial, and above all, embodied.

Cyborg Gender

Looking at the list of binaries Haraway includes in versions of the 'Manifesto', we can see that these terms tend to be associated with gender. Mind, human, machine, public, culture, civilized have become aligned with the male, while the female aligns with body, animal, organism, private, nature, primitive. It is especially problematic for analyses of technology and the cyborg that 'nature', 'body' and 'female' are linked together, and so placed in opposition to 'machine' and 'mind'. Such combinations can make the construction of female cyborg bodies a difficult business, and the resulting cyborg embodiment can be read as especially monstrous and transgressive. Additionally, there is a tendency for 'the body' of the cyborg to be seen to refer to the *female* body rather than the *human* body, and it is true that female cyborgs abound in literary, cinematic and television fictions; two more-or-less random examples from literature and cinema are Molly in William Gibson's *Neuromancer* and Trinity in the Wachowskis' *Matrix* trilogy, and this book will focus on several female cyborgs of television.

The image of the female cyborg does complicate the relationship between women and technology. If machinery is conventionally associated with the masculine, while the body is associated with the feminine, how is the cyborg gendered or associated? If the body of the cyborg is female, does it follow that the body overcomes the machine? Because of the tendency to read 'the human/machine interrelation configured through a female body' as 'not mind/machine but body/machine', this connection 'conveys a very ambiguous message for women' (Cranny-Francis 2000: 155–6), notwithstanding the equally troublesome and problematic connection of 'mind/machine'. The construction of the female cyborg means that, paradoxically, 'it is the woman who becomes the model of the perfect machine' in a process of 'not production, but reproduction' (Doane 2013: 164). Some critics simply conclude that '[f]emale cyborgs […] perpetuate oppressive gender stereotypes' (Balsamo 1988: 336). Yet cyborgs can be gendered male or female, and both are subject to the tensions and alterations of technology.

It is evident that fictional male- and female-gendered cyborgs attract particular kinds of critical comment. If the cyborg is gendered female, it/she is often seen to embody the problematic relationship of the female to (monstrous) technology. She is viewed as 'hypersexual', presenting an exaggerated version of femininity that reinscribes gender markers onto a constructed, artificial body. If the cyborg is gendered male, it/he is categorized as a hypermasculine 'hard body' or – if the cyborg does not fit this category – is viewed as 'feminized' through his engagement with 'penetrating' technology. Some critics view the hypermasculine male cyborg as fixed within a gender category, while the female cyborg's identity is 'more malleable and dexterous'; though she may be 'hyperfeminine' she may also possess 'tough-girl strength, allowing her to transcend the patriarchal limits of female identity/femininity' (Genz and Brabon 2009: 149). Stacy Gillis' analysis outlines a typical viewpoint:

> [...] it is the figure of the female cyborg which has been positioned as potentially most disruptive with its simultaneous lack (the technology or metal obscuring its human or meat components) and excess of meaning achieved through its femininity (which is overtly sexualized). (2007b: 11)

This type of summary makes cyborg embodiment and representation appear very straightforward, but the cyborg is not so easily contained in such categories. It is quite easy to note that 'the figure of the [female] cyborg – as witnessed in a number of contemporary popular manifestations [...] – is problematic, often reinstating a traditional, sexualized and hyperfeminine body' and so to close off the discussion (Genz and Brabon 2009: 146); it is more challenging, but ultimately more rewarding, to argue that, despite the reinstatement of sexualized aspects (which most certainly does occur), both female and male cyborgs can still be read in ways that resist and complicate embodied existence. A female-gendered cyborg might show 'aggression'; a male-gendered cyborg might combine its/his apparent strength with plasticity or fluidity of embodiment, so that both have potential for hybrid and boundary-crossing forms of embodiment.

Haraway's cyborg shows us some ways to cut through such binary tangles. Using Haraway's model, I look for examples of boundary-crossing and confusion in the cyborg images I analyse in this book. These may not always be straightforward or unproblematic: a cyborg image may show evidence of stereotypical or even exaggerated gender markers, especially as regards female cyborgs. *Voyager*'s Seven of Nine is frequently cited as an example of this kind of hyperfeminine presentation (Johnson-Smith 2005: 270, note 9; Genz and Brabon 2009: 146) and critics tend to dismiss such characters as nothing more than 'eye candy for the boys' (Short 2011: 191). That is unfortunate, since cyborg characters, even hyperfeminine ones, may still undercut or complicate aspects of gender (and this is certainly true of Seven, as Chapter 2 shows). It is possible for a fictional cyborg to be depicted as unemotional, machinelike and linear in some respects, but at the same time such a character may develop modes of embodiment that are very close to the human/organic, as well as forging bonds of friendship or family. In keeping with Haraway's notion of the boundary-crossing figure, I aim to resist any absolute classification or taxonomy of the cyborg figure. Both female and male cyborgs offer a variety of transformative possibilities that trouble, cross and complicate binaries, boundaries and categories.

Cyborg Virtuality

In addition to these analyses of cyborg corporeality, the image of the cyborg intersects with theories of virtuality. Paradoxically, the cyborg body offers a form of augmentation that suggests the possibility of escape from embodiment. This is especially prevalent in the work of theorists of cyberculture and 'posthumanism' such as Marvin Minsky, Hans Moravec, and Arthur and Marilouise Kroker. Ideas of bodily transcendence and of immortality are strongly present in these works; Moravec, for example, posits a future – a real-world future, not a science fiction one – in which the human mind can be downloaded, like so much data, into an artificial shell, a process that somehow preserves the identity or 'being' of the individual. Other theorists show similar hyperbolic attitudes towards the possibility of disembodied life that could allow the self to range with complete freedom throughout a virtual space. Arthur and Marilouise Kroker insist that the body 'has *already* disappeared' and is on its way to being 'reborn in its technofied forms' (1988: 21–2, 31). In encounters with virtual reality, both fictional and actual, we find '[c]onfusion over the boundaries between the self and technological systems' (Springer 1991: 314); the embodied self may find freedom in virtual technologies, but the organic body is constantly on the verge of being overpowered by technology.

Much of this theory displays a dislocation from (at worst, a denial of) the physical, embodied world and from the systems that embodied individuals live within. For example, when questioned on the socioeconomic implications of these ideas, Moravec says that this is 'irrelevant. It doesn't matter what people do because they're going to be left behind' (in Dery 1996: 307). Similarly, computer designer W. Daniel Hillis theorizes that:

> [I]f this artificial mind can sustain itself and grow of its own accord, then for the first time human thought will live free of bones and flesh, giving this child of mind an earthly immortality denied to us. (in Haraway 1991b: 253, note 7)

For Hillis, Moravec and others, virtuality brings immortality, and embodiment is of no importance. However, what is emphasized by Haraway in her *Manifesto*, by Grosz and Butler in their thinking around 'corporeal feminism' and the performance of gender, and by many other critics writing on cyberculture and virtuality, is the individual, the self which is acted upon by power, politics, economics, and the physical world, which is not a code or a decaying shell but a being of flesh, a corporeal body.

We do need to question what virtuality offers the cyborg body and, in thinking about the gendered cyborg, to think too whether ideas of virtuality have different implications for female or male cyborg bodies. In some respects, virtuality offers 'the promise of total control and complete mobility' (Sofia 1992: 57), where 'technology serves fundamentally as a prosthesis of the human body, one that ultimately displaces the human body' (Woodward 1994: 50). Virtuality in its fictional representations is often connected with the body's disappearance – or with a wish for such a disappearance – that will bring total freedom. The classic example is William Gibson's *Neuromancer*, where the character Case yearns for the 'bodiless exultation' of pure data in the realm of cyberspace (1993: 12). The apparent promise of transcendence for Case, as for so many cyborg characters, remains forever beyond his reach, and instead he experiences a reconnection with his own body and his experiences of corporeal existence. Gibson reprises many ideas from his cyberpunk novels in the episodes he wrote for *The X-Files*, in which virtuality, especially, remains a problematic attraction ('Kill Switch' 5.11; 'First Person Shooter' 7.13). Rather than reading such characters as disappearing, virtual bodies, I see Case and others as excellent examples of the 'crucial role that the body plays in constructing cyberspace […] [I]t is obvious that we can see, hear, feel, and interact with virtual worlds only because we are embodied' (Hayles 1996: 1).

Some critics view female characters as unequivocally shut off from the (supposed) transcendent liberation of virtuality: this form of cyborg embodiment is only available to male characters. Scott Bukatman, for instance, notes that

> When the cybernetic cyborg is female, transcendence does not await her in the form of bodiless – or embodied – exultations nor in the satisfying multiplicity of subjectivities […]. In her interface with the electronic landscape, the woman is reconstituted as a figure of subjugation, and her body exists only as a sign of her own repression and incompleteness. (1993: 320)

But this interpretation ignores the point that there are plenty of female characters in cyber-fiction who do discover empowering transformations through cyborg embodiment, although such characters are often more keenly aware than their male counterparts that their transformations are, if not problematic, certainly not completely 'free'. In fiction, such female characters typically achieve only a brief 'transcendence' in virtual space before being reconstituted in the narrative according to fixed gender boundaries (see Pat Cadigan's *Synners*, Marge Piercy's *Body of Glass*, and Justina Robson's *Silver Screen*, for example) but 'transcendence' is, in any case, generally viewed as equally problematic and temporary for male characters. Alongside this, cyber-fictions show 'male bodies now become vulnerable to the technological penetration, leaky boundaries, and pregnancy-like status that have long been part of women's history and ontological condition' (Sofia 1992: 61). This is especially true in those literary, cinematic or televisual representations that situate the cyborg as a dangerous and monstrous entity that threatens the human/organic body with the prospect of technological augmentation.

Cyborg Television

The cyborg has been viewed for some time as a 'dominant figure' in science fiction cinema (Bukatman 1993: 43; Cornea 2003: 4). Its status as a body overlaid or incorporated with technology brings it into the realm of the visual and of performance, and it is often analysed in terms of cinematic spectacle. In this book, I want to move from the cyborg's cinematic image to consider how television depicts the cyborg, and there are a number of distinctions to be made. Television's longer serial narrative and story arcs allow cyborg characters, whether they are villains or hero figures, to become embedded in the ongoing story; while such characters are often introduced as distant, different, possibly threatening individuals, over time they can be drawn in more closely to a regular series cast and portrayed more sympathetically. Television's more limited budgets for big special effects alter the way cyborg characters are presented. The television cyborg is often shown in a subtle fashion, identifying for most of the time as primarily organic/human, while the narrative focuses on ideas and concepts around cyborg embodiment, exploring questions such as whether the cyborg has a soul, whether its identity is programmed, how far it is like and unlike a human. Television cyborg characters may also demonstrate that they are cyborg through particular feats of strength, skill and power in fight scenes, and through limited special-effects displays of their mechanical/technological working parts. The hybridity of the cyborg body intersects with television's genre hybridity, so that we see cyborgs not only in science fiction television (*Battlestar Galactica*, *Doctor Who*) but also in action-adventure shows (*Dollhouse*) and in hybrid police procedural drama (*Fringe*). Furthermore, many of the series explored in this book could be very loosely classified as family drama (*Terminator: The Sarah Connor Chronicles*, *Bionic Woman*, *Caprica*) giving another dimension to the hybridity of the cyborg character. This allows for further complexities in explorations of the cyborg on television.

In each chapter of this book, I examine a different television text, with different – sometimes complementary, sometimes contradictory – versions of the cyborg. Each chapter's analysis can stand alone, but I refer to connections and common threads that link together different versions of cyborgs and different television texts. Different critical and theoretical perspectives help to illuminate each television text. The texts themselves show development in how they present cyborg characters. Although many series may begin with cyborgs situated as straightforward enemies of humanity, the depiction of the cyborg tends to become more complex, contradictory and problematic, eroding and compromising divisions and boundaries.

I begin with the classic BBC television series *Doctor Who* and its early (1960s) examples of the television cyborg. The series presents two types of cyborg, and in the classic series both types are consistently cast as villains and adversaries for the Doctor and his companions. In this introduction,

Introduction: Troubled Boundaries and Transformative Cyborgs

I examine some initial appearances of the cyborg characters the Daleks and the Cybermen, and I look at some of the ways in which the classic serials represent the cyborg as an enemy of humanity. Both cyborg adversaries are reimagined in the new *Doctor Who* series. In this more recent series (with showrunners Russell T. Davies and Steven Moffat), the divisions between cyborg and human become more complex and the narrative goes so far as to make both Daleks and Cybermen into (occasional) sympathetic individuals. This is particularly evident in those episodes which make connections between cyborgs and strong female characters. The presentation of the TARDIS as a sentient being and (briefly) physically represented as a woman allows for a further examination of the sympathetic cyborg.

Chapter 2 focuses on the recurring *Star Trek* adversaries, the Borg. From their initial appearance in *Star Trek: The Next Generation* as a foreboding nemesis that comes to take a central role in particular episodes and story arcs, to the introduction of a regular Borg character as a crew member in *Star Trek: Voyager*, the Borg reflect fears of technological supremacy and of assimilation and loss of individuality. These fears are dramatized through narrative moments like the (temporary) assimilation of Captain Jean-Luc Picard in *Next Generation* and the 'rescue' of Borg entity Seven of Nine in *Voyager*. Picard's transformation presents a breakdown of boundaries and of the established narrative format, with a series' central authority figure stripped of power and control and turned into the spokesperson for a long-standing adversary. The representation of Seven of Nine foregrounds the paradoxical visual representation of the female cyborg, with an apparently artificial and asexual character costumed and presented in a body-revealing, sexualized way. Meanwhile her presence as a regular crew member troubles the classification of cyborg as 'other'. Key points within the narrative (and across more than one *Star Trek* series) complicate a simple reading of Borg assimilation as a negative process.

In the reimagined *Battlestar Galactica* the cyborg plays key roles across the entire series narrative, and this is my focus in Chapter 3. These cyborgs, the Cylons, appear in different modes and provoke different reactions. Imposing metal models maintain a sense of dread and fear, but are recognizably artificial and non-human; the series also introduces a humanoid Cylon model that overturns many of the divisions between human and 'other'. Since the newer-model Cylons are identical in appearance to human beings, their presence redefines and probes the complicated connections between humanity and Cylons throughout the series. The Cylons' ability to duplicate their bodies and to resurrect themselves also play on themes of individuality and mortality. These work alongside examinations of community and society in the series to further complicate the relationships between human and cyborg. Though the Cylons are situated as 'other' and as 'enemy' for much of the narrative, which chimes with real-world fears of insurgency and terrorism from within (something we see explored in a more realistic format in a series like *Homeland*), this opposition is continually undercut, as the narrative also offers a range of Cylon viewpoints.

The focus of Chapter 4 is the *Battlestar Galactica* prequel *Caprica*. This narrative traces the invention/creation of the Cylons with a storyline that, once again, troubles oppositions of life and death, real and virtual. In many ways, this narrative can be viewed as an origin story for the Cylons, and so as a commentary or alternative viewpoint on *Battlestar Galactica*. In *Caprica*, human Zoe Graystone's existence as a virtual copy allows her to continue to exist after her physical self is blown up by a terrorist bomb, and her downloaded consciousness located in the body of a Cylon foregrounds debates about the nature of consciousness, identity, embodiment and the positive possibilities of the cyborg body. I look at the way Zoe's physical self is represented on-screen, with the use of cuts that show her physical body (as cyborg) and her identity (as a human body); these directing and editing decisions help the viewer to engage with a cyborg character. I explore cyborg virtuality through character interactions in the virtual game-world which forms a significant thread of the series. Zoe's presence as virtual self and as cyborg assists the narrative development, so that a view of cyborgs/Cylons as enemy and thus 'other' develops into a more complex consideration of the cyborg as a version of ourselves.

The cyborgs examined in Chapters 5 to 7 can all be seen as representations of the female action hero. In Chapter 5, the reimagined *Bionic Woman* presents both bionic women, central character Jaime and her adversary Sarah, in the action hero role. Aspects of powerful, superhero embodiment connect in this narrative with views of the damaged body repaired by means of technology. So, I analyse Jaime and Sarah as examples of disabled embodiment, considering how the series presents the body made 'whole' by the addition of artificial cyborg prostheses. This series also situates the central character in a maternal role/relationship within a family unit. Thus, a further area of analysis for this chapter is how this series presents the cyborg as protagonist, and whether Jaime's cyborg character is made more acceptable to the viewer through the narrative emphasis on family connections and other links to a 'normally' embodied self. In many ways, Jaime is represented as a hybrid – cyborg/human – and there are possibilities here for comparison with other television narratives that present the action heroine as hybrid in various ways, such as *Buffy the Vampire Slayer*, *Alias*, or *Dark Angel*.

Family connections are also central in Chapter 6, with my examination of *Terminator: The Sarah Connor Chronicles*. Once again, the storylines are focused on a family unit, the Connors and their allies. The narrative offers male and female cyborg characters in central roles, and links together cinematic and televisual representations with the 'hard-body' male Terminator contrasted with more flexible female models. The series maintains the concept of the 'muscular cyborg' in the character of the Terminator Cromartie, but undercuts this with the resurrected cyborg body of Cromartie 'reborn' as the child-like John Henry (both characters played by the same actor, Garret Dillahunt). These examples reference the film franchise and, in particular, offer comparisons with the cinematic cyborg embodiment created by Arnold Schwarzenegger.

Dollhouse is not at first glance an obvious 'cyborg' narrative, but Chapter 7 argues that characters in this series are physically altered in ways that add technological components to their organic bodies. The series follows a range of individuals who have technological augmentations known as 'Active architecture' embedded in their brains. The purpose of this technology is to enable the individuals' personalities to be removed and their bodies 'imprinted' with other, created personalities. 'Active' technology allows them to be created and recreated in a multiplicity of identities. These characters' identities are continually reset with new personalities, undermining the notion that a person possesses a unified and constant identity. The narrative, which presents the same character in different personalities from episode to episode, provokes viewers to observe the 'simulacra' of personality, and the imitative qualities of multiple identities. I consider aspects of mind/body separation, programming, simulacra and authenticity in this chapter.

In Chapter 8, I turn to *Fringe*. Cyborg embodiment is just one strand of this generically hybrid series which mixes elements of the police procedural with science fiction. Across several seasons, the narrative follows cybernetic 'shapeshifters' that duplicate human bodies in a nightmare vision of technological domination. However, the series resists oppositional constructions by including characters from the regular cast – Nina Sharp and Peter Bishop – as alternative versions of the cyborg body. An important plot strand with regard to this discussion is the fifth season's storyline that explores futuristic developments of the human body. The series' mysterious twenty-fifth-century humans possess technological modifications that alter the organic body to the extent that it approaches the 'posthuman'. The process by which a central character, Peter Bishop, becomes augmented and changed through technology further dramatizes the tension between organic and cybernetic.

As I examine the television cyborg through the following chapters, I am aware that some readers will have seen all of the series I talk about, some will have seen a few and others none. My discussion necessarily looks at series narrative and development, and there are some episodes and whole series that it would be best to have watched before you read the relevant section or chapter so as not to find out plot twists and narrative shocks (quite a lot of *Battlestar Galactica* and all of *Dollhouse* falls into this category). As Matt Hills observes, television studies tends not to take note of such things. 'Television studies likens TV to bits of literature, which can be contained [...] and treated as fixed or finished. At the same time, it downplays the emotional experience of a "first viewing"' (2010: 9). This is an aspect that Sue Turnbull addresses through her work on 'ekphrasis' in relation to TV studies. 'Ekphrasis' attempts 'to recover in language the effect which a particular performance, moment or TV series may have had on us' (Turnbull 2005: 368). It is within this context that the characters I analyse act and interact, and I attempt to remain aware that '[i]t is by shocking, surprising and moving audiences that the programme comes alive affectively' (Hills 2010: 11). The television texts I examine in this book are, in one sense, finished or complete – the series have ended, or the self-contained story of the episode has ended. I can look at them as whole texts. In another sense, these texts are forever unfinished or open, and full of potential for new and different perspectives. I hope to add one such perspective with this focus on the transformative and boundary-crossing possibilities of television cyborgs.

1

Exterminate, Upgrade: *Doctor Who*

Doctor Who is a well-established part of British television history. The classic (1963–89) and the new series (2005–present) follow the adventures of the Doctor, a Time Lord from the planet Gallifrey, who has the ability to regenerate into new bodies – a particularly clever and convenient invention, which allows different actors to portray the same character. With a selection of (usually human) companions, he travels through time and space in the TARDIS, which takes the form of a blue police telephone box. Over the half-century of the Doctor's existence, he has encountered a huge variety of alien life forms, often hostile to others and especially to humans and the Earth. Among these adversaries are two distinct versions of the cyborg, and these beings appear repeatedly in both classic and new series narratives. Donna Haraway's vision of the cyborg is as a positive, liberatory, boundary-crossing figure. The cyborgs of *Doctor Who*, however, appear fairly consistently as figures of horror, representing boundaries that are not 'crossed' but violently breached. The recurring cyborgs in this series offer versions of the cyborg 'other' that reconfigure organic body boundaries in abject ways. These cyborgs are menacing and monstrous, depicting technophobic anxieties about powerful twentieth- and twenty-first-century technologies.

The classic *Doctor Who* series gives us two very early examples of television cyborgs. On 23 November 1963, in the episode 'The Dead Planet', a cyborg – that became known to audiences as a Dalek – rolled into view on the screen, waved a rubber-plunger arm and electronically barked 'Exterminate!' In 1966, the Cybermen joined the legion of the Doctor's monstrous adversaries in the serial 'The Tenth Planet' (broadcast 8–9 October), and both Daleks and Cybermen persist as adversaries from the 1960s to the present. These figures reflect a shifting series of concerns, which in the classic series include postwar trauma – specifically focused on the aftermath of World War II – and anxiety about technological-medical advancements. In the new series, both kinds of cyborg reappear as enemy figures, and are a means to interrogate such things as the nature of heroism; war and genocide; religious mania and intolerance; uniformity and conformity – all problems that a twenty-first-century Western world meditates on with some regularity. Perhaps also befitting the uncertainties of the twenty-first century, the new series continually subverts and questions the monster status of both Daleks and Cybermen. All these concerns are mapped onto the monstrous cyborg body with its impulse to 'exterminate' or to 'upgrade' human embodiment into something approaching its own monstrosity.

Created by Terry Nation, the Daleks were 'intended to be uncannily monstrous' (Bignell 2005: 80) and, in a sense, straightforward enemies: 'they were bad, bad guys and you could absolutely…know they were bad' ('Terry Nation' 2014). Nation wanted to design a non-humanoid monster (that did not look like 'a guy dressed up') and achieved this with the Daleks by 'get[ting] rid of the legs' ('Terry Nation' 2014). Nation's idea of a rounded metal shell with protruding appendages, including an eye-stalk and a weapons array, makes 'their appearance and their silent movement […] both menacing and plausible' (Chapman 2013: 29). They certainly captured the viewers' attention. By Boxing Day 1964, when the Daleks made their second appearance in the final episode of 'The Dalek Invasion of Earth', these monsters were already household names in Britain and could boast their first *Radio Times* cover (21–27 November 1964). Nation suggests that their popularity was helped by the fact that they could be imitated 'by any child with a cardboard box', and there is early evidence that children picked up on this, play-acting parts of the serial (Cook 2002: 123) and so demonstrating that, despite their terrifying onscreen personae, the Daleks were and 'continue to be popular monsters' (Unruh 2013).

Although '[t]he Daleks represent an extreme form of technocracy' (Chapman 2013: 28), the fact that the Daleks are *cyborg* monsters is almost an aside in many of the classic serials. Their cyborg embodiment and their status as *technological* monsters are not generally explored in much detail; they are simply presented as radically other in their embodiment. One exception is the 'Genesis of the Daleks' storyline (1975) which examines the Daleks' origins, and reveals that they were made from scientific/technological manipulation of the humanoid race of Kaleds.

The Daleks of the classic series 'belong to a lineage of apocalyptic fantasy in which civilisation is destroyed by atomic war' (Chapman 2013: 27). In the serial stories that focus on their origins as Kaleds ('The Daleks' 12 December 1963–1 February 1964; 'Genesis of the Daleks' 8 March–12 April 1975), we see references to classic science fiction texts, especially H.G. Wells' *The Time Machine* (1895). These cyborg monsters allowed the series to allegorize the World War II Holocaust and nuclear holocaust (Chapman 2013: 28), as well as British wartime experiences more generally. The 1964 serial used London locations to dramatize an alien invasion of Britain using the framework of the Pathé newsreel: 'Shots of Dalek patrols against familiar [London] landmarks [...] remind[ed] audiences of how close Britain came to invasion only 24 years earlier' (Chapman 2013: 43). Indeed, for their appearances through the 1960s and 70s, the Daleks appear as a 'thinly veiled re-incarnation of the Nazis', especially in 'Genesis of the Daleks' when 'the Daleks were revealed to be the creations of a culture whose uniforms and salutes echoed the Nazis' (Cull 2001: 101). This was a deliberate reference on Nation's part (Fleming 2011). In these serials, the Daleks feature as emblems of a totalitarian state and the storylines explore the population's possible responses to such a state, outlining 'difficult issues such as the level of violence justifiable to destroy the Daleks, and such taboo issues as the question of whether British people would have collaborated [in World War II]' (Cull 2001: 101).

While Terry Nation created the Daleks simply in order to include a monster in his story, the Cybermen were introduced as a specific response to real-world developments in medical technology. Kit Pedler, *Doctor Who*'s 'unofficial scientific advisor' (Chapman 2013: 61) introduced the Cybermen in order to comment on the potential effects of advancements such as pacemakers, transplants and artificial body parts, especially the fears and anxieties associated with such non-organic augmentations. The Cybermen 'represented the nightmarish possibilities of "dehumanized medicine"' with the body augmented to such a degree that it has lost any connection to the organic (Chapman 2013: 63). In this respect, the Cybermen reference other science fiction texts that reflect on medical technology running out of control, like Mary Shelley's *Frankenstein* (1818). Besides their technological enhancements, 'certain weaknesses', for example, human emotions, have been eradicated from the Cybermen, so that nothing interferes with 'survival as their primary goal' (Geraghty 2008: 89). While the Daleks are more obviously and overtly non-human or 'other' in their appearance – they do not possess human-like bodies/shells, their appendages do not look like human hands, they have no feet, and their voices do not sound human – Cybermen are recognizably human-shaped, despite their rejection of the organic body. As critics have noted, the appearance of the Cybermen has altered over time, 'showing the evolution of the Cyber race as they shed their remaining human parts and became increasingly robotic in appearance' (Chapman 2013: 64). Their silver/steely exterior ensures that pliable human flesh gives way to solid metal, 'the last vestiges of the human body (skin) are completely hidden or eradicated' (Geraghty 2008: 92). Perhaps because of this, there is evidence that viewers find Cybermen more alarming than Daleks. One commentator notes that 'the Cybermen looked like terrible human beings, whereas the Daleks were just Daleks' (in Chapman 2013: 64). These examples give us two different ways in which both types of cyborgs are 'uncannily monstrous' (Bignell 2005: 80): similarity to the human figure adds to the Cybermen's uncanny representation, while the sense of the uncanny is produced for the Daleks through their lack of a human shape.

Both cyborg adversaries are reimagined in the new *Doctor Who* series (2005–present). Under showrunners Russell T. Davies and Steven Moffat, Daleks and Cybermen have made very regular appearances, to the point that the series attracted criticism for repetition and overuse of the 'big enemies' (*Radio Times* 2011; Rozeman 2014). Undoubtedly, the new series' writers wish to make use of popular monsters from *Doctor Who*'s history, partly to appeal to new, young viewers, but also to play on the nostalgic memories of viewers old enough to have seen the classic series (Hills 2010: 222).

What these recurring storylines demonstrate, too, is the persistence of anxieties about technology and the human body's interaction with it;

cyborg monsters like Daleks and Cybermen serve as a means to explore these anxieties. Nicholas Cull argues that by 1989 'Doctor Who had outlived its cultural purpose'; that society no longer needed to explore issues associated with technology, diversity, identity or invasion (2001: 107). However, in its near-constant engagement with these very themes, the new series has demonstrated that there is still a need to engage with figures of cyborg monstrosity.

Versions of artificial embodiment proliferate throughout the new series. The first new episode features the Autons ('Rose' 1.1); other examples include clockwork people ('The Girl in the Fireplace' 2.4), virtual worlds ('Silence in the Library' and 'Forest of the Dead' 4.8–9) and the Tesselector, a replica body powered by miniaturized humans ('Let's Kill Hitler' 6.8 and 'The Wedding of River Song' 6.13). Even the TARDIS is reimagined as a woman, or at least, as a female body ('The Doctor's Wife' 6.4). Season 8 is especially well populated with examples of artificial embodiment, featuring a version in almost every episode, including the reappearance of Daleks ('Into the Dalek' 8.2), clockwork people ('Deep Breath' 8.1), robots ('Robot of Sherwood' 8.3) and Cybermen ('Dark Water'/'Death in Heaven' 8.11–12). So many stories featuring forms of artificial embodiment underline the point that the artificial body is still the repository of fears, anxieties and fascination.[1]

The new series develops the Doctor as a contested hero-figure through 'a particular archetype of masculinity: the traumatised war veteran' (Chapman 2013: 190; see also Gibbs 2013); his potential for heroism is often in doubt, and occasionally complicated to the extent that he seems poised to become an anti-hero or even a villain. Within this framework, it is appropriate that the series arcs also contest the positioning of long-standing monster figures like the Daleks and the Cybermen, as the new series' scripts play on nearly fifty years of back-story and develop the mythology of the series for the twenty-first century.

Inside/Outside: *Doctor Who's* Technological Monsters

As I have noted, Haraway and other critics view the cyborg as a 'liberatory' figure which transcends boundaries and oppositions, offering freedom from embodied limitations (Silvio 1999: 54). Yet the cyborg as presented in

Doctor Who is most often a figure of horror, an entity that reveals boundaries breached and ruptured through violence. These cyborgs are associated with the abject re-configuring of organic bodies and the violation of any organic body's boundaries in upgrading, in conversion, or in extermination – all of which result in the death of the organic body. The possibilities of cyborg upgrading/conversion suggest that the mind and body can be easily separated, but this is regularly presented as more difficult than Daleks or Cybermen anticipate. In many examples, the mind and body resist separation, suggesting that, as Elizabeth Grosz states, '[b]odies and minds are not two distinct substances or two attributes of a single substance, but somewhere in between these two alternatives' (Grosz 1994: xii). She emphasizes the connection of inside and outside, different aspects of embodiment that coexist in a similar way to the continuous surface of the Möbius strip. This notion allows 'a way of problematizing and rethinking the relations between the inside and the outside of the subject, its psychical interior and its corporeal exterior, by showing […] the torsion of one into the other, the passage, vector or uncontrollable drift of the inside into the outside and the outside into the inside' (Grosz 1994: xii). In similar ways, *Doctor Who*'s narratives depict the organic (human) body and especially its brain as resistant to mechanisation despite the cyborgs' attempts at violent reconfigurations. This is evident in episodes involving both Daleks and Cybermen, like 'Asylum of the Daleks' (7.01) and 'Doomsday' (2.13). Here, we see humans endeavouring to retain their humanity despite their forced re-embodiment as cyborgs.

The construction of Daleks and Cybermen disrupts embodied integrity in several similar ways. The Daleks have an inner organic component within their metal casing; the organic part is fleshy and defenceless while the metal exterior is impenetrable and bristles with weaponry and technological apparatus. This is displayed in great detail when a microscopic Doctor ends up inside a damaged Dalek and encounters its digestive and immune systems ('Into the Dalek'). The construction process for Cybermen as portrayed in the new series involves a rupture between inside and outside: the human brain taken out of, and separated from, its organic body. For both Daleks and Cybermen, the uniformity of their existence creates a further layer of 'the monstrous': these monsters are not organic, and not wholly machine, but they do appear to be exactly alike, especially when they are shown in large numbers; CGI processes certainly allow 'the creation of believable epic-scale settings' (Britton 2013: 41) in the new series. Storylines that follow attempts by Daleks or Cybermen to make other lifeforms like themselves – and so, in a sense, to duplicate themselves – add another layer to their cyborg monstrosity. Not only do they aim to gain control over worlds, they aim to control and transform the embodiment of other beings. These cyborgs co-opt other embodied selves and destroy others' embodied integrity (in a similar way to the Borg in the *Star Trek* series, see Chapter 2). This is consistent in both classic and new series' portrayals; Cybermen in 'The Tenth Planet' declare that humans 'will become like us' and new series episodes like 'Rise of the Cybermen' (2.5) and 'Doomsday' show this process in action, while in 'Revelation of the Daleks' (1985) and 'Parting of the Ways' (1.13) human bodies are used to create new Daleks.

Both classic and new series foreground the horror of the uniformity that results from cyborg augmentation, and present cyborg transformation as enslavement. This is especially evident with regard to the Cybermen who drive out difference and cause those they assimilate to celebrate that very lack of difference. Their transformation is framed as an uncomplicated improvement, thanks to the unfailingly logical Cyber thought-processes. In 'The Tenth Planet' Cybermen refer to their 'freedom from disease, protection against heat and cold […]' and question, 'Do you prefer to die in misery?' Similarly, new-series Cybermen insist on their 'positive' qualities: 'Cybermen will remove fear. Cybermen will remove sex and class and colour and creed. You will become identical. You will become like us' ('Doomsday'). Cybermen do unite the world, after a fashion: after they take over a parallel-world Earth, they 'delete' the President of Great Britain who attempts to resist them ('Rise'); when Torchwood head Yvonne Hartman tells them, 'we don't have a global world authority' their retort is, 'You do now', and include Hartman with other humans who are 'upgraded' to a Cyber-body ('Doomsday'). With the 'upgrade' process, the Cybermen do create 'pain-free immortality' and so 'are actually fulfilling the ambition of many humans' but they 'ride roughshod over the autonomy of their convertees' (Green and Willmott 2013: 68). In a sense, then, the Cybermen bring about a utopian, unified world where difference is erased, or at least 'upgraded' into identical metal bodies, but this is clearly presented as a horrifying fate for the human race.

Anything for an Upgrade: 'Rise of the Cybermen'/ 'Age of Steel'

In the double episode 'Rise of the Cybermen'/'Age of Steel' (2.5–6), the Doctor, Rose and Mickey crash-land in what appears to be contemporary London, but is a parallel-world version of Earth. In this world, scientist John Lumic is working to create artificial bodies ('Cybermen') as a means to improve on organic human bodies. Once again, the new narrative references the classic series, and assumes knowledge on the part of the viewers, while taking the classic series' storyline in a new direction with the shift to a parallel Earth. That shift allows the episode to feature new and different forms of technology, from the zap-gun wielded by Mickey's parallel-world double, to the zeppelins flying instead of aeroplanes (a shift that is also seen in the alternate-world 'Manhatan' in *Fringe*) and to the ear-piece, similar to a Bluetooth headset, which is worn by almost every person in the parallel world, demonstrating its ubiquity and availability to any- and everyone. Russell T. Davies acknowledges that the series is '[t]apping into modern paranoias and modern obsessions' and adds, 'People *want* to relate to technology, that's […]what they're after. And, you know, how many people do you see walking round with the Bluetooth attachment now?' ('*Doctor Who* Confidential: Cybermen' 2006). Even before the Cybermen are revealed in the last few minutes of 'Rise', a sense of unease prevails at the way in which, because of their personal, near-invisible technology, people behave as though they are already programmed.

This is demonstrated in a long scene early in 'Rise of the Cybermen', in which Rose and the Doctor explore the streets of parallel-London. They observe a crowd's behaviour as, following a three-note tone similar to a mobile phone text-message alert, everyone on the street stands motionless and expressionless, staring into space. Rose's own mobile phone acts as an interface to show that data is being downloaded directly into the brains of the people around them.[2] The crowd 'receives' a news bulletin, lottery numbers, the weather report, and a joke, after which they laugh in unison and begin to disperse. Rose looks troubled while the Doctor remarks: 'You lot, you'll do anything for an upgrade'. His comment mocks the contemporary rush for newer and newer versions of technology, but by the end of the episode, it has a more sinister twist as the narrative begins to reveal scientist John Lumic's plans to 'upgrade' the world's population into Cybermen. Lumic's headset technology is 'compatible', designed specifically for ease of use and quick incorporation into everyday life. This allows him to exploit the technology in order to achieve his aims. In the sequel episode 'Age of Steel', Lumic uses the universally compatible headset technology to turn humans into obedient drones who will follow orders. Walking in an orderly fashion and in straight lines, the rows of humans appear to be already part-cyborg as they are directed into a factory to receive their cybernetic 'upgrades'. These examples show humans' reliance on technological appendages such as mobile phones, tablets, headsets and wireless technologies as potentially dangerous because of their very ubiquity: 'this whole idea that it will slowly creep up on us and we won't quite notice it happening' (David Tennant, in '*Doctor Who* Confidential: Cybermen' 2006). The cyborg monstrosity presented here is implicit in the embodied presence of the Cybermen, but it is easy to view the exterior hard-body of the Cyberman as integral and unified with its interior, and to forget the human aspect of this cyborg. Humanity's 'free upgrade' comes in the form of identical tall 'hard-bodies' in reflective steel, bodies that will not age or die.

Lumic himself has a complicated position regarding the Cybermen. They are his creation, his 'children', 'a miracle', with 'skin of metal and a body that will never age or die' ('Rise'). They are invented out of his wish to cure his own diseased body; Lumic is shown in a technologically-modified wheelchair with attachments for an oxygen mask and other aids, and there are clear references throughout these episodes to his own failing health. The creation of the Cybermen is thus a means for Lumic himself to overcome disease and death by replacing the organic body with a metal one. Looking on at his metal creation, he says 'I envy it', showing the kind of technophilic mindset outlined by Hans Moravec's theories that would allow the human brain – or its data – to be 'rescued from the limitations of a mortal body' (1988: 5) and downloaded into an indestructible, immortal body. Yet, Lumic resists the 'upgrade' himself, declaring that he will only allow himself to be modified into a 'Cyberform' 'with my last breath' ('Age of Steel'). This comment complicates his otherwise triumphal attitude towards his cybernetic creations, suggesting that such a transformation *is* a last resort for him and that, despite all its obvious limitations, he *would* rather remain in his own imperfect body. This contradicts his previous declaration which privileges the brain: 'We're all flesh and blood, but the brain is what makes us human. And my mind is more creative than ever.' The behaviour of various Cybermen contests this. The very fact that each 'upgraded' Cyberman must have an emotional inhibitor installed to stop them going mad gives the lie to Lumic's suggestion that the brain has primary importance.

'It was a woman': Experience of Cyborg Embodiment

Some Cybermen appear to remember their original embodied forms and personalities, and in 'Rise of the Cybermen' and 'Age of Steel' all such examples are of *female* embodiment. The Doctor and resistance fighter Mrs Moore discover that a damaged Cyberman can remember its previous human life as Sally Phelan, who was preparing for her wedding. Another tells Pete and Rose, 'I was Jacqueline Tyler' (Pete's wife in this parallel world; another version of Jackie Tyler is Rose's mother in our universe). The discovery of the Sally-Cyberman is framed as a moment of horror for the organically-embodied witnesses. While this scene is in part horrific because it emphasizes the un-gendering of the human body once it is transformed into a Cyber-body, at the same time the horror is enhanced – for the characters, certainly – because they discover that 'it was a woman'. Technically of no gender, the tall, powerful, squarely-built Cybermen do still give the 'visual impression of heightened masculinity' (and retain a gendered name) and as a result, once 'upgraded' herself, Sally 'is no longer gendered as female'; she is 'cut off and separated from the experiences of the body' (Rose 2010: 293). A similar process occurs with the parallel-world Jackie Tyler, who is consistently portrayed in these episodes through stereotypically feminine form-fitting dresses, elaborate hairstyles and makeup, and high-heeled shoes, until she is 'upgraded'. There is an enormous visual contrast between human Jackie and the metal-bodied Cyberman (sic) that announces 'I was Jacqueline Tyler' ('Age of Steel'). While the Cyberman maintains and calls on a link between its present embodiment and its past – it has Jackie's brain, part of that past embodiment (Green and Willmott 2013: 66) – it does so in an emotionless manner, with no sign that it can remember the physical experience of *being* Jacqueline Tyler. Moreover, everything about its cyborg embodiment, its visual appearance and its 'flattened vocal tone' (Cranny-Francis 2009: 133), emphasizes its difference from Jackie. This moment is presented as a deeply emotional one for both Pete and Rose as they are confronted with the evidence of Jackie's death told (in a sense) from Jackie herself. However, they also cling to the hope that this is false information, because they lack any physical proof that this 'Cyberform' *is* Jackie. The difference between human Jackie and her Cyberman upgrade is clear, too, when Pete and Rose look for the Jackie-Cyberman to question it further, only to find a crowd of identical silver-metal faces looking back at them. This is Lumic's ideal – 'uniformity, unity' – played out on a human-family scale.

The *Doctor Who* spin-off *Torchwood* offers a further example of a female in Cyber-form. 'Cyberwoman' (1.4) continues the events of *Doctor Who*'s 'Doomsday' and examines the aftermath of the Cyberman attack. In this story, human Lisa has been subject to a 'partial upgrade' which, instead of encasing her brain in metal, has added cybernetic parts to her organic form. This female cyborg embodiment differs from the examples in the *Doctor Who* Season 2 storylines, in that Lisa still exists in a female body, and does not become a metal-suited hard-body. Lisa's cyborg embodiment could offer more positive possibilities; her body could be shown adapting to additional abilities gained from her cyborg transformation and embracing a boundary-crossing hybrid identity. However, Lisa's embodiment as cyborg is consistently presented as a horrific aberration, and Lisa is as much a threatening monster as any of the metal-suited Cybermen. As cyborg, Lisa threatens other humans' embodied integrity, as she attempts to continue her 'upgrade'. This *Torchwood* example results in a much more sexualized, and therefore more problematic, cyborg representation. Lisa's is described as a 'partial' conversion, but this does not explain why Cyber-Lisa has been 'upgraded' to wear a metal bikini and high-heeled silver boots 'with her midriff exposed' (Dunn 2010: 114). Further, Lisa is a cyborg woman of colour, which renders 'her difference doubly obvious in comparison to the all-white Torchwood men' (Dunn 2010: 114). A sexualized representation is reserved for the black, *female* cyborg; in *Doctor Who*'s Season 8 Danny Pink undergoes a partial conversion into a Cyberman ('Death in Heaven'), but he appears with a metal casing covering his whole body, and only a mask-like aperture showing his organic face. Lisa's actions suggest that her aim is to 'upgrade' herself back to an organic status, but by putting her own brain into a human body that is female, white, and blonde, she erases some of her difference. At the same time, her murderous actions emphasize the monstrosity of her technological 'upgrade' and its horrific and bloody consequences for her victims and for Lisa herself.

Who is the Monster?: Going Into the Dalek

If the presence of Cybermen in the new series signals explorations of human identity, conformity and free will, the presence of Daleks is slightly more complex. While Cybermen are, on the whole, presented as cyborg monsters, the new series' re-examination of the Daleks follows a more generally ambivalent characterization of 'hero' and 'villain' figures. The Daleks 'are no longer always and only horror monsters' and indeed, their monstrosity is queried in the new series (Hills 2010: 128). The Daleks themselves are allowed more individual characterization than in the classic series; instead of a series of identical metal-shelled enemies, the new series offers individual Daleks with original, possibly unique, characteristics: Daleks who are tasked with imagining the impossible, who see themselves as gods or saviour-figures, who have become mentally unstable. In a sense, these Daleks exhibit non-Dalek behaviour and so trouble their category definition as Daleks. Several examples in the new series fit this description. The Supreme Dalek has a concept of blasphemy, hitherto unknown to Daleks ('Parting of the Ways'). Dalek Sec's plan for a new kind of Dalek embodiment is a monstrous transformation according to Dalek thought, so dreadful that they reject him: 'you are no longer a Dalek!' ('Evolution of the Daleks' 3.5). A tortured Dalek sees itself as fatally 'contaminated' by human DNA ('Dalek' 1.6); Dalek Caan works against all other Daleks in a plan to destroy them ('Journey's End' 4.13). Such individual Daleks are monstrous to their own kind.

The Daleks begin the new series as uncompromising monsters, beings that terrify the Doctor as well as (potentially) the viewers; their aggression culminates in a seemingly unstoppable attack in the first season's finale ('The Parting of the Ways'). Yet their potential for terror and menace is undercut early in this first season, in 'Dalek', the first 'story [...] explicitly to reference the old' (Chapman 2013: 195). Writer Robert Shearman and director Joe Ahearne use this first appearance of a Dalek in the new series to play on *Doctor Who*'s adult audience's knowledge of the classic series. The episode offers a slow unveiling of the mystery creature known as the 'Metaltron', which forms part of billionaire Van Straten's museum of 2012 (seven years in the future of the 2005 air date), and is only a mystery to the characters. Paradoxically, this episode 'successfully reinvented the Dalek as a formidable and menacing antagonist' (Chapman 2013: 196) and simultaneously presents both Doctor and Dalek in new ways, incorporating alien points of view from both characters into its narrative, and giving the Dalek point of view a growing significance. Such point of view is emphasized in the episode's opening. The screen displays the blue-tinged, Dalek-eye viewpoint, referencing cinematic depictions of the cyborg's-eye view (as seen in films like *The Terminator*) and the audio presents its electronic voice. We witness the Dalek screaming while soldiers are commanded to 'make it talk'; the Doctor, generally someone to take a moral stance on such matters, here uses Dalek terminology as he insists that this Dalek should be 'exterminated'. The story gives us the opportunity to see a terrifying monster in a new way: Rose's horrified reaction offers an altered viewpoint through which we might recognize that the Dalek is a suffering individual. While viewers with background information from the classic series (and from British culture more generally) might find Rose's questions to the Dalek such as 'Do you feel pain?' naïve and ridiculous, she does approach the monster from a completely fresh standpoint. This new perspective accommodates a changing status for both Dalek and Doctor: while the Doctor realizes he is losing touch with himself, becoming more like a Dalek (Chen 2008: 57), the Dalek incorporates human DNA from Rose into its organic/metal body, and becomes more like a human. The likeness between the two is explicitly acknowledged: the Dalek says, 'I am alone in the universe…so are you [the Doctor]. We are the same.' This underlines the point that, following the apocalyptic Time Wars, both Dalek and Time Lord are the last of their kind. As it becomes possible to see the Dalek – or at least, its inner self, its psyche – as a suffering individual, so too it becomes possible to see how the Doctor is becoming more Dalek-like, focused on anger, revenge and death.

Parallels between the Daleks and the Doctor continue with recurring Dalek appearances in Seasons 7 and 8, which again stress the point that these beings are more alike than either would care to recognize. Exchanges between the Doctor and Dalek leaders throughout the new series redefine 'good' and 'evil' and position both Doctor and Daleks as monstrous. The Supreme Dalek considers himself 'god' and describes his creation; he also taunts the Doctor for his willingness to destroy the Earth and probably all human beings in order to destroy the Daleks ('Parting of the Ways'). Davros, the Daleks' creator, repeatedly casts the Doctor as a villain, naming him 'the destroyer of worlds' ('Journey's End'). As a radiation-damaged Dalek, which seems to have discovered morality and a sense of right and wrong, tells the Doctor, 'I am not a good Dalek. *You* are a good Dalek' ('Into the Dalek'). A further possibility is that the Doctor's division of things into 'good' and 'bad' is flawed. A cyborg, after all, breaks through such boundaries. In 'Into the Dalek' the Doctor makes the discovery that a change of perspective can occur, even for Daleks: '[t]he radiation allowed it to expand its consciousness – to consider things beyond its natural frame of reference – it became good. That means a good Dalek is possible.' However, in his attempt to 'save [its] soul' the Doctor shows it his own, which is still full of hate for the Daleks. At this point in the narrative, it is unclear whether Time Lord or Dalek is a worse option.

'Remember me': 'Asylum of the Daleks'

'Asylum of the Daleks' develops the sympathetic cyborg of 'Dalek' and looks ahead to 'Into the Dalek', making a Dalek the point of view through which much of the story is told. Oswin Oswald is a human who has been 'converted' into a Dalek after crash-landing on the asylum planet where defective Daleks are abandoned.[3] Oswin hides her conversion from herself (and the audience) by fantasising a virtual world where she retains human form. Aspects of Oswin's virtual world, transmitted to the Parliament of the Daleks, are perceived as a threat; the Daleks 'acquire' the Doctor and companions Amy and Rory to 'save the Daleks' from that threat. Sent to the asylum planet, Amy, Rory and the Doctor have to contend with Dalek technology in the form of 'nanocytes', 'micro-organisms that automatically process any organic matter, living or dead, into a Dalek puppet.'

The narrative switches between two main threads which are both concerned with embodied integrity: Amy, Rory and the Doctor struggle to avoid contamination by the nanocytes, and Oswin struggles to conceal her contamination from herself.

The mise-en-scène for Oswin's sections of 'Asylum' is the home: she is depicted in a small space (an escape pod) that contains a bed, a sofa, and a kitchen. Here, she makes soufflés, listens to music and records an audio diary which includes a *Big Brother*-style tally of the number of days she has spent inside the pod, and digresses to send birthday greetings to her mother. Oswin's space looks inviting, but it is also framed as a refuge from something frightening; the camera lingers on a barricade of wooden boards nailed over the escape pod door, and several times, as in Figure 2, we see Oswin maintaining and reinforcing this defence. Visually, this homely interior is bright and attractive; Oswin's dress and trainers provide colourful red accents and there is comfortable furniture. The bright interior contrasts strongly with the real 'outside', represented as a monochrome space containing a dust-covered Dalek – Oswin's true exterior. This comments on the embodiment of all Daleks, composed of a fleshy interior and an armoured, metal exterior. This narrative, again, troubles the oppositions of inside/outside and organic/metal in the cyborg body. It reveals truths about cyborg embodiment while it constructs its story through an interior viewpoint, Oswin's own mind.

Figure 2: Oswin Oswald, 'Asylum of the Daleks', *Doctor Who* (7.1)

This episode covers a lot of ground in forty minutes, and with her pacy dialogue, humour and inventiveness Oswin becomes likeable very quickly. This is necessary for an effective denouement; the revelation of Oswin's true embodied state as a cyborg is intended to shock and frighten, and to create uncanny resonances: 'That which we already know – what we have known all along – but which we are not yet aware that we know' (Charles 2011: 3). There are ample clues in the episode that point to Oswin's true form. How does she know so much about the asylum planet and the facility's geography? How can she manipulate technology within the asylum, and (an especially revealing point) how is it possible that she can 'delete' the Doctor from the collective hive mind of the Daleks, unless she is herself connected to that hive mind? Oswin's explanation – 'I'm a genius' – itself becomes the explanation for her fate. 'You're right,' the Doctor tells her. 'You're a genius. And the Daleks need geniuses. They didn't just make you a puppet. They did a full conversion.' At this point, script, camera work and special effects underline the point that Oswin's consciousness (and presumably the remnants of her organic self) is part of the metal-cased Dalek standing before the Doctor. The camera cuts from Oswin's face to the Dalek tied up in chains. Both, in turn, ask 'Where am I?' and in the sentence which follows – 'I am not a Dalek – I am not a Dalek' – the screen shows Oswin speaking the words 'I am not' while the mechanical Dalek voice speaks the rest of the sentence; the screen cuts back to Oswin insisting, 'I'm human'. The sequence looks as though it is arranged as shot-countershot: Oswin and the Dalek are both in close-up, and the sequence suggests a conversation between two separate characters. Only the continuous line of dialogue undermines any separation between Oswin and the Dalek, so that instead the shots show the *inside* and the *outside* of the same character. In this dramatic rendering of Oswin's transformation, the sentence is neatly divided so that the camera is on the Dalek as it speaks its own name, 'a Dalek', before the camera cuts to Oswin saying, 'I'm human'. However, the coda to this sequence disturbs this inside/outside contrast, with a fast cut from Oswin saying 'I'm' to the Dalek saying, 'Human!' It is particularly unsettling to hear the word 'human' uttered in the voice of a Dalek and the fast and choppy cutting accentuates Oswin's confusion and incomprehension; she has, after all, created an entire fantasy domain in order to escape the reality of what was done to her.

Oswin provides a focus on female embodiment in relation to the Daleks, which is similar to the process that reveals aspects of female embodiment within Cyberman bodies. In 'Asylum', the narrative's back-and-forth switching between interior and exterior creates contrast between the now-imaginary body of Oswin and the genderless metal shell and mechanized vocal register of the Dalek. And yet, it is Oswin's humanity, her individuality, her memory of who she is, as well as her command to the Doctor to 'remember me', that enables her to act independently. If she were a fully-converted Dalek, she would simply exterminate the Doctor and his companions. It seems appropriate that at its end this episode re-embodies Oswin and returns her to her cosy (imaginary) home.[4] Re-embodying Oswin emphasizes one of *Doctor Who*'s key themes: the importance of individuality, uniqueness, the quirky, the unusual, the original working with other originals in a community.

'I gave them back their souls': Individuality and the Cyborg

Although *Doctor Who*'s cyborgs are consistently presented as a group, a mass, or a species, and although both Daleks and Cybermen prize uniformity, conformity and the continuation of a certain kind of collective vision, Oswin's story highlights the recurring theme of the persistence of (human) individuality. The Doctor is shown to value imagination and the individual, describing the Cybermen, for example, as 'metal men with metal thoughts' ('Age of Steel'), devoid of inventiveness, beings that can only obey orders and conform. While Lumic insists that his cyborg processes 'can set you free [...] give you] a life without pain' the Doctor and his allies reject such an existence. The conclusion to 'Age of Steel' turns on a counterpoint between body, brain and soul. The ideal, utopian future of a world populated by Cybermen is not achieved through simply stuffing a human brain into an (apparently) indestructible metal casing. No individual willingly volunteers for the upgrade and those who have been upgraded must be 'dampened' into obedience for without it, their human feelings will override their cybernetic circuitry. The Doctor defeats the Cybermen by destroying their emotional dampener to reconnect them to their human selves: he says, 'I gave them back their souls. They can see what you've done, Lumic, and it's killing them.' It is human emotion and feeling that defeats the Cybermen; 'the soul' here is the link between the human brain and its former organic body.

In certain key examples, as in 'Asylum of the Daleks', human identity asserts itself despite all attempts to assimilate, upgrade, convert, or exterminate. The case of Yvonne Hartman, the head of Torchwood, in 'Doomsday' demonstrates this assertion of identity, and does so in a way that is distinct from the examples of Sally Phelan or Jacqueline Tyler who refer to their previous embodied existence. As she is taken away for upgrading as a Cyberman, Yvonne repeats, 'I did my duty for Queen and country'. Later in the episode, a single Cyber-form confronts a group of attacking Cybermen, and repeats the same phrase, making it clear that, somehow, aspects of Yvonne's human identity remain, even with her brain in a metal suit. Unlike Sally Phelan and the other Cybermen in the new series episodes, Yvonne's emotional inhibitor is intact; nevertheless, she is able to retain her sense of self and to act independently of any Cyberman programming, and even to fight against other Cybermen. Oswin and Yvonne both manage to retain aspects of human/embodied identity despite traumatic enforced transformation into a new cyborg embodiment. In a sense, they fight against their cyborg embodiment, and against other cyborgs (Daleks or Cybermen). Once again, becoming cyborg offers no improvement or benefit; what is emphasized in all these storylines is the possibility of a continuing existence for the core, 'real' self, despite any cyborg augmentation.

The Season 8 finale 'Death in Heaven' returns again to this theme, killing off companion Clara's boyfriend Danny, and making him a key part of the ensuing story. The Doctor's nemesis The Master – now regenerated as a woman, so becoming the Mistress/'Missy' – creates an army of Cybermen in a dramatically different fashion from John Lumic's process. Instead of putting a human brain into a metal body, Missy's Cybermen are resurrected from dead bodies. The story's central conceit is that Missy has used Time Lord technology to store the minds of the dead, returning them to their bodies with 'a bit of an upgrade' in the form of 'shiny and new' Cyberman armour. Because Missy has moved through time to capture the dead, her resulting army is vast – 'everyone who ever lived […] is now at my command'. These Cybermen are a different form of cyborg than Lumic's creations; they are a combination of organic (resurrected/reconstituted) flesh and metal/technological shell. The narrative suggests that the saved and restored minds (or possibly 'souls') are a vital ingredient in the creation of this Cyber-army; it is necessary to animate the metal/organic bodies with the saved mind/soul. These Cybermen still need to have emotional inhibitors activated in order to eliminate human feelings.

In this scenario, Danny functions as the series' best example of a boundary-confusing cyborg. He is on the threshold between human and cyborg life: neither alive nor dead, he does not show obedience to Missy or to the Doctor. He is 'not under cyber control' but he begs Clara to activate his emotional inhibitor so that he can stop his human feelings. He evokes his human life as a soldier and veteran of Afghanistan, and gives the clearest articulation of the Doctor's complicated involvement in 'battle', calling him 'the blood-soaked general'. Danny is able to connect to the Cyberman hive mind and reveal their plans to make Earth into a world of cyborgs. In his embodiment, too, Danny is both human and Cyberman, removing part of his helmet to show his own face beneath the steel armour. Even after his emotional inhibitor is activated, Danny is still 'the one soldier not obeying' Missy, who is able to override Cyberman programming and command the army to destroy itself and save the people of Earth.

The episode was broadcast in November 2014 at a time of national commemoration of the World War I centenary, and it clearly draws on themes of war, sacrifice and loss – the ranks of Cybermen are described as 'an army' and the setting of a significant part of the episode in a graveyard underlines the aspects of remembrance. It also draws on series history and commemorates a long-standing classic-series character, the Brigadier (played by Nicholas Courtney, who died in 2011). Like Danny, even though he is made into a Cyberman, the Brigadier is able to act against his programming to save his daughter Kate. The Doctor's acknowledgement of his actions, as he formally salutes the Cyber-Brigadier in a poignant moment at the end of the episode, makes this cyborg resurrection an opportunity to celebrate a beloved character and the actor who played him. But the Brigadier as cyborg is a disturbing example of boundary-crossing, something that appeared to unsettle fans of the series more than Danny's transformation (Delgado 2014).[5] As Missy explains, her plan is to transform 'everyone who ever lived' into a Cyberman – and no individual is exempt, including beloved characters like the Brigadier.

In their actions, which are specifically directed at loved ones (Clara, Kate), the cyborg Danny and Brigadier maintain links to their human selves and so complicate and confuse their cyborg identities/bodies. This episode places great emphasis on the possibility that a continuing mind/spirit/soul of an individual might persist through death and into non-human, technological bodies. In this respect, it echoes Moravec's concept of the continuation of organic memory and identity within an entirely technological/mechanical embodiment. Yet it rejects Moravec's theories, because the cyborg embodiment presented here is not a replacement for the organic or for human life. Danny stresses the point that his resurrection into a metal body does not mean that he is alive ('I'm already dead') and he demonstrates no desire to continue to exist as a cyborg.

'When we talked': the TARDIS as Cyborg

The series offers a further possibility for cyborg embodiment, one that is, for once, emphatically not framed as an enemy/adversary. In the Neil Gaiman-authored episode 'The Doctor's Wife', the TARDIS temporarily becomes a human being. The new series has maintained a concept of the TARDIS as a thinking being rather than a machine. It is described as 'telepathic', 'alive' ('The Parting of the Ways'); its powers go beyond what is possible for a mechanical object. Even before 'The Doctor's Wife', cyborg possibilities or potentialities are suggested for the TARDIS. At its simplest, the TARDIS' organic components are the living beings that interact with it; the Doctor and the TARDIS are represented as a partnership, two beings working together. Human beings interact with the TARDIS from time to time, and often create dramatic transformations. In 'Journey's End', with another example of engagement with the classic series, 'a playful, respectful, affectionate dialogue with the myth of *Doctor Who*' (Brooker 2013: 86), a collection of past and present companions become the TARDIS' pilots. In 'Parting of the Ways', companion Rose Tyler's bond with the TARDIS matrix creates a cyborg embodiment that allows Rose's human body to access the technological power of the TARDIS. This cyborg embodiment connects Rose to 'the whole of time and space [...]... all that is... all that was... all that ever could be' and allows her abilities that are, quite literally, super-human (she is able to destroy a Dalek army and to bring Captain Jack Harkness back to life).

The central conceit of 'The Doctor's Wife' is similar to the Rose-TARDIS connection in 'The Parting of the Ways'. The TARDIS matrix – essentially, its 'mind' – is transferred into the body of a woman, Idris. With the TARDIS represented as a 'beautiful' woman wearing 'a wrecked Victorian party dress' as shown in Figure 3 (Gaiman script, in 'Doctor Who Confidential: Bigger on the Inside' 2011), the cybernetic entity is specifically feminized. The notion of the TARDIS as female is noted elsewhere in the series; in 'The Time Warrior' (1973), for example, the Doctor begins to call his ship 'old girl' (Capettini 2012: 148). In the new series, however, the TARDIS is not only feminized but represented as sexually alluring: the Doctor breathes, 'Oh you sexy thing' when he discovers a newly repaired TARDIS in 'The Eleventh Hour' (5.1); Idris reminds the Doctor that when he first encountered the TARDIS, he called it 'the most beautiful thing I'd ever known'; comparing notes with Rose, former companion Sarah Jane Smith asks, 'Does he still stroke bits of the TARDIS?' ('School Reunion' 2.3). Showrunner Steven Moffat reinforces these perceptions, commenting, '[if] the TARDIS

Figure 3: The TARDIS takes embodied form as Idris, 'The Doctor's Wife', *Doctor Who* (6.4)

was a woman [the Doctor]'d be very happy wouldn't he?' ('*Doctor Who* Confidential: Bigger on the Inside' 2011), and indeed, when the Doctor attempts to explain to his current companions that Idris is 'a woman – and she's the TARDIS', Amy wryly retorts, 'Did you wish *really* hard?' Idris is not only an embodiment of the TARDIS but, according to the episode title, the 'wife' of the Doctor. In one sense, this chimes with the sense of 'intimacy' in the 'close, highly privatized relationship' depicted between the Doctor and the TARDIS (Capettini 2012: 157). Emily Capettini argues that the term 'wife' gives the Doctor/TARDIS pairing the sense of 'a constant, loving relationship between equals' (2012: 158). However, the title 'wife' 'cloud[s] feelings of female empowerment by contributing to the stereotype that a woman's status is measured by close relationships to men' (Coile 2013: 94), and it certainly reinforces heteronormativity in the relationship. We can only speculate on how this story might be told differently if the TARDIS were perceived as male or had been transferred into a male body.

Still, the embodiment of the TARDIS in the form of Idris does present a view of the cyborg that is more positive than the examples of Daleks and Cybermen. This female cyborg embodiment allows some of the fundamental aspects of the Doctor's world to be undermined and overturned. Where the Doctor has previously confessed to stealing (or borrowing) the TARDIS ('The Name of the Doctor' 7.13, 'The Big Bang' 5.13), Idris says, 'I stole a Time Lord'; she describes people as 'bigger on the inside', using the recurring comment and terminology that explains the TARDIS. This gives a strong sense of Idris as a personality and intelligence in 'her' own right, which in turn counteracts the notion that the TARDIS is a mechanical device that operates according to the Doctor's authority (Capettini 2012: 153). When the Doctor comments that 'you never took me where I wanted to go' Idris retorts, 'I always took you where you *needed* to go', further overturning the idea of the TARDIS as a broken machine with faulty navigation.

Furthermore, embodiment in a human (female) form allows new experiences for both the Doctor and Idris. This is focused on their ability to communicate: as the Doctor exclaims, 'Look at us – talking! Wouldn't it be amazing if we could always talk?' This ability is so 'amazing' that at the end of the episode, the TARDIS matrix – now restored to the blue police box – briefly reappears in the form of Idris especially to commemorate 'when we talked'. What Gaiman's script emphasizes is the sense that embodied interaction (existence as a living body) allows for more than is available to an entity that is disembodied and 'in the box', despite the powerful nature of that box and the possibilities it allows. This depiction may appear to suggest an essentialist return to the 'pure' organic body; however, the experience of 'when we talked' is only possible because Idris contains technological power, and/or because the TARDIS is contained in a human body – because of cyborg embodiment. It is more unfortunate that some of the positive cyborg embodiment here is undermined through Gaiman's presentation of Idris-as-TARDIS as mentally unstable. The 'wrecked Victorian' costuming lends the character the air of a stereotypical gothic madwoman-in-the-attic, while her confused utterances cause other characters (including the Doctor) to belittle and dismiss her (the Doctor tells her, 'you're just a bitey mad lady').[6] In this episode, while Idris' cyborg embodiment does emphasize the point that a human body is too small to contain the power of the TARDIS, and human language too limiting for such a being, this is filtered through her depiction as a mad, female body.

The embodied TARDIS is a version of cyborg embodiment that can only ever be temporary; so, as with the example of Lisa in *Torchwood*, there are limited possibilities here for more positive representations of the cyborg. Idris remarks that 'I'm not constructed that way [as a person who can talk to another person]. I exist across all space and time and *you* talk and run around and bring home strays.' It is clear that the TARDIS matrix cannot exist *within* a body, or can only do so temporarily; the matrix will destroy an organic host. This is demonstrated in Rose's near-fatal interaction with the TARDIS in 'The Parting of the Ways' as well as in Idris' embodiment of the TARDIS matrix. Rose and Idris each demonstrate the limits of becoming cyborg in this fashion. Rose's bond with the TARDIS gives her power over 'the whole of time and space', but this will kill her, because a human body cannot contain the power of the TARDIS. Similarly, Idris' bond reveals both the limitations of the human body and its extraordinary abilities in the 'amazing' example of embodied speech. It seems to me that 'The Doctor's Wife' does attempt to present a positive version of the cyborg, even though this is overlaid with strong gendered expectations and assumptions. At the same time, this cyborg embodiment maintains the distinction (and returns to the separation) between a fragile human body and a powerful mechanical/technological device.

The examples of cyborg embodiment in this chapter reveal the limitations of the image within the long-standing *Doctor Who* narrative. The frightening, threatening cyborgs in the forms of Daleks and Cybermen are certainly not examples of 'boundary-crossing' freedom. Instead, they represent uncontrollable technology that does not respect boundaries, but violently breaches them through upgrading, conversion or death. The few instances of different kinds of cyborg embodiment still only offer the potential for positive engagement with the image. Oswin as Dalek is not a positive representation, although she is an active female character who displays clever, resourceful and powerful traits (especially in her connection to the Dalek hive mind). Idris as TARDIS is not wholly positive either, partly because of her cyborg embodiment is finite and partly because of her depiction as a Victorian madwoman. Her cyborg representation does trouble some established boundaries, however, especially with regard to customary ways of describing the TARDIS and its functions.

At the same time, the Daleks and Cybermen remain paradoxically popular monsters that recur over and over again in different storylines throughout the new series. The Daleks do not take long to reappear in the opening double episode of the ninth season. Jenna Coleman has an opportunity to revisit her Dalek embodiment as her character Clara is tricked into occupying a Dalek's metal casing ('The Witch's Familiar' 9.2). This, once again, allows some exploration of the sympathetic cyborg – the viewers know that the apparently hostile Dalek is Clara, desperately trying to communicate with the Doctor. This episode recalls Oswin's story from 'Asylum of the Daleks', particularly in the dialogue sequences in which Clara's human utterances – 'it's Clara', 'I am your friend' – are translated through her telepathic link with the Dalek shell and vocalized as 'I am a Dalek' and 'I am your enemy.' Clara's temporary cyborg embodiment here also recalls the many other examples of individuals forcibly embodied as cyborg – Yvonne, Sally, Jackie, Danny and the Brigadier – who still work to assert their distinctive abilities and personalities in the face of technological dominance and the erasure of difference. The vision of cyborg embodiment as a conversion or upgrade into 'total technological assimilation' (Geraghty 2008: 87) connects *Doctor Who*'s cyborgs with those of Chapter 2. In the next chapter, I examine the ways in which *Star Trek*'s narrative confronts the Borg, a literal and ironic embodiment of 'collective' cyborg community and cooperation.

2

Resistance, Assimilation and the Collective: *Star Trek: The Next Generation* and *Voyager*

> We are the Borg. Existence, as you know it, is over. We will add your biological and technological distinctiveness to our own. Resistance is futile. (*Voyager*, 'Scorpion Part I' 3.26)

The recurring *Star Trek* adversaries, the Borg, are the focus of this chapter. From their initial appearance in *Star Trek: The Next Generation* ('Q Who?' 2.16) as a foreboding nemesis, this cyborg race takes on a central antagonistic role within the *Star Trek* series mythology. In their first appearance in *Next Generation*, the Borg figure as one more among the many unfamiliar beings encountered by successive Starfleet crews. The purpose of the original series' 'voyages of the Starship *Enterprise*' was precisely 'to seek out new life and new civilizations', and *Star Trek*'s narrative construction around the ship's 'five-year mission' allowed the storylines to explore meetings between the individuals of Starfleet and a variety of alien life forms. This narrative format continues in the later series *Next Generation* and *Voyager*, setting up viewer expectation that different aliens will continue to be introduced.

In the original series, while specifically cyborg characters do not appear, examples of artificial bodies are present in the storylines of 'What Are Little Girls Made Of?' (1.7) with android duplicates of organic bodies, and 'I, Mudd' (2.8) which features an android-populated planet. Either the androids ('I, Mudd') or their creators ('What Are Little Girls...') have things in common with the Borg of the later *Star Trek* series; in both storylines, the androids threaten to subdue organic life forms and take control of the galaxy. The original series tends to present a more consistently negative view of human interaction with technological beings like robots or androids, in which the latter are beings to be feared, or at least mistrusted. This is evident in the episode 'The Changeling' (2.3) in which a robot spaceprobe is reprogrammed to destroy 'imperfect beings': organic life forms. In such episodes, the *Enterprise*'s Captain Kirk frequently contrasts the mechanical or technological with the organic/human, and the narrative celebrates human (or human-like) creative abilities in the ways Kirk and his fellow officers defeat their technological aggressors.

The representation of the Borg and of other human-machine constructs (especially the character of Data) in more recent *Star Trek* series does complicate these black-and-white divisions of machine and human in the original series. Data, the android Starfleet officer of *Next Generation* and several of the *Star Trek* franchise feature films, is written as a futuristic Pinocchio whose quest to become progressively more human makes him an appealing and sympathetic character. In contrast to the sympathetic portrayal of Data's character, the Borg first appear in *Next Generation* as fearsome adversaries, introduced into the Star Trek narrative as uncomplicated enemy figures. There are similarities to some of *Doctor Who*'s presentations of Cybermen and Daleks in the way the Borg are depicted as the literal embodiment of human fears of technological supremacy and of assimilation and loss of individuality. However, *Star Trek: Voyager* enables a closer examination of the Borg by introducing a former Borg character as a regular Starfleet crew member.

Early encounters between the United Federation of Planets, Starfleet, and these cyborg aliens is framed extremely negatively. Picard's rash boast in 'Q Who?', and Q's retort – bringing the crew forcibly into contact with the Borg – positions the crew of the *Enterprise* (and by extension humanity and its interplanetary allies) as unprepared for the terrifying dangers of the unknown universe, represented by the implacable, relentless Borg. The spin-off series *Voyager* emphasizes this still more strongly: *Voyager* is not simply on a journey of exploration but, after an encounter with alien technology, is stranded in the Delta Quadrant, an unexplored, unknown part of the universe, some 70,000 light years from Federation space. It is estimated that their journey 'home' will take them 75 years. Where Picard's initial encounter with the Borg underlined the point that Starfleet and the Federation of Planets is small and defenceless in comparison with the Borg, *Voyager*'s narrative reduces Starfleet and the Federation to the crew of a single ship, potentially at the mercy of aggressive aliens.

Since *Voyager*'s premise locates the starship literally *outside* Federation space after it is stranded in the Delta Quadrant, its narrative, as Elaine Graham notes, unfolds in 'a more complex universe [...] where the confidence of earlier humanist precepts is beginning to disintegrate' and its narratives offer a 'more ambivalent attitude [...] towards many of the assumptions of earlier series' (2002: 149). The series presents a slightly more diverse crew, for example, with a woman in command of the ship, and people of different races and species in key roles of authority: Native American Chakotay as First Officer, human/Klingon Torres as Chief Engineer, Vulcan Tuvok as Science Officer.[1] *Voyager*'s casting and its storylines illuminate the way the earlier *Star Trek* series were founded 'on a particular constellation of concepts – progress, perfection and social harmony – that all revolve around essentialist definitions of the self and of human nature' which tend to 'efface difference between people, classes, and genders' (Boyd 1996: 95). It is evident that, while 'pluralism and peaceful coexistence amid cultural and racial diversity are [...] the core themes of the original series', this 'vision of exemplary humanity [...] is ultimately a vision of homogeneity, rather than radical diversity' (Graham 2002: 135)[2] – and a 'homogeneity' that is 'bourgeois, white, rational masculinity' (Graham 2002: 141), 'humanity [...] coded predominantly as white' (Ott and Aoki 2015: 54). Katrina Boyd notes that *Next Generation* 'has difficulty addressing contemporary issues of radical difference' (1996: 95) and this is a difficulty that extends to other *Star Trek* series. The tendency to approach 'exemplary humanity' from a homogenized, white, masculine viewpoint encourages a treatment of different forms of embodiment – perhaps especially cyborg embodiment – as threatening and dangerous, rather than as potentially liberating or transforming.

The context of *Next Generation* and *Voyager* places cyborg characters within a futuristic setting. This is a point of contrast with other series I look at in this book, such as *Bionic Woman* and *Terminator: The Sarah Connor Chronicles*, in which cyborg characters appear in a contemporary, real-world setting. Cyborgs in such narratives may possess cutting-edge technological augmentations (like Jaime, the Bionic Woman), or may embody future possibilities (like the time-travelling Terminators). In the *Star Trek* narratives, the technology used and incorporated by the Borg is more advanced than that used by Starfleet or by the Federation of Planets, but Starfleet and the Federation use technology that is advanced by twentieth and twenty-first century standards. It is perhaps curious that in *Next Generation* and *Voyager*, '[t]wenty-fourth century humanity displays a remarkable retrogressive resistance to the encroachment of digital, prosthetic and medical technologies on the integrity of the human body' (Graham 2002: 148). We might expect to see such technologies in use in a science fiction narrative set in the future; indeed, in *Next Generation*, we see the character Geordi using a technological prosthesis that stimulates his optic nerve, and gives him sight (though Geordi is an exception; it is difficult to locate other examples of characters who incorporate, use or add technological or mechanical parts to their organic bodies). The assimilation carried out by the Borg is imagined as an assault of technological devices on the organic body. In the example of Geordi's use of optic-nerve stimulation technology, Geordi is (for the most part) in control of his technological augmentation: he can choose not to wear it, for example. This technology is imperfect; it causes him pain, and so is not presented as an improvement on human/organic sight – or even as its equal. In contrast, those assimilated as Borg do not choose to have technological augmentation or mechanical appendages; those aspects of their Borg embodiment seem to be added according to the decision of the hive mind.

Elaine Graham describes '[the Borg's] corruption of the ontological hygiene of the body [...] achieved by means of invasive technological implanting, and the mind by the immersion of the individual in a collective consciousness' (2002: 133). *Voyager*, especially, frames Borg embodiment as the infection of the body by technology. The Borg's technology does not replace the organic body as with *Doctor Who*'s Cybermen or Daleks; Borg technology acts as a literal additional appendage. These cyborgs 'assimilate' technology into – or more accurately, *onto* – the organic body. These augmentations are very obviously displayed on the body in the form of mechanical arms or legs, ear- and eye-pieces allowing augmented hearing and vision, and other forms of technological hardware such as wiring and tubing. Although the Borg statement of intent upon attacking any likely-looking species cites that species' 'distinctiveness' as the factor that interests the Borg, the visual representation of these cyborgs is not as amalgamations of different organic forms but as amalgamations of the organic and the technological. Despite their proliferation of technological appendages, the organic body remains as a kind of foundation for the embodiment of all Borg drones. Visually, the Borg appear as monster cyborgs caught between the technological and the organic.

Some critics find puzzling the Borg's popularity as recurring adversaries in the *Star Trek* universe. Mark Dery, for example, explains their popularity as symptomatic of 'a creeping body loathing congruent with the growing awareness that wires are twined through all our lives' (in Collado-Rodriguez 2002: 73–4, note 4). This does not quite ring true; a viewer may well be fascinated by the Borg characters for many different reasons, and, as we know from discussions about television horror, it is possible to enjoy the experience of watching characters and situations that are troubling and frightening (Hills 2005; Jowett and Abbott 2013). The Borg speak to particular anxieties about the relationship between body and technology in similar ways to *Doctor Who*'s Cybermen, though with important distinctions. While the Cybermen's 'creeping technology' assimilates gradually, so that humans become automatons by degrees (Tennant, in '*Doctor Who Confidential: Cybermen*,' 2006), with the Borg, technology pounces without warning. It is paradoxical that viewers do find enjoyment in watching the Borg in *Star Trek*, even though the aims and society of these threatening characters are entirely opposed to the series' themes of exploration and freedom. The threat of assimilation and re-embodiment as cyborg drones is something that all *Star Trek* narratives present as repulsive and fearful. However, what the series' narratives depict with 'loathing' is not cyborg embodiment per se but the process by which individuals are assimilated as cyborg drones, bound in a collective 'hive mind'. The threat of being joined in a Borg Collective and the resulting loss of individual selfhood is frequently portrayed as more terrifying than the prospect of cyborg embodiment itself.

In some respects, *Voyager*'s introduction of a Borg character as a series regular, and eventually as a crew member, fits with the presentation of the starship *Voyager* as a place that allows very different individuals to band together in collaboration and cooperation against unknown adversaries. *Voyager*'s representation of Seven of Nine foregrounds the paradoxical visual representation of the female cyborg, with an apparently artificial and asexual character costumed and presented in a body-revealing, sexualized way. Her presence over several seasons enables her to be seen as an individual, as a regular, trusted crew member, and as part of the *Voyager* community, all of which troubles the classification of cyborg as 'other'. Such key points within the narratives of more than one series complicate a simple reading of Borg assimilation as a negative process.

Despite the issues of homogeneity and difficulties with difference, and the fears surrounding technology and loss of individuality that connect with the Borg, it is possible to look at Borg embodiment in a different way. The Borg are embodied with organic flesh as well as technological appendages, and they 'still need some fleshly parts to go on living and assimilating people and planets in their never ending quest for galactic supremacy' (Collado-Rodriguez 2002: 74). We can certainly read the Borg as examples of 'alienation from the [organic] body' (Consalvo 2004: 191), but a counter-argument is possible because the Borg are body as well as mind, and flesh as well as technology: they experience technology through and within the body. They are not separated from technology, nor are they separate from each other. The hive mind connects them, and Borg bodies join together in patterns dictated by the hive, the work unit, or the Borg Queen, 'constituted and reconstituted in different configurations in relation of the discursive arrangement of the occasion' (Gunkel 2000: 345). Their collective status might then be seen as 'offering a way out of solitary existence' (Consalvo 2004: 199), a possibility that *Voyager* explores in several episodes. It is possible, then, to read some examples of Borg existence, including that of Seven of Nine, in ways that run counter to the primary *Star Trek* narrative, giving a more positive view of this form of cyborg embodiment. *Next Generation*, however, has a more consistent perception of the Borg as technological threat.

Locutus of Borg: Embodiment on the Technological Borderline

The Borg appear in *The Next Generation* as fearsome, terrifying and entirely alien adversaries, viewed from the standpoint of the homogenized society represented by the Federation. In the now-famous double episode 'The Best of Both Worlds' (3.26/4.1), the order of that universe is overturned when the *Enterprise*'s captain, the urbane and cultured Jean-Luc Picard, is captured by the Borg and assimilated. As 'Locutus of Borg,' he becomes the Borg spokes-entity; his knowledge of Starfleet logistics is exploited. With Picard's knowledge, the Borg are able to mount a large-scale attack on Starfleet and the Federation, resulting in a comprehensive defeat for Starfleet (the Borg's single cube destroys all but one of the opposing fleet, dramatized in *Star Trek: Deep Space Nine*, 'Emissary' 1.1–2). The fact that the end of 'The Best of Both Worlds, Part 1' is also the second season finale leaves Picard in cyborg limbo, with even the series writers unsure of the conclusion to his story (Couch 2015).

In 'Best of Both Worlds' the male body becomes the site of trauma and breakdown; the Collective and the hive mind subsume the individual. Picard is presented in the *Next Generation* narrative as a very individual character indeed, with distinctive traits – such as reading Shakespeare or drinking tea – that are coded as European (although, of course, such distinctions of nationality are supposed to have been left behind in the *Star Trek* universe). However, Picard, though individual and distinctive, is part of the hierarchy, an insider, a leader, authority figure and role model to his crew. His transformation creates a breakdown of boundaries and of the established series narrative, as he is stripped of power and control and made to embody a key adversary.

As Borg, Locutus/Picard is a figure located *on* the boundary between the organic and the technological. Louis J. Kern points out that 'Locutus is a kind of half-breed', a partly-technological cyborg retaining more organic flesh than is usual for a Borg drone (2000: 103). Ultimately, though, this narrative turns away from the concept of the cyborg as organic/technological embodiment to a notion of cyborg existence 'based in a Cartesian conception of "the human" as "will" or "mind", which enables Picard to overcome his bodily transformation' since his mind/will takes precedence over anything that has been done to his organic body (Cranny-Francis 2013: 47). Despite his cyborg embodiment, Picard's mind/will persists and is able to communicate with the other officers, 'initiat[ing] contact' with Data and 'suggest[ing] a course of action' to defeat the Borg, so that in fact, Picard continues to captain the *Enterprise* from within his cyborg body. Indeed, once rescued and restored to a fully organic state, Picard reveals that he remembers 'everything' from his time as Borg. In the film *Star Trek: First Contact*, there is a suggestion that his connection to the Borg hive mind also persists, in some way; he 'can still hear [the Borg] song' and tells the Borg Queen, 'I remember you'. In this sense, Picard remains on the border between human and Borg, the 'half-breed' that the Borg Queen intended: 'You wanted more than just another Borg drone. You wanted a human being with a mind of his own, who could bridge the gulf between humanity and the Borg. You wanted a counterpart, but I resisted. I fought you.' It appears that this aspect of the Borg narrative persists in *Voyager*, in episodes where the Borg Queen attempts to coerce Seven into performing the same function, 'bridging' – or indeed, boundary-crossing – the divisions of human and cyborg.

We might compare Picard's partial transformation and restoration with *Voyager* captain Kathryn Janeway's in 'Unimatrix Zero II' (7.1) and 'Endgame' (7.25–26). In 'Unimatrix Zero', as illustrated in Figure 4, Janeway is partly assimilated and augmented with Borg technological components, as are her officers Tuvok and Torres. Thanks to a 'neural suppressant', the three officers do not succumb to the Borg hive mind, and they make use of the Borg modifications to carry out their own plans. Torres uses the metal spines issuing from her hand to interface with the Borg ship's 'central plexus' and inject a virus designed to restore individuality to some Borg drones. In 'Endgame', Janeway allows herself to be injected with Borg nanoprobes in order to infect the Borg Queen – and the whole Collective – with a virus designed to destroy them all. In these two examples, partial assimilation is a route to tactical success. Furthermore, the characters who allow themselves to become cyborg in this way are women and alien species played by actors of colour, disrupting the established hierarchies of Starfleet and the *Star Trek* universe.

figure 4: Captain Janeway allows herself to become Borg to carry out her mission, 'Unimatrix Zero II', *Voyager* (7.1)

Seven of Nine: Embodiment as Borg, Embodiment as Female

Seven of Nine first appears as a Borg representative, carrying out a similar role to Locutus/Picard, during a period of truce between Borg and *Voyager* while they battle the fearsome and mysterious Species 8472 ('Scorpion, Parts I and II' 3.26/4.1). As a Borg drone, the character exhibits what viewers know are typical Borg characteristics of logic, technological ability and a ruthless drive to assimilate other species, something the drone attempts at the conclusion of the double episode. After being 'severed from the Collective' ('The Gift' 4.2), Seven presents a unique combination of cyborg embodiment in conjunction with human characteristics. In *Voyager*, Seven of Nine has the potential to embody difference and 'a disruptive – at least in part – radical performativity' (Leaver 2015: 71) that cuts across the *Star Trek* series' tendency to refuse and reject technological transformations of the body. Even so, and as Tama Leaver notes, Seven's potential as a radical cyborg is itself undercut in later seasons of *Voyager*, almost as though the series could not support such a boundary-crossing transformation of the *Star Trek* universe's status quo.

As Borg, Seven of Nine's body is integrated with technological modifications with a metal plate over one ear and a laser implant jutting out from one eye socket; the head is bald and the skin lacks pigmentation. The body is encased in metal armour and the feet in heavy boots; Figure 5 shows this Borg representation. Seven has some internal modifications too, chiefly the 'cortical node' that prevents drones from redeveloping individuality, by dampening emotions. Once Seven's connection to the Collective is broken, the character's appearance changes to reflect her transition from Borg to human, a process that continues for the remainder of the series. Now represented as female, she no longer has ear, head or eye implants, but even with '82% of Borg hardware' removed she retains some Borg technology on her cheekbone, temple and hand ('The Gift') and retains her cortical node ('Imperfection' 7.2; 'Human Error' 7.18). Seven is still able

Figure 5: Seven of Nine first appears as Borg, 'Scorpion Parts I and II', *Voyager* (3.26/4.1)

to interface with technological devices or to puncture the skin of other beings with metal prongs or 'tubules' that occasionally emerge from the back of her hand. In these respects, Seven's visual representation situates the character – like Picard – between the organic and the technological/mechanical.

Seven's physical appearance in *Voyager* is a point of contrast with all other Borg characters in the *Star Trek* universe. In *Next Generation*, the Borg are portrayed as gender-neutral, 'not a he, not a she, not like anything you've ever seen' ('Q Who?'), although their portrayal tends to default to the masculine since male actors portray them (Consalvo 2004: 179, 183). In *Voyager*, Borg drones played by female actors do appear more frequently (for instance, in 'Survival Instinct', 6.2, and 'Unimatrix Zero').[3] By contrast, the Borg Queen appears in the film *First Contact* and in occasional *Voyager* episodes with a shapely 'techno-femme fatale body' that is overtly sexualized and feminized (Consalvo 2004: 184). Seven's embodiment as part-cyborg, yet not Borg, allows the character to retain an all-over bodysuit that is tight fitting and revealing, despite the fact that it covers most of her flesh. Seven of Nine's visual appearance informs and, in some cases, closes off critical analysis. Stacy Gillis cites Seven as an example of stereotypically female-gendered cyborg embodiment with her 'sexualized, sometimes hysterical [female] body' (2007a: 209), but does not comment further; similarly, Sue Short dismisses the character, noting only that Seven is 'clearly intended as eye candy for the boys' (2011: 191) – and possibly for some girls, too. There is certainly a purpose in the character's creation and casting; Kate Mulgrew, reflecting on her first sight of actor Jeri Ryan in costume as Seven, describes the result as, 'va-va-va-voom […] I knew our ratings were going to go *up*' ('Seven of Nine Jeri Ryan Interview' 2013). There is much more to say than Short allows about the character's physical representation, which is similar in many ways to the gender-neutral character Illyria in the series *Angel* (Calvert 2012). Seven's character in no way follows the Borg Queen in terms of her performance of gender. While Seven is costumed as a hypersexualized female, as Borg she is asexual, and as human she is immature, with the psychology of a six-year-old girl, the age she was when the Borg assimilated her. The series, then, manages to have it both ways: the 'va-va-va-voom' of the actor in costume, and the contrast of that body-revealing costume with a character who does not conform to human categories of gender – who does not think of displaying her body in a provocative way. Mia Consalvo argues that 'for Seven, redeveloping her humanity is accomplished through the appropriate gendering of her body and self' (2004: 185) but this is a slow process. For much of *Voyager*, Seven's appearance is at odds with her logical, mechanical cyborg character.

Seven's process of becoming or re-becoming human is complicated by the means by which she is 'rescued' from the Borg. Acting as a single speaker for the Borg – and so with the status of an ambassador – she is 'severed from the Collective' following an attempt to assimilate *Voyager*'s crew ('Scorpion Part II'). It has been established through examples in *Next Generation* that a single Borg drone, once separated from the Collective, can regain its previous organic characteristics and memories. Picard, following his temporary assimilation, resumes his life as Starfleet officer ('Best of Both Worlds Part 2'); a separated Borg becomes an individual with a name ('I, Borg' 5.23). In the aftermath of Seven's separation from the Collective, we are offered the opportunity to consider Borg embodiment from Seven's point of view, as well as from the point of view of Janeway and the others on *Voyager*. For Janeway and the others, this is a rescue and their positive action will restore Seven to her 'true' human self. For Seven, this is a second assimilation resulting in the loss of abilities and connections that she values. Elaine Graham notes, 'Seven of Nine is resistant to a transformation that involves the acquisition of what she regards as human imperfection' (2002: 151). We can interpret Seven's refusal in stronger terms, and from her own point of view, not as 'acquisition' but as regression. As human, Seven will lose most of her cyborg enhancement and, crucially, her link to the Collective.

Seven's example further highlights the parallels between the Federation and the Borg. As noted, the *Star Trek* universe's 'vision of exemplary humanity [...] is ultimately a vision of homogeneity, rather than radical diversity' (Graham 2002: 135). The Federation requires other species to conform – or assimilate – to its ways. In a sense, both the Federation and the Borg occupy 'the same moral plane' (Consalvo 2004: 197) though with a twist: '[t]he colonising and assimilation [sic] functions of the Federation and the colonising and assimilating functions of the Borg are inverse reflections of one another' (Russell and Wolski 2001). Seven readily identifies this point when she challenges Janeway, 'You are no different than the

Borg' ('The Gift'). Janeway requires Seven to assimilate; 'she will become human, even if it requires force to achieve this object' (Russell and Wolski 2001). Immediately following Seven's separation from the Collective, the character is obviously distressed at her changed embodiment, and states her wishes very clearly: 'We [Seven] do not want to be what you are. Return us to the Collective!' ('The Gift'). In writing about Seven as 'she', it is worth noting that this is the gender designation given or assigned to Seven by Janeway and the others on *Voyager*; it is likely not the designation Seven would choose.[4] In 'The Gift', her Borg identity is particularly evident in her pronoun use: having no concept of the single, individual self, Seven says, 'we', while Janeway, the Doctor, and others use 'she'. Similarly, Seven refers to her child self as 'the girl' or 'her', marking a distinction between the two identities. She refuses to adopt her human name, Annika, but consistently refers to herself as Seven of Nine for the rest of the series narrative, making a conscious choice to do so ('Collective' 6.16). The continuation of her 'designation' as Seven of Nine, like her continued cyborg embodiment, puts the character on the boundary between Borg and human identities.

Community and Collective: Cyborg and Non-Cyborg Connections

Seven's presence on *Voyager* (both ship and series) troubles established Starfleet, Federation or series concepts, and allows them to be explored in new ways. In this sense, Seven can be viewed as a transgressive cyborg that crosses and recrosses boundaries between human and machine, organic and technological, and in so doing illuminates both sides of the divide. We see in the debates of 'The Gift' that Seven offers a new perspective on cyborg existence as part of the Borg hive mind. While the narratives of *Next Generation* and *Voyager* frame assimilation into the hive mind as a catastrophic loss of identity and individuality, Seven's perspective cuts across this. For Seven, the hive mind has been a source of strength and community. Indeed, from such a perspective 'Borg assimilation offers the opportunity for upgrading the fragile human species' and 'promises vast improvements in human life' (Gunkel 2000: 93). Other *Voyager* episodes offer new insights into similar cyborg communities, and in some episodes the process of cyborg assimilation, with its access to the hive mind, is revealed to offer some positive potential.

We might consider ways in which the episode 'Unity' (3.17), located midway through the series' third season, and so pre-dating Seven's first appearance, works to pave the way for the inclusion of Seven's sympathetic Borg character as a regular series cast member at the beginning of the following season. 'Unity' focuses on a group of people who are attempting to establish a new society on an isolated planet. A former scientist, the human (and female) Riley Frasier, acts as the society's spokesperson, introducing Chakotay to their 'cooperative' existence based 'on tolerance, shared responsibility and mutual respect'. As the episode continues, Chakotay discovers that the people of the cooperative are former Borg, severed from the Collective after they crash-landed on the planet.

While their rediscovered physical embodiment is represented as positive – 'we were free', 'everything was new again' – the loss of the cyborg hive mind has returned these individuals to the entrenched attitudes of their own species. Antagonism between species threatens the whole society; as Riley tells Chakotay, 'It's not exactly a United Federation.' 'Unity' makes the point that individuals can be programmed in certain ways whether they are cyborg or not, and the violence between different factions of the supposed 'cooperative' shows that this programming can be difficult or impossible to overcome. The example of Oram, a Romulan, working with Riley, a human, offers hope that different species can cooperate, despite their past tradition or programming. However, this episode offers a more complex view on cyborg community, whether Collective or 'Cooperative'. These former Borg wish to recreate a version of the hive mind, using a 'neural network' that will unite them in harmony. This is a realization, in a slightly different form, of the Borg's 'utopian' collective project. Riley describes the former hive mind in strongly utopian terms: 'we had no ethnic conflict, there was no crime, no hunger, no health problems, we lived as one harmonious family' with a 'unique ability to cooperate and problem solve'. Janeway reacts with scepticism, noting that Riley's 'family' was 'bent on the violent assimilation of innocent cultures', and she refuses to assist them. Viewers are likely to have a more sympathetic reaction, since we have seen a version of the hive mind in action, when members of the cooperative create a temporary neuroelectric field to heal Chakotay's injuries near the beginning of the episode. In this way, the hive mind has been shown as benevolent, but the new Cooperative only achieve their aim by using their established link to take control of Chakotay's mind. Their permanent link includes those who fought against the Cooperative as well as those who wished to restore the connection, and so they make their new Cooperative through other kinds of force or assimilation. The reinstated hive mind is emphasized when the Cooperative speaks with one voice at the conclusion of the episode, underlining the point that their return to this form of cyborg embodiment means a loss of individuality even as it enables a return to unity.

'Survival Instinct' (6.2) further troubles the supposed utopian vision of a perfect life as an assimilated cyborg with a hive mind. As in 'Unity', a group of four former Borg have been severed from the Collective and separated from the hive mind; however, they continue to be able to hear each other's thoughts. This time, their mental proximity is a source of conflict and distress; each individual longs to be alone, separate and silent, to the point that they choose death over a continuing existence in their collective of four. Flashback sequences reveal that the four, with Seven, were temporarily marooned without a connection to the Collective, and that Seven, regressed to her age at assimilation, returned them all to the security of the hive mind by forcibly re-bonding them. Seven comes to realize that her action created their permanent bond, and ensured that they could never be separated. This episode dramatizes the Borg society's erasure of public and private space: no Borg space is private, and Borg do not engage in 'activities that would be considered private' (Consalvo 2004: 188). Seven's actions create a complete erasure of private space for these four individuals.

Cyborg Monstrosity: 'Unimatrix Zero'

A further development on the idea of cyborg community offers yet another viewpoint on the monstrous cyborg nature of the Borg. The 'Unimatrix Zero' double episode (6.26/7.1) reveals a virtual world that is accessible only to Borg who possess a certain mutation. Once in the virtual world – which these mutated individuals visit while in regeneration mode, or, in human equivalent, in sleep – they regain their organic embodiment from before their assimilation as Borg. They are not bound by the hive mind but are free to be individuals. '[Unimatrix Zero is] our sanctuary. When we are here, our thoughts are our own.'

Unimatrix Zero is a virtual scenario that can be read as a utopian 'no-place' or a dream space. In cyberfictions and writings on cyberculture, virtual reality tends to exhibit disengagement from the physical world and from concrete embodiment. In cyberpunk narratives like William Gibson's *Neuromancer* or the Wachowskis' *The Matrix*, a virtual world allows individuals to move beyond their abilities in the physical world, and in some cases to escape their physical bodies and corporeal limitations altogether. Connection with a virtual space makes an individual into a cyborg, and a virtual self becomes 'a version of and a container for the self' (Hayles 1994: 176), but that version is not able to reproduce embodied experience (Sofia 1992: 57). What, then, happens to cyborgs who access a virtual space? For the mutated Borg, Unimatrix Zero is the antithesis of cyborg embodiment. It appears as a natural outdoor space, visualized as a beautiful forest leading on to a beach. The individuals who meet there have no technological appendages or augmentations, or any sign of their cyborg embodiment in the physical world. In this way, too, Unimatrix Zero functions as a utopian space allowing individuals to be their 'true' selves, unaffected by their physical aspect as Borg. The mutation that connects Borg drones in Unimatrix Zero is monstrosity from a Borg viewpoint, in particular because it causes disengagement from the Collective. With the help of *Voyager*'s crew, the mutated Borg can be separated from the hive mind and restored to an individual identity in the physical world, but in order to escape detection and death, they must give up their connection to their virtual utopia-world, and to the others who are like them. The mutated drones become fully monstrous within the Collective as individuals who are in control of their own thoughts and actions, but who retain Borg augmentation and abilities.

When Seven first appears in the virtual space of Unimatrix Zero, she retains her real-world appearance, her Borg implants and sleek, formal hairstyle. In that virtual space, however, individuals can choose how to appear, and they tend not to appear as cyborg, but as their organic embodied selves. As Seven returns repeatedly to Unimatrix Zero over the time-period of the double episode, her appearance changes. The virtual world allows her to return to her human identity as Annika Hansen. Seven's virtual representation as Annika has a softer and, arguably, more traditionally feminine look, her loose, flowing blonde hair a particular contrast to Seven's usual severe chignon style (Consalvo 2004: 186). Although her clothing is more 'feminine' in colour, with purples and mauves predominant, paradoxically less of Annika's body is on display in her virtual-world outfit of trousers and loose top. Unimatrix Zero provides a space for the asexual, mechanized Borg to be embodied in different ways, to take on the appearance of their original species and genders, and so be their 'true selves' in bodily terms as well as in their minds. This offers a different reading of cyborg embodiment, one that allows the individual to experience both freedom in a virtual space and the rediscovery of aspects of their corporeal existence. In this sense, the mutated Borg enact Elizabeth Grosz's description of corporeality as 'an open materiality, a set of (possibly infinite) tendencies and potentialities which may be developed' within or upon bodies that are 'neither "blank" nor programmed'; these boundary-crossing cyborgs turn towards corporeality as a means of expressing individuality and personhood (1994: 191, 190). In her previous visits to Unimatrix Zero, while she was still a Borg drone, Seven/Annika developed a close relationship with another mutated Borg, Axum, who appears as a male humanoid in the virtual space. This aspect of the storyline shows that Seven/Annika has been able to develop as an adult woman through her experiences in virtual space. In virtuality, Annika and Axum are able to have a romantic relationship: while they are *not* embodied, they are able to have experiences that connect or reconnect with the body (friendship, love, sex). These examples stand as positive reconnections to embodied life; however, this episode narrative revises or rewrites some of Seven's established character traits and presents her in more conventionally gendered ways. She sees the error of her ways in rejecting a heterosexual romantic relationship, and is able to rekindle her relationship with Axum – a relationship which has only ever existed in a virtual environment. By the end of the double episode, Unimatrix Zero is not quite the replacement for embodied life that it had been: 'it seemed sufficient, before' says Seven. She is humanized (feminized) through her virtual identity as Annika, and through her romantic, thwarted love affair with Axum whose embodied form is separated from hers by a considerable distance (he is in a Borg cube on the edge of 'fluidic space' – the *Voyager* equivalent of 'here be dragons'). However, this storyline begins to erode Seven's cyborg embodiment, especially the potential she has for 'radical performativity' (Leaver 2015: 66).

The presentation of Seven as Annika in the virtual utopia of Unimatrix Zero reinscribes her as stereotypically feminine, and distances her from her cyborg embodiment. This persists through the remainder of the series. Seven continues to experiment with romantic possibilities in virtual spaces, using *Voyager*'s holodeck programming to enter other imaginary worlds and play out romantic scenarios. Here, she develops an imaginary, virtual, very feminine persona with loose, flowing hair and a figure-hugging red dress ('Human Error' 7.18). Seven's behaviour in the series finale, in which she sets out a picnic for Chakotay, is uncharacteristic enough that the viewer may well expect to discover that she is once more experimenting with an imaginary holodeck scenario; it is bewildering to discover that this scene happens in the physical world, and to hear Seven declare that she is willing to experience human emotions ('Endgame'). Examples such as these 'contradict and/or undermine the strong reading of Seven of Nine' especially in regard to 'her relationship with [...] Chakotay (the normalizing heterosexual male love interest)' (Leaver 2015: 66). By the end of the series, Seven is no longer the gender-neutral cyborg but a fully-functioning human female. The narrative links this final stage in her human development to her experiences in Unimatrix Zero, but we can see that Seven is 'assimilated' back into humanity through other relationships that position her as child and as parent.

Re-assimilating the Cyborg: Seven of Nine as Parent and as Child

In contrast to Seven's highly feminized physical representation, her psychological representation is often presented as immature or childlike. This is fitting for a character who was assimilated as Borg at an early age, and never developed mentally; it is shown in examples of child and adolescent Borg characters like Icheb ('Child's Play' 6.19, 'Collective'). In her first appearances in Season 4, 'Seven is immediately positioned by the Captain as a wayward child, needing to be brought into line with the "family's" goals and beliefs' (Leaver 2015: 70) and viewed as incapable of making her own decisions ('The Gift'). Seven undertakes relationships with others in a child-identity; it is significant that she spends a good deal of time with the mixed-species human–Ktarian child Naomi Wildman. While Seven is read as solitary and friendless, 'unable to connect with *any* individual for friendship or solace' (Consalvo 2004: 186), this is only true if we look for adult friendships and romantic/sexual relationships. Seven's relationship with Naomi can be read as a friendship between two children. It is framed in this way quite clearly when Seven involuntarily regresses to a child identity, one of those she assimilated while a Borg, and spends time playing a board game with Naomi ('Infinite Regress' 5.7). At the conclusion of that episode, returned to her single identity once more, Seven expresses an interest in learning the same board game, something that suggests she would like to spend more time playing with Naomi. The bond of friendship between the two is also strongly in evidence when Naomi comes to Janeway with suggestions for ways to rescue Seven when she has returned to the Borg under duress ('Dark Frontier I and II' 5.15/16). Seven is, similarly, in the position of child in her relationship with Janeway, and this relationship develops into a mentor/mentee connection as well as what is arguably a mother/daughter bond with Janeway figuring as 'the once absent and rediscovered mother figure' (Leaver 2015: 66).[5]

In later *Voyager* episodes, Seven is repositioned as adult or parent in regard to other Borg or former Borg characters. This adult repositioning shifts Seven's child–child friendship with Naomi. When Seven is placed in the position of parent/carer for a group of young former Borg, the human-Ktarian Naomi is included as one of the group of children ('Collective'). Seven cannot continue to be one of the children if she is supposed to be the adult, parent figure in charge of guiding them. In an earlier episode, Seven is very clearly positioned as a mother-figure to a Borg drone, and the narrative just as clearly pushes her character towards a possibly 'feminine' identity as teacher and nurturer ('Drone' 5.2).

'Drone' is especially interesting for the ways in which it reexamines Seven's cyborg being in relation to her developing humanity (and thus her femininity). Seven is positioned as one of the 'parents' of a being that is grown from Borg and hologram components combined with human DNA, although 'parentage' is a loose definition of the events that lead to the creation of this being. Unknown to the *Voyager* crew, the Doctor's hologram 'mobile emitter' – the device that allows his hologram to move from place to place – is contaminated with Seven's nanoprobes after a transporter malfunction. These Borg nanoprobes begin to assimilate the emitter and parts of the science lab, then extract a tissue sample from a passing crew member, and create a maturation chamber to incubate a Borg drone. The new drone, 'One', emerges from the chamber as a fully-grown cyborg like Seven; it behaves and speaks in Borg fashion, 'We are Borg. State our designation.' Having refused to kill the drone while it incubated,[6] Janeway charges Seven with its education and socialization.[7] Throughout the episode, Seven is very clearly identified as 'mother' (and the hologram Doctor as 'father') to One; for example, Neelix tells One 'You have your mother's sense of humour.' Seven, the being who exists between human and cyborg, is usually the different, alien 'other' on *Voyager*. In 'Drone', she becomes the point of connection between human and Borg – between the rest of the crew and One.

Indeed, the episode highlights Seven's positioning with regard to the rest of the wholly-organic individuals on *Voyager*. The beginning and end of the episode finds Seven looking into a mirror. At these points in the narrative, Seven is a lone cyborg, the only individual on the ship who exists on the borderline between organic and machine embodiment, and the only individual who possesses her combination of organic and machine. In the episode's middle section, though, Seven is in a group of two, as she acts as mentor, teacher and mother-figure for One. Again, a bond is clearly in evidence. When the drone insists on sacrificing himself to save the *Voyager* crew, Seven begs him not to, repeating 'You are hurting me' – an unusual statement from Seven. Like the mirror scenes, this scene of One's sacrifice echoes and parallels an earlier scene. On its activation, Seven struggles to communicate with the drone until she establishes a direct 'neural interface' with it, at which point it attempts to assimilate all of her knowledge. Seven commands it to disengage, saying, 'You must comply…you are hurting me'. In the later scene, as Seven begs One not to sacrifice himself, she repeats, 'You must comply…please, you are hurting me'. The physical hurt of the first scene becomes mental/psychological grief in the last, and it seems that this aspect of the narrative is intended to be read as a development in Seven's emotional state. She comes closer to her human, organic self, and this is achieved through the process of parenting, specifically mothering.

To return to the opening and closing mirror scenes, we can read emotional development here too. In the opening scene, Seven looks into the mirror while forcing her face into a smile. That is not a customary expression for Seven, who usually maintains a neutral or more serious expression, and on her face the smile looks artificial and unnatural. In the closing scene, Seven turns off the Borg regeneration alcove that One had used, then passes in front of the mirror, stops, and looks at her own face: she is crying. This expression of grief appears authentic and authentically *human* as she responds to the loss of her fellow individual Borg who was constructed as her child. 'Drone' encourages a view of Seven as parent and as mother, and suggests – however problematically – that such experiences will enable Seven to reconnect with her identity as a human being. In the terms of the series narrative, such progress would see Seven crossing the human/machine boundary, leaving her cyborg embodiment to return to a fully human/organic mode, and the fact that at the series finale she decides to have her cortical node removed indicates that Seven is actively contemplating such a return.

Seven takes on the child role in other relationships. The double episode 'Dark Frontier I and II' positions Seven as child in her connection with the Borg Queen, and contrasts this with the example of Janeway as surrogate mother. Flashbacks in these episodes show Seven's real childhood, too, her human identity as six-year-old Annika, and her life with her scientist parents. 'Dark Frontier' fills in her human history, allowing Seven to reveal feelings of grief, anger and fear associated with this part of her life. Her parents' scientific study of the Borg ended with the family being assimilated: 'Because of their arrogance I was raised by Borg'. The Borg Queen attempts to reclaim Seven, not to reassimilate her, but to make use of her uniqueness; she is 'valuable with [her] individuality intact'. The Queen singles out Seven and initiates special, secret communication with her – secret as it occurs while Seven is regenerating (in human terms, asleep) ('Dark Frontier I'), and calls Seven 'still mine' ('Dark Frontier II'). As I have discussed, the closeness of the Borg existence is imagined as a heightened and utopian version of the family group that is 'so close that we can hear each other's thoughts' ('Unimatrix Zero II'). For Seven, the possibility of rediscovering her family is literally true: the Queen tells Seven that her father is still with them, and shows Seven his embodied form, a Borg among the other drones ('Dark Frontier II'). Seven's rejection of her drone father, and of the Queen and her plans to make Seven into an intermediary in the process of assimilating human beings into the Collective, is phrased in standard Borg terms, but with a twist: Seven's 'our thoughts are one' expresses her alliance with Janeway, and her rejection of the Borg Queen (Dark Frontier II').

Seven is viewed as unique and special to Janeway as well as to the Queen; Seven's death during *Voyager*'s return to Earth is a – possibly *the* – motivating factor for Janeway's journey to the past and attempt to rewrite the future ('Endgame'). The confrontation between Janeway and the Queen in the series finale can be read as a battle of the mothers, with points of contrast throughout their confrontation. The Queen's 'physically fragmented body and overtly sexualized performance "code" her character as representatively seductive and threatening' (Leaver 2015: 66), while Janeway maintains a more controlled physical presentation that is not overtly feminized. Admiral Janeway's final confrontation with the Queen parallels the Queen's confrontation with Janeway in 'Dark Frontier'. In the earlier episode, Janeway's embodied integrity was under attack with the threat of infection and incorporation into the 'body' of the Borg Collective. In the series finale, Janeway is the carrier of the virus that will infect and destroy the Borg. The respective infections are dramatized in similar, though opposing, ways: in 'Dark Frontier' Janeway's organic body is injected with Borg nanoprobes and overlaid with technological implants including eye-socket modifications, and mechanical implants on her shaved head; once infected with the virus in 'Endgame', the Queen's organic body appears to reject her Borg appendages, which cease to function. In a visually spectacular moment near the conclusion of the series finale, as the Queen's mechanical limbs begin to fail she removes them and throws them aside, as though she is attempting to halt the disintegration of her cyborg body by taking it apart herself. Janeway's action resets history so that *Voyager* is able to return to Earth sooner, missing the confrontation that would have killed Seven. This aspect of the series finale may seem reductive, with Janeway as yet another sacrificial heroine (Crosby 2004: 176, note 1), but reading Janeway as mother – and specifically, as *Seven*'s mother – gives us opportunities to look at this aspect of the narrative in a different way.

Alongside the Collectives, Cooperatives or communities of existing and former Borg, the series offers the example of *Voyager* as a different kind of collective, one that both contrasts with and illuminates the Borg's Collective. The collective space and identification of *Voyager* and its crew unite a disparate collection of individuals within a network, with access to webs of information, and with a common purpose in their attempts to navigate their way out of the Delta Quadrant. Ultimately, Seven is assimilated as a member of *Voyager*'s crew, and allies herself with them, declaring, '*Voyager* is my collective' ('Drone'). The representation of Seven and Janeway as mother-figures is not necessarily essentialist or regressive, but could be seen as a way of emphasizing the importance of community, of relationships that are a vital part of being or becoming human. The fact that, by the end of the series, Seven declares a wish to become fully human may indicate that she cannot continue to exist in isolation as a single cyborg. She must declare her allegiance to her new collective, and she intends to do so by altering or removing something that has been part of her embodiment: her cortical node. In my next chapter I turn to a different kind of cyborg collective, one that parallels much of the Borg's quasi-utopian ideals. The Cylons of *Battlestar Galactica* struggle in what can only be described as a love–hate relationship with humanity, and in this narrative we can see a continuation of some of the questions I have posed in this chapter around the feminized cyborg and the possibilities for 'radical' cyborg embodiment and transformation.

3

Toasters and Replicas: *Battlestar Galactica*

In the reimagined *Battlestar Galactica*, cyborgs are both terrifying aggressors and hybrid boundary-crossers at different points across the entire series narrative. The reimagined series was launched with a two-part Miniseries that ended on a cliffhanger, and continued with a four-season run. Its plot follows that of the original *Battlestar Galactica* series (1978–79), with storylines centred on the ongoing struggle between the human race and their adversaries, the Cylons. However, the reimagined *Battlestar Galactica* presents a much more complex narrative, both in the sometimes tortuous story arcs of multiple seasons, and in the darker mood of the entire show, which allows for subtle character portrayals. The complexity and subtlety extends to the series' Cylon characters, too. In the original series, the Cylon enemies were a race of reptile-like creatures and their robot creations were known as Centurions. In the new series, the Cylons are a cyborg race created by humans. Several different models of Cylons offer a variety of perspectives on cyborg embodiment, and we see shifts in the positioning of cyborg characters, moving from the cyborg as hostile other to the cyborg as version of ourselves.

At the opening of the reimagined series, the extent of the hostility between humans and Cylons is made clear when a Cylon Basestar attacks and destroys a space station intended to serve as neutral territory for the two warring factions. The Miniseries' opening titles – and the opening titles of the rest of the series – summarize the history of human and Cylon. Humans created the Cylons 'to make life easier on the Twelve Colonies' or, to put the Cylon viewpoint, as slave labour. Forty years before the events of the series, the Cylons instigated a war against humanity, beginning 'a long and bloody struggle'; following an armistice, the Cylons left the Twelve Colonies 'for another world to call their own' (Miniseries Part 1). The Miniseries dramatizes the Cylons' return and their destruction of the Twelve Colonies, an act that leaves a remnant of the Colonial Fleet, and a small number of civilian vessels, in exile (and that follows the main plotline of the original series). The reimagined series narrative follows the surviving humans from the Twelve Colonies as they travel in a random assortment of spacecraft, struggle to survive amid continued attacks from the Cylons, and search for another planet that can support human life. Although the series is positioned as science fiction, and maintains many science fiction tropes and themes, its narrative takes up political, religious, legal, medical and social-justice storylines that could equally appear in realist dramas like *Homeland* and *The West Wing*. The friendship between the Fleet Commander Bill Adama and the President Laura Roslin anchors story arcs that follow the struggle between military and civilian governance. The continuing threat from Cylon forces, especially from the newer-model humanoid Cylons that are physically identical to humans, makes narrative connections to real-world fears of insurgency and terrorism from within. To complicate matters further, the reimagined *Battlestar Galactica* includes the Cylon Final Five, the original Cylons who are the creators of all other models, who have been exiled among the human race with no memory or knowledge of their Cylon identities, and believe they are human. The narrative centres on certain key characters from Colonial and Cylon factions, including Colonial pilots Kara Thrace (call sign 'Starbuck'), Lee Adama ('Apollo'), Sharon Valerii ('Boomer') and Karl Agathon ('Helo'), their Executive Officer Saul Tigh and maintenance chief Galen Tyrol, and scientist Gaius Baltar who is rescued from Caprica during the Cylon attack. At the end of the Miniseries, Boomer is revealed to be a Cylon, one of the humanoid models; Season 1 introduces her double, who comes to be known as Athena, and other Cylon characters have important roles in the unfolding narrative.

The presence of the Cylon Centurions in the first moments of the Miniseries links the rebooted series to its 1980s original, but the Centurions are one of several reimagined Cylon models. Cylon Raiders, small attack ships, are shown to possess intelligence and stand as yet another example of cyborg embodiment in the series. Cylon Hybrids have organic, humanoid form, which is compromised and destabilized through their close interactions with technology as they navigate the large Cylon vessels, the Basestars, through faster-than-light travel. The metal Centurions maintain a sense of dread and fear, but also are recognizably artificial and non-human. The humanoid Cylon model, thanks to the difficulty in distinguishing it from organic humans, overturns many of the divisions between human and 'other'. The humanoid Cylons redefine and probe the complicated connections between human beings and Cylons throughout the series. Humanoids, Centurions, Raiders and Hybrids are ranked in a cyborg hierarchy in which those Cylons that most closely resemble humans have authority over all other types or models of Cylons (Shipman 2008), and this, alongside examinations of community and society, further complicates the connections between human and cyborg. Though the Cylons are situated as 'other' and as 'enemy' for much of the narrative, this opposition is continually undercut, as the narrative also offers viewpoints from this 'other side'.

The humanoid Cylon characters have attracted much critical attention, with ample critical commentary examining their portrayal in the series according to aspects of gender and sexuality (George 2008; Jowett 2010) their position as other (Deis 2008; Ott 2008), cyborg embodiment (Heinricy 2008; Kind 2011), orientalism (Pegues 2008; Bennett 2012), individuality (Moore 2008; Hawk 2011), justice and punishment (Johnson-Lewis 2008; Randell 2011), and horror and the double/doppelgänger (Peirse 2008). Considering 'what Cylons represent on the show', Brian L. Ott concludes that, '[t]he Cylons do not signify technology; they do signify a human enemy that is culturally different to the colonists' (2008: 19). The creators of *Battlestar Galactica* position Cylon characters in the role of 'culturally different' enemy other. The series uses the distance of science fiction to fictionalize and comment on real-world events like 9/11, the War on Terror, incarceration and torture in Guantanamo Bay and Abu Graib, and other 'allegor[ies] of contemporary politics' (Tranter 2007: 49); religious distinctions are also apparent, the humans following a polytheistic religion, while the Cylons are monotheists, and worship 'the One True God'.[1] The humanoid Cylons become the hidden or invisible enemy, the other that 'look[s] like us now'. They are especially dangerous because that lack of distinction allows them to pose as humans, to infiltrate human institutions and to plant 'sleeper agents' – Cylons who do not know they are Cylons – in key areas of human society, including within the Colonial Fleet (as has been done with Boomer). As the series progresses, characters who seem the very epitome of what it is to be flawed human beings are revealed to be Cylons: the rough-speaking, hard-drinking, honest and loyal Colonel Tigh, for example, turns out to be one of the Final Five. Still, the humanoid Cylons do not remain fixed in the role of enemy other. Their development through all four seasons encourages far more complex analyses of these cyborgs, pushing critics – and viewers in general – to move beyond a simple, binary view of allies and enemies, us and them, self and other.

Technology itself is involved in generating fear, discomfort and alienation in *Battlestar Galactica*, where the first Cylon War has revealed the potential for any cyborgs to co-opt technology for their own purposes. Human characters tend to hold a more technophobic stance than we might expect of a science fiction series in which faster-then-light space travel is possible. In early seasons, the humans show a clear resistance to technological developments and a reluctance to embrace technological solutions because of the likelihood that the Cylons would hijack them. The *Galactica* itself is an outmoded antique, about to be decommissioned and turned into a museum ('Miniseries Part 1'). It stands as an emblem of justified technophobia, since its lack of a computer network saves it from the Cylon virus that incapacitates most of the rest of the Colonial Fleet. This faster-than-light spacecraft requires its officers to maintain communications through analogue wired telephones and messages on pieces of paper.

To return to Ott's point that '[t]he Cylons do not signify technology', while the Cylons do stand as examples of cyborg characters that allow for – and even encourage – a variety of different readings and real-world parallels, this most certainly extends to include readings and parallels focusing on technology. The Cylon Centurions' metal-covered cyborg bodies mirror aspects of the human body but are clearly artificial and exaggerated, accentuating the difference between human and Cylon. The Raiders trouble distinctions between organic and machine as well as those between machine and animal. Cylon Hybrids are, of all the models, the example that demonstrates an embodiment that is almost entirely in service to technology. These Cylon models trouble critics, too, who struggle to define and place them as machine, cyborg and/or other. Marshall and Wheland suggest that despite the presence of 'organic components' inside the Raiders and Basestars 'they are not cyborgs in the traditional scientific sense, in that there is no indication that there is, or ever was, a biological original' (2008: 96). But these models certainly combine machine and organic parts, in ways that parallel the humanoid Cylons' embodiment. The biomechanical nature of both Raiders and Basestars suggests equivalent cyborg embodiment – and consequently, associated fear and unease – for the vessels, even if they have no vestige of human physicality. The Raiders, Centurions and Hybrids are compelling examples of cyborg embodiment, and these models, as well as the humanoid models, demonstrate difference, represent 'otherness' and encourage explorations of cyborg embodiment and individuality.

The humanoid Cylons accentuate the differences between Cylon models, and they allow for the development of points of contrast between human and Cylon, too. There are even divisions among the humanoid Cylons, making it very evident that they have no common cyborg mindset, even within their own Number group. (There are twelve humanoid Cylon models and individuals are frequently referred to by their respective model numbers, especially the Six and Eight models.) The humanoid One model, represented in the narrative as an older, white male, is an atheist with an uncompromising anti-human stance. He rejects his own human aspects, and longs instead for a pure machine form: 'I don't want to be human. I want to see gamma rays, I want to hear X-rays, and I want to smell dark matter. [...] I'm a machine, and I can know much more, I could experience so much more' ('No Exit' 4.17). This Cylon, Cavil, allies himself with other male-gendered Cylons, like the Four model Simon, adopts a rational standpoint and makes use of scientific and medical technology in attempts to transcend his humanoid cyborg embodiment (Jowett 2010: 63). In contrast, the Six and Eight models, especially Caprica Six and the Eights Boomer and Athena, are gendered as female; they adopt closer ties to humanity through their relationships with human men, and tend to show evidence of empathy and emotion.

The Cylons' ability to duplicate their cyborg bodies and to resurrect themselves also plays on themes of individuality and mortality. The Miniseries opens with a scene in which one of the female-gendered Six models confronts the Colonial officer acting as the human envoy in a diplomatically-neutral space station. Coming close to him the Six asks, 'Are you alive?' When he replies, 'Yes' she counters, 'Prove it.' The 'proof' of being alive 'and thus different from the Cylon, is not by dying, but by dying without resurrection' (Giardina 2006: 48). Cylon identities continue, since their cyborg bodies, once dead or destroyed, are resurrected with all their previous memories and experiences intact ('Downloaded' 2.18).

Fears associated with the humanoid Cylons have more to do with their very *likeness* to human beings, to the way their embodiment duplicates human embodiment in uncanny ways (Peirse 2008), to their ability to 'pass' as human (Koistinen 2011), to the fact that their 'otherness' still means they 'look like us'. Throughout the series, they are both humanized and dehumanized; their status as persons is constantly shifting, and the boundary between 'them' and 'us' destabilized (Ott 2008: 18–9). By way of contrast, the metal-bodied Centurions evoke fear or unease that relates to the artificial techno-body, to the body of the muscular cyborg that is obviously stronger and more powerful than an organic human body. The Raiders and Hybrids generate further unease: the Raiders complicate distinctions between human and machine and between machine and animal, while the Hybrids 'look like us' in that they retain a human appearance, but they present a very different interface between the body and technology, and so create a unique version of cyborg embodiment.

The Cylon Centurions: Muscular Cyborgs

The Centurion model Cylons evoke dread and fear that is connected to their monumental appearance, and in this respect they are similar to film and television cyborgs like the Terminator, RoboCop, or *Doctor Who*'s Cybermen. These cyborg types share a monolithic stature. They are not human-sized, but appear as tall and muscular mechanical men. In many respects, they echo the shapes of (male) bodybuilders whose arms, shoulders and torsos are bulked-up and muscular in comparison to the rest of their frame. Cylon Centurions have a metal outer covering with large heads, hips and legs and small, disproportionately slender waists. These exaggerated shapes and lack of proportion emphasize their artificial nature. Their shiny metal casing with its chrome appearance stresses their manufactured state and connects these cyborgs to mass-manufacturing and factory processes; these are cyborgs that are made to look identical, and are produced in large numbers. There are similarities between the Centurions and *Doctor Who*'s Cybermen, especially in view of the point that their metal exterior appearance encourages many to read them as robots, that is, as entirely mechanical/technological beings. Both Cybermen and Centurions, however, are cyborg; while the Cybermen are created out of a combination of human and machine that requires existing human bodies to be transformed or 'upgraded' with technological parts, the Cylons (like the cinematic and televisual Terminators) are created out of organic and technological components.

Their height and their imposing exterior is often displayed through special-effects sequences that use long-shots or extended tracking shots, and feature marching rows of Centurions, often in large numbers. This is evident in the opening scene in the Miniseries, when two Centurions accompany the Six model onto the space station, creating the impression of a guard of honour for what is supposed to be a diplomatic meeting on neutral territory. In a similar way, rows of marching Centurions emphasize the Colonials' defeat by the Cylons at the end of Season 2 ('Lay Down Your Burdens' 2.20). An overhead shot reveals a seemingly endless line of Centurions, all with an identical appearance. Their movements and military-style close-order formation are similarly coordinated, down to the clanging of their synchronized steps. (Again, this connects with the presentation of the Cybermen in the rebooted *Doctor Who*, as discussed in Chapter 1.) The sheer numbers of these cyborgs, their metal exteriors and their excessive height all produce an overwhelming effect, showing that they have completely overpowered the surviving humans.

As these examples suggest, the metal Centurions have very specific roles within Cylon society. As their designation indicates, they are used as military troops and 'perform the duties of foot soldiers' providing strength and firepower (Shipman 2008: 159). This role is thoroughly displayed in the Miniseries and in other episodes which depict combat situations between humans and Cylons. In episodes following the human resistance force on Caprica, the Centurions are both the targets of attack ('Downloaded') and the soldiers deployed to battle the humans ('Lay Down Your Burdens Part 2'); they are used as a raiding party in 'Valley of Darkness' (2.2) when they manage to board *Galactica*. The Centurion model is also shown carrying out other kinds of duties; in 'Downloaded' we see them working as security guards and involved in heavy work like building or landscaping, for example, they are shown planting trees. This suggests that the Centurion model can be used for any task needing strength or stamina, or for straightforward mechanical or tactical tasks, but not for tasks requiring special skill, dexterity or brainpower.

The opening credits of each episode repeat the history of the Cylons: 'The Cylons were made by man [sic]; they evolved – they rebelled…' but, while this history appears to refer to all types or models of Cylons, continuing storylines reveal that this is not the case. Conversations between the humanoid Cylon models make it clear that the humanoid Cylons do not intend the Centurions to 'evolve' but to be 'improved' or 'upgraded' as the humanoid models decide. These discussions indicate that intervention by the humanoid Cylons has reduced the Centurions' capacity for intelligence ('Six of One' 4.2). Similarly, Centurion models once had the ability to speak (*Battlestar Galactica: Razor*, and see Shipman 2008: 158–9), but in *Battlestar Galactica*'s series narrative they are mute. So, their 'upgrades' have not improved, but have reduced or removed aspects of their embodiment. The removal of intelligence and of speech marks a lack of agency for these otherwise powerful cyborgs: 'they are not able to articulate their thoughts and desires' (Shipman 2008: 159). Historically, humans used the Cylons as slave labour 'to make life easier on the Twelve Colonies' ('Miniseries Part 1'), and as with so many aspects of human society, the Cylons adopt humans' use of Centurions, using them as muscle/might. This aspect of their status troubles their apparent impregnability; despite their powerful appearance they are slaves among their own cyborg kind. As David Roden notes, they are 'treated as mere instruments for achieving human [and other Cylon] goals' (2008: 114).

Roden's point opens up a further area for exploration. Roden describes the Centurions as 'instruments', 'like *toasters*' (2008: 114, emphasis in original). In the series, 'toaster' is a pejorative name humans give to any Cylon, of whatever model.[2] The usage is closer to racial slur than nickname; both Six and Helo react to the term in this way ('Resistance' 2.4, 'Flight of the

Phoenix' 2.9). Toasters are, of course, machines – a toaster does not choose to make toast; making toast is its function. Centurions operate in the same way: they are machines with no choice in how they act; they can only fulfill particular functions. A sequence at the end of Season 1 demonstrates this point. Helo and the Cylon Eight we come to know as Athena (who at this point in the storyline is masquerading as Boomer) are hiding from Cylons in a restaurant building ('You Can't Go Home Again' 1.5). Helo is preparing breakfast in the kitchen area and is in the middle of making some toast when he is surprised by a Centurion patrolling the area. The toaster finishes its function and pops up the toast, causing the Centurion to detect Helo's presence. The chrome-plated toaster and the metal-encased cyborg Centurion are paralleled visually with shots that cut between the Centurion's metal body and glowing red eye, and the toaster's metal casing and glowing red switch. Each one carries out the function appropriate to its machine existence; having detected Helo, the Centurion attempts to kill him, because it is its function to do so.

Cylon Raiders: Machine, Animal, Cyborg

On the basis of early appearances, the Cylon Raiders – small fighter spaceships – appear to be similar in construction to the Centurions. They look more mechanical than organic, and their appearance is very far from human. Raiders are small, saucer-shaped fighter ships, with a complete metal covering, and a glowing red eye-piece that is similar to the Centurions'. Despite this appearance, the Raiders are conceptualized in animalistic terms. Boomer examines a captured Raider and muses, 'It's probably a Cylon itself – more of an animal maybe than the human models. Maybe they genetically design it to perform a task – to be a fighter' ('Six Degrees of Separation' 1.7). While she speaks, Boomer strokes the 'head' part of the Raider as though stroking a horse's nose (an action also noted by Shipman, 2008:161, and demonstrated in Figure 6). Athena confirms the Raiders' status: '[they are] much like a trained animal with a basic consciousness and survival instinct' ('Scar' 2.15). Like the Centurions, the Raiders lack agency within the Cylon hierarchy, and are treated as lower beings, unable to 'correct themselves' and needing to be 'reconfigure[d]' – or 'lobotomize[d]' when they do not perform as required ('Six of One'). Cavil even denies

figure 6: Boomer with the Cylon Raider, 'Six Degrees of Separation', *Battlestar Galactica* (1.7)

their animal aspects, calling them 'tools, not pets' ('Six of One'). As I noted, Marshall and Wheland view the Raiders as an 'intermediary evolutionary step, not quite deserving of individual personhood' (2008: 96), but evidence from 'Scar' and 'Six of One' 'shows there is a sophisticated awareness at work in the Raiders, far beyond what we would consider animalistic or instinctive' (Shipman 2008: 161).

The Raiders' cyborg nature is revealed most spectacularly in 'You Can't Go Home Again', in which Starbuck gains access to the inside of a crashed Raider. Starbuck's encounter is the first in which a human manages to penetrate a Raider's metal exterior and reveal its organic (and graphically bloody) interior that contains technological and mechanical components; as Tyrol comments later on, 'this whole thing is a bunch of veins and ligaments and sacs and goo!' ('Six Degrees of Separation'). Further, Starbuck's adaptation of the Raider makes her body into part of its components – in effect, she turns *herself* into a Cylon-hybrid cyborg. The series has a tendency to conceptualize the Colonials' human pilots as flesh extensions of their machines, bodies working in harmony with technology. The Colonial Fleet emphasizes the importance of a fully-functioning, fit body as well as a well-maintained machine. For example, Starbuck is unable to fly while she is recovering from a leg injury because the act of piloting a Viper fighter needs physical strength ('Hand of God' 1.10); Lee Adama puts on weight and must work to regain his fitness ('Lay Down Your Burdens, Part 2', 'Torn'); Starbuck and Helo train by boxing and lifting weights ('Scar'). In a sense, then, the Colonial Viper pilots are aspiring to the perfect combination or blend of organic and machinic which is so effective and so dangerous in the Raiders. This is the aspect of cyborg embodiment that Starbuck taps into when she hotwires herself into the downed Raider. She becomes part of its organic system which is fleshy, bleeds, and needs oxygen. And she understands its machine system, the factors necessary for it to fly effectively: 'Every flying machine has four basic controls: power, pitch, yaw and roll. Where are yours?' ('You Can't Go Home Again'). Starbuck remakes the Raider, and literally marks it with her own name to ensure that the Fleet will recognize her and not shoot her down. Starbuck creates an individual and unique cyborg identity, not a copy or a duplicate.

In the case of the Raider nicknamed 'Scar', its repeated downloads into a succession of new cyborg bodies preserve its knowledge of combat against the human forces, making it difficult to defeat. Despite its 'animal' programming, this particular Raider, at least, uses intelligent strategy; for example, it hides behind asteroids before pouncing on Colonial Vipers, demonstrating, as Hal Shipman notes, 'a sophisticated awareness at work' (2008: 161). Scar even evidences feelings; Athena warns Starbuck, 'Be careful of Scar [...]. He's filled with rage.' This cyborg experiences hatred, which fuels its attacks on the Colonial fleet.

In contrast to Scar's embodiment and knowledge preserved through Cylon resurrection, death for the humans brings no such continuation, but instead the irretrievable loss of their personhood, and the prospect that they will be forgotten by the living. The problem of remembering the dead is highlighted at key points in the episode 'Scar'. Several Viper pilots puzzle over the name of a dead comrade's girlfriend when they find her photograph; Lee Adama says he forgets dead pilots' faces and Starbuck insists she cannot remember their names. Even so, they find ways to remember the dead: Kat pins the unnamed girl's photograph to the memorial wall on *Galactica*, while Starbuck commemorates the dead pilots by reciting their call signs which, it turns out, she remembers perfectly. For the Cylons in their final battle of the episode, death is also final, as they are out of range of any resurrection ships. Scar's death ends its cycle of rebirth into renewed hatred and bitterness.

Cylon Resurrection: Doubles, Duplicates and the Uncanny

As Alison Peirse notes, the Cylon resurrection process features as a monstrous duplication of uncanny cyborg bodies. Freud connects 'the uncanny' with 'the doubling, dividing and interchanging of the self' (1961: 233), and these duplications mean that '[t]he presence of the double calls into question the authenticity of either individual' (Peirse 2008: 119). But for the resurrected Cylon body the process goes beyond doubling; in its very creation the Cylon body is multiplied – in the forms of Centurions, Raiders and humanoid models – so that 'the double is endlessly repeated'; in death and resurrection we find both horror and the uncanny through the 'disintegration and renewal of Cylon bodies' (Peirse 2008: 119, 129).

The Cylon ability to resurrect their consciousness into new bodies shows a further level of cyborg embodiment. The survival of consciousness from one cyborg body to another implies a separation of body and mind – something we see in relation to many imaginary cyborgs – and allows the Cylons a form of immortality. This is yet another way in which the cyborgs in *Battlestar Galactica* differ from their human adversaries. Some episodes emphasize potential advantages of the Cylon resurrection process. Since it allows an individual consciousness to retain all its experience and knowledge as it moves from body to body, Cylon resurrection ensures that knowledge builds and expands. Athena contrasts this preservation of knowledge with human death, 'you lose their experience, their knowledge, their skill sets. It's gone forever. So if you could bring them back and put them in a new body [...] death becomes a learning experience' ('Scar'). In the case of the Raider Scar, this preservation of knowledge allows it to become a formidable and almost unstoppable fighter. Cylon resurrection has more negative qualities too. Again, Athena explains, 'Dying's a painful and traumatic experience. Every time [Scar]'s reborn, he's filled with more bitter memories' ('Scar'). So the resurrection process preserves all aspects of an individual personality, but it also has lasting effects that are clearly problematic and detrimental to the resurrected individual.

The preservation of an individual through successive incarnations in identical cyborg bodies complicates the Cylon assertion that, even though Cylons are created as different forms and models, they are otherwise identical. Cavil, for example, makes the point that individual humanoid Cylons do not – or should not – deviate in opinion from the opinion of their model ('Six of One'). The Raider Scar is clearly not identical in consciousness to all the other Cylon Raiders. Similarly, the humanoid Cylons Boomer (an Eight model) and Caprica Six are shown to develop in fundamentally different ways from others of their model, as does Athena, another Eight. Amy Kind examines '[w]hat makes a Cylon the same Cylon over time' in the context of 'experiential memory', concluding that it is the individual Cylon's very different embodied experiences that combine to create distinct personalities (2011: 64, 66). Thus, Boomer's experiences make her a very different individual from Athena, though both are Eight models.[3]

The episode 'Downloaded' foregrounds the psychological cost of resurrection, especially the trauma around retained memories of death, which is to say, of the *physical* remembrance of the process of death. For many Cylons fighting a war against humanity, death is often violent. Caprica Six retains memories of being blown up in the Cylon attack ('Miniseries Part 1') and Boomer has memories of being shot ('Resistance' 2.4). After their respective resurrections, they retain their individuality. Boomer continues to call herself Sharon, identifying herself with her sleeper identity, and Caprica Six is singled out by name, untypically, by other Cylons 'like you're the only Six on the planet'. Other Cylons refer to this particular Six and Eight as 'the heroes of the Cylons'. Boomer maintains her old apartment in Caprica City (Pegues 2008: 201; Bennett 2012: 29), dresses as though she were still a member of the *Galactica* crew and carries out military-style fitness training. Furthermore, she describes her former crewmates on *Galactica* as people she loves, and so maintains her psychological connection with them. She dismisses her memories of her parents as a fiction, 'none of it's real' ('Downloaded'), but she does develop a connection with Commander Adama as an 'adoptive father figure' (Pegues 2008: 201). Caprica Six, too, maintains a connection to her previous body, to the extent that after her resurrection she complains that she 'can't get used to *this* body', even though it is identical. As well as her struggle with the memory of her violent death, she, like Boomer, holds on to her experiences and connection with individuals (notably with Gaius Baltar) that she forged in her previous existence.

The individuality of Caprica Six and Boomer makes them aberrations within Cylon society, but gives them authority and power within that society. They are able to persuade the other humanoid Cylons that 'the occupation of the Colonies was an error' (an understatement, to say the least, spoken by one of the Cavil models, 'Lay Down Your Burdens Part 2') and that instead their aim should be 'to change things for the better […] our people [the Cylons] need a new beginning' ('Downloaded'). Their memories of time spent with humans alters them to the extent that they wish to make peace with humanity, and although their apparent aim of coexistence fails ('Lay Down Your Burdens Part 2', 'Exodus Parts 1 and 2' 3.3–4) it continues to motivate and complicate their behaviour for the remainder of the narrative.

Humanoid Cylons: Cyborg Femininity and the Femme Fatale

The humanoid Cylons appear both as monstrous others and as indistinguishable from human beings. The oscillation between these viewpoints adds a certain instability to all the encounters between humans and Cylons over the series narrative. Cylons are 'othered' through emphasis on aspects like their identical duplication, and their ability to resurrect and preserve their consciousness after death. But the difference between Cylons and humans is also eroded through particular encounters and extended development of individual Cylon characters. We see Number Eight and Number Six models in the identities of Boomer, Athena, Caprica Six, Shelly Godfrey and more, who integrate themselves into the community of the Colonial Fleet, developing alliances and relationships with humans. The narrative examines humans' treatment of Cylons just as it examines Cylons' treatment of humans, often finding similar tendencies for humans and Cylons to lose compassion and decency when faced with what each perceives as 'the other'.

Because the Number Eight model known as Boomer/Sharon Valerii is revealed early on to be a Cylon 'sleeper agent', a Cylon who does not know that she is a Cylon ('Miniseries Part 2'), Boomer's character is doubled from the start of the narrative. Her identities as 'the team player' and the 'alien other' are in conflict (Pegues 2008: 196), displaying an 'oscillation between "robotic" and "human" parts of herself' (Bennett 2012: 30, note 4). As Eve Bennett notes, Boomer is 'duplicitous' in her plotting against humans *and* Cylons (2012: 36), which makes her a traitor to both sides at different times. In Season 1, her doubled self, and her terror that she could be a Cylon without knowing it, is clearly displayed for the viewer; for instance, she carries out actions of sabotage without remembering them ('Water' 1.2), or falls into a reverie in which she accesses information about Cylons ('Six Degrees of Separation'). Such examples reinforce a sense that Boomer's body and its actions are programmed, which also reinforces the cyborg-Cylon aspect of this character. As the narrative progresses, Boomer's character becomes other to Cylons as well as to humans. For example, Boomer is the only humanoid Cylon to vote against her own model, an action that is greeted with incomprehension by the majority of Cylons ('Six of One').

Boomer's double, who comes to be known in the Fleet as Athena, is in many ways her opposite. Athena is conscious of her orders to lure and seduce Helo, and she does perform this specific task ('Six Degrees of Separation'). However, she later overcomes her programming and falls in love, joins the Colonial fleet as a Viper pilot, and forms a family group with Helo and their daughter Hera. There are some suggestions that because 'Athena shares many of Boomer's memories [...] her love for Helo is in many ways shaped by Boomer's experiences with him' (Kind 2011: 65). We see further evidence of the way Cylons of a particular Number can identify with each other; for instance, watching the documentary film of the *Galactica* in 'Final Cut' (2.8), Boomer exclaims 'I'm alive!' as the camera pans across the crew and focuses on Athena (Kind 2011: 71). Despite such examples, it is very clear that Athena is meant to be viewed as a distinct and different *person*, not as any sort of copy; Athena is 'learning to be an individual, and not merely another Number Eight' (Moore 2008: 109). And Athena's individuality is as a Cylon. Her cyborg embodiment is not forgotten or minimized, and is key to the outcome of several episodes. This is often shown in dramatic and visually arresting examples, such as her use of her own body as an interface to rescue the *Galactica* from a virus ('Flight of the Phoenix'). Over time, she becomes a trusted fellow crew member to the

Galactica personnel, who know she is a Cylon, and, more importantly for the series narrative as a whole, she is the mother of Hera the Cylon-human hybrid child who is to become the ancestor of the human race on Earth.

The humanoid Cylons are both male and female-gendered, appear to represent different age groups, and include Black and Asian characteristics among their models (Fours, Eights), acknowledging the possibility – or perhaps, desirability – of difference for cyborg embodiment. However, individuals from the female Number Six and Number Eight models, Boomer, Athena and Caprica Six, dominate the series narrative. Their gender places them in the context of other 'female-gendered cyborgs [that] inhabit traditional feminine roles – as objects of man's desire and his helpmate in distress' (Balsamo 1988: 151). Susan George contends that these female Cylons enact both 'object of desire' and 'helpmate' roles (2008: 160), and that *Battlestar Galactica* as a whole 'continues what Claudia Springer has described as "a misogynistic tradition…of associating technology with women's bodies to represent the threat of unleashed female sexuality"' (Springer 1996: 114; George 2008: 164). We can certainly read *Battlestar Galactica*'s key female Cylon characters as desirable bodies – indeed, we are cued to do so on the appearance of a Number Six model in the first moments of the series, walking into the Colonial space station with white-blonde hair, wearing knee-high boots and a bright red tailored suit ('Miniseries Part 1'). That Six model may well work as an example of technology associated with the female body in order 'to represent the threat of unleashed female sexuality', but the representation of female humanoid Cylons generally is far more complex and nuanced than Springer's quotation or George's analysis suggest.

Tricia Helfer's portrayal of the various incarnations of the Number Six model includes a variety of identities and individualities: as Shelly Godfrey ('Six Degrees of Separation'), the tortured Gina ('Pegasus' 2.10), Cylon rebel Natalie ('Six of One'), and the 'hero' Caprica Six ('Downloaded'). All these Cylons have concrete embodiment in the physical world, and their embodiment is also differentiated and individual; the Sixes change their hair colour, some wear glasses, and they dress in distinctive and different ways. The Virtual Six, visible only to Gaius Baltar, does provide an exaggerated representation of a particular type of feminine embodiment: the glamorous femme fatale. It is Virtual Six who 'parades around the ship in heels and a red, form-fitting halter dress'

(George 2008: 166); other Six models do not appear in any such clothing. The costuming and overall presentation of this Virtual Six is as a blonde, statuesque temptress. However, presenting Virtual Six visually as a classic or cinematic femme fatale heightens the sense of artificiality and suggestion of performance around this character, which is something that potentially attaches to every humanoid Cylon character. An equivalent representation would see an Eight model costumed as Madama Butterfly – as a fantasy, extra-textual representation of an Asian female body.[4] Further, Virtual Six does not possess a corporeal body, something that highlights the involvement of fantasy in her appearance.[5] And while Virtual Six takes on the 'exaggerated body' of the femme fatale or pinup (Kakoudaki 2000: 165), her incorporeal body is otherwise identical to the corporeal cyborg bodies of the Six model Cylons, none of which take on such exaggerated feminine costume.

In other ways, these female cyborgs refuse what George evaluates as the 'traditional representation of the feminine [… a] helpmate, not only to her man but to the human race in its distress' (2008: 169). Both Juliana Hu Pegues and Eve Bennett offer more nuanced readings of Boomer and Athena, drawing on the characters' presentation of race and gender in connection with the *Madama Butterfly* trope of the Asian woman's sacrifice. Bennett, for example, highlights the storyline in which Athena commits 'suicide' ('Rapture' 3.12) in order to download onto the Cylon resurrection ship and rescue Hera: '[c]arrying out this plan with determination and efficiency, Athena reworks the suicide motif of the Butterfly tale, turning it from a submissive, pointless act into an active, productive one' (2012: 41). While these characters remain complex, complicated, and are often caught between internal and external tensions, they are part of – integral to – the narrative as much as any of the human characters. In this way, *Battlestar Galactica* allows some of its cyborg characters an equal status with its human characters, who are shown as complex and contradictory.

Reproduction and Hybridity

Battlestar Galactica offers several different interpretations of hybridity. Cylon–human relationships are seen as hybrid, as are the children of such relationships. A different model of Cylon embodiment is also designated 'a Hybrid'. The Cylon obsession with human reproduction leads them to attempt to create hybrid human-Cylon children. This is represented in various ways, running from the horror and coercion of mechanized Cylon–human reproduction, to the loving hybrid family composed of Helo, Athena and Hera. The inability to procreate obsesses the Cylons; as Athena explains, 'It's one of God's commandments…we can't fulfill it, we've tried' ('The Farm' 2.5). So although in terms of their embodiment 'the Cylons […] negate the need for reproduction at all' (Jones 2010: 179), and although they proclaim their utter opposition to humanity, paradoxically they are engaged in attempts to replicate human procreation. The drive to procreate is framed here as a religious imperative, but giving birth, like dying without resurrection, is a human, organic attribute, another way to show that one is alive.

Efforts to make human women part of a Cylon birth project are very clearly presented as a technological nightmare, and the project in effect turns women into mechanized living wombs, yet another form of cyborg embodiment. Technology in this instance makes the women's bodies hybrid and monstrous, a source of terror for Starbuck when she discovers them ('The Farm'). In the same episode, the Cylon Simon, posing as a Resistance doctor, frames the female body as a resource, as he tells Starbuck, 'Finding healthy childbearing women your age is a top priority for the Resistance […] you are a very precious commodity to us.' The human women Starbuck discovers in a hospital ward are connected by tubes and wires to various machines, with some of the wires fixed to their heads, their legs in stirrups mimicking gynecological or obstetric medical examinations. One of the women – Sue-Shaun, another Resistance fighter – accurately sums up their new cyborg embodiment, 'we're baby machines', and she begs Starbuck to disconnect her from the technological interface, preferring to die than embody the birth machine, and so graphically demonstrating an absolute refusal of Cylon–human hybridity.

Athena and Helo are the sole example of a Cylon–human couple who are able to have children, and their daughter Hera is a key character for several reasons. Hera can be viewed as 'the ultimate contamination of both human and Cylon bodies' (Heinricy 2008: 102), and she is certainly treated in this way by both humans and Cylons. Even before she is born, she is seen as a dangerous threat to the Fleet and to human existence; President Laura Roslin plans to force Athena to abort her child ('Epiphanies' 2.13). Once she is born, the Fleet's authorities act to remove Hera from Athena and conspire to keep her existence secret ('Downloaded', 'Exodus Part 1'). The humans view Hera as other, but so do the Cylons; as Lorna Jowett points out, Cavil sees Hera as 'a half-human, half-machine object of curiosity' and not as a being in her own right (2010: 63; 'Daybreak Part 1'). In other respects, however, Hera's unique form of cyborg embodiment offers more hopeful possibilities. Hera is the only known Cylon–human hybrid child, but her existence suggests that it might be possible for Cylon–human couples to reproduce and so finally fulfil their commandment. The discovery that Hera's foetal blood has curative properties saves Laura Roslin from death and puts her terminal cancer into remission ('Epiphanies'). And Hera is instrumental in guiding the Fleet to a habitable planet: her drawing shows Starbuck a sequence of musical notes that represent the coordinates for Earth ('Someone To Watch Over Me' 4.19, 'Daybreak Part 2' 4.22).

In more subtle ways, Hera's existence as Cylon–human hybrid, and specifically as the child of Athena, another Number Eight model, informs and transforms Boomer's motivations. Bennett suggests that Boomer reveals true feelings to Tyrol when she shows him her 'projection' of an imagined future in which she and Tyrol have a home and a child (Bennett 2012: 36, 'Someone To Watch Over Me'). This imaginary future, and the love it represents, influences her connection with Hera, and motivates her to return Hera to her parents, even though this means sacrificing herself ('Daybreak Part 2'). Here is a complex representation of hybridity: Boomer imagines herself and Tyrol – who is revealed to be one of the Cylon Final Five – as a hybrid couple who bridge the human–Cylon divide. Boomer's double, Athena, actually realizes Boomer's imagined hybrid future in her partnership with Helo. That hybrid future is made corporeal in the human–Cylon child Hera, who becomes the ultimate representation of hybridity as 'Mitochondrial Eve', the mother/ancestor of humanity.

A different mode of hybridity is shown in the character of the Cylon Hybrid, the final type of Cylon embodiment shown in the series. The Hybrid is humanoid, but interacts with technology to create an interface that enables Cylon Basestars to achieve faster-than-light travel. Cylon

Hybrids are represented visually as both male and female bodies (*Battlestar Galactica: Razor*, 'Torn' 3.06), although the Season 4 narrative focuses more closely on one female-embodied Hybrid ('Six of One'; 'Faith' 4.08). Looking at the Hybrid as another example of a cyborg body, we see a close, though problematic connection between the organic and the technological. As Shana Heinricy notes, this connection is 'perhaps too intense' since 'while the hybrid has superior control of technology, the technology appears to overpower the organic parts' resulting in a 'struggle to achieve balance' (2008: 101). Also problematic is the way in which the Cylon Hybrid acts as 'an oracle of sorts' (Marshall and Wheeland 2008: 96), speaking a combination of technological commands and observations, and prophetic utterances:

> Please, cut the fuse. They will not harm their own. End of line. Limiting diffusions to two dimensions increases the number of evolutionary jumps within the species. Rise and measure the temple of the five. Transformation is the goal. They will not harm their own. Data-font synchronization complete. ('Six of One')

Although the Cylon Hybrids possess speech and intelligence, 'they are characterized as insane and their speech is, therefore, dismissed' (Shipman 2008: 159). Shipman compares the relatively lucid Hybrid of *Battlestar Galactica: Razor* with the examples in episodes like 'Torn' or 'Six of One', arguing that the Hybrids 'are not "born" insane, but are driven so by their [faster-than-light] travel' (2008: 160). The contradiction between the Hybrid intelligence, connected technologically to the Basestar and able to control its complex navigational functions, and the Hybrid body, static and unmoving in a vat of liquid similar to that of the Cylon regeneration tanks, emphasizes the division of organic and machinic/technological in this mode of embodiment. As an example of cyborg embodiment standing alongside those of the Raiders, Centurions and humanoid Cylons, it embodies and wields technological cyborg power while it suffers and experiences lack of control because of that power. Although it would make sense to read the Hybrid as asexual or neuter, Lorna Jowett points out that 'gender is signaled here in several ways,' not least in the presence of a 'female actor' in the role of the Hybrid (2010: 70).[6] Jowett is alert to the feminized space the Cylon Hybrid inhabits, noting its 'womb-like' tank and means of connection to the Basestar 'as a foetus is connected to the mother', and further, she reads the Cylon Hybrid's speech as 'semiotic', which fits with its 'representation as a kind of Kristevan archaic mother (or pre-Oedipal child)' (2010: 71). Positioning the Hybrid in this way connects it with abject bodies of horror as well as with bodies that exist outside the symbolic order; despite its likeness to human bodies – or even to the bodies of the humanoid Cylons – its separation and difference, its otherness, is signaled repeatedly.

If the embodied status of the Cylon Hybrid is a feminized one, then it is tempting to read Sam Anders' hybridization at the conclusion of the series as a loss of masculinity, as well as a loss of humanity. One of the Final Five, the Cylons who created all other types and models, Anders has spent most of the narrative completely unaware of his cyborg nature. Indeed, he has appeared as a solidly, almost stereotypically brave and resourceful, physical and human fighter. Anders is 'hybridized' in an attempt to wake him from a coma after he is shot in the head. He is put into a liquid-filled tank identical to the one occupied by the Cylon Basestar's Hybrid, and his brain is connected first to the Basestar datastream and then to the *Galactica*'s control system ('Someone to Watch Over Me'). This makes Anders' formerly active body 'a neutered and blank conduit: one way to read this is that his hybridization feminizes him' (Jowett 2010: 71–2). Matthew Jones' reading aligns with this: 'the only option left for the series is to both emasculate and feminize [Anders], erecting new boundaries to separate him from the traditional masculinity that he had previously been allowed to exhibit' (Jones 2010: 163). These views of Anders as 'feminized' and as 'emasculated' (which Jones conflates) demonstrate the implicit gendering of the Cylon Hybrid model as female despite the appearance of at least one Hybrid that could be gendered male.[7]

Anders' corporeal status at the end of the series is indeed troubling, but it 'potentially offer[s] a challenge to the feminized trend' (Jowett 2010: 71). Anders as Hybrid presents a version of cyborg embodiment that troubles, breaks down and obliterates binaries and boundaries as much as the humanoid Six and Eight models, the Raiders, or the metal Centurions. Anders the active fighter becomes inactive; as we can see from Figure 7, his powerful male body is inert and occupies the same kind of 'womb-like', 'foetal' space as the female-embodied Cylon Hybrid (Jowett 2010: 71). However, if the female Hybrid is not entirely powerless in her cyborg embodiment, neither is Anders. As the *Galactica*'s Hybrid he has a pivotal role in the final battle,

figure 7: Sam as Cylon Hybrid, 'Islanded in a Stream of Stars', *Battlestar Galactica* (4.18)

as he is able to interface with the Basestar Hybrid and shut down the Cylon weapons systems. He performs a vital task at the conclusion of the series as he pilots the *Galactica* into the sun ('Daybreak Part 2'). Rather than becoming preoccupied about which side of the (human) gender boundary Anders occupies, we might read his example more productively as an ultimate form of boundary-crossing hybridization; certainly the fact that a highly masculine male in the *Battlestar* narrative can cross organic and technological boundaries is a striking narrative point.

Hybridity and a Cyborg Future

As with several other television cyborg narratives I examine in this book (see Chapter 6, *Terminator: The Sarah Connor Chronicles* and Chapter 8, *Fringe*), at the conclusion of *Battlestar Galactica* hybridity becomes the way forward for humanity. It is hybridity in the networks and relationships between humans and Cylons that is seen to overthrow divisions and binaries. These networks and relationships gain strength in the final season. Here Cylons and humans mix aboard *Galactica*, even in its military personnel: in 'Someone to Watch over Me', Starbuck briefs a mixed assembly of humans and Cylons before a flying mission. Alliances form between

Cylon factions and humans, as in the joint plan to destroy the Resurrection Hub ('Sine Qua Non' 4.10, 'The Hub' 4.11), and ironically such alliances are much more in evidence after a mutiny on the *Galactica* ('The Oath' 4.13) when loss of human and Cylon lives makes it imperative that the two work together in order to survive. Cylon biotechnology becomes part of the very fabric of the *Galactica*, as it is used in repairs ('No Exit', 'Deadlock' 4.18), and, after the Resurrection Hub is destroyed, Cylons too show that they are 'alive' by dying without resurrection. By the time of the final battle between the Colonial Fleet and the rest of the Cylons, the Fleet itself includes Cylons who are sympathetic to humans and who wish to coexist. With such examples, we can see the boundary between Cylon and human becoming less distinct. In the climactic battle of the series, the narrative highlights human-Cylon pairs who work together for a common goal. Helo and Athena form part of the team that attack the Basestar to retrieve Hera; Caprica Six and Baltar fight side-by-side against Centurions; Adama and Tigh face each other on the bridge of *Galactica*, each with a key role in the planned battle and the operation of the ship. All surviving Cylons and humans, including the remaining Final Five, colonize the Earth of 150,000 years ago.

The different examples of Cylons – the Centurions, the Raiders, the Hybrids and the humanoid models – may seem to represent a cyborg embodiment that is antagonistic to humans, one that represents a dangerous form of technological evolution. Such a representation also suggests that these cyborgs can only be positioned in opposition to human forms of embodiment. However, the unfolding narrative of *Battlestar Galactica* reveals that Cylons are constantly in a process of negotiation with their human counterparts. The Cylons themselves aspire to human biological processes, death as well as birth, and show themselves capable of difference and individuality. In Chapter 3, we turn to *Battlestar Galactica*'s prequel series, *Caprica*, which revisits the troubled connections between humans and cyborgs, while reconsidering some key aspects of *Battlestar Galactica*'s narrative, and offering some new perspectives on cyborg embodiment and boundary-crossing.

4

'Between Life and Death': Embodiment and Virtuality in *Caprica*

Chapters 1 and 2 follow cyborg characters that recur and reappear over different, interconnected series, as in *Star Trek*, or over a lengthy time period, as in classic and new *Doctor Who*. *Caprica* – a spin-off of *Battlestar Galactica* – offers a slightly different perspective on the reappearance of established cyborg characters. In many ways, its narrative can be viewed as an 'origin story' for the adversary cyborg Cylons of *Battlestar Galactica*, and thus it functions as a commentary or alternative viewpoint on the entire rebooted *Battlestar Galactica* series. *Caprica*'s storyline troubles oppositions of life and death, the real and the virtual. It explores possibilities for virtually-embodied life in a parallel digital world, and follows the emergence of Cylons as defined individuals with independent consciousness. In one respect, this chapter serves as a case study of a short-lived spin-off series, a 'marvellous failure' (Kapica 2014: 612), but – perhaps because of its brief existence – *Caprica* nevertheless offers a concentrated insight into and fuller examination of concepts that are central to the original series. *Caprica* maintains and develops *Battlestar Galactica*'s focus on cyborg embodiment, especially the ways in which Cylons function as monstrous others, and considers cyborg personhood and authenticity. At the same time as it makes connections with its parent series, it presents these themes in a fashion that chimes with other fictional commentaries and critical writing on contemporary Western technological development.

The *Caprica* storylines that follow experiences in virtual worlds and negotiations of cyborg identity mesh with late twentieth and twenty-first century fictions that are concerned with cyborgs and with virtuality, such as the cyberpunk novels of William Gibson, Pat Cadigan and Neal Stephenson, and the films *Blade Runner* and the *Matrix* trilogy. These fictions share an interest in the liberatory possibilities, problematic effects and enduring influences of human beings' exposure to virtual worlds and to artificial versions of the human. *Caprica* follows some of the key problems of cyberpunk and academic cyberculture so well that it makes a rich source for closer examination. It is puzzling that more critical comment on *Caprica* has not appeared; although there are some thoughtful analyses, in number they fall far short of the explosion of articles and full-length collections of academic writing that have focused on *Battlestar Galactica*. Since this series directly addresses aspects of our contemporary fears about personhood, artificial life and the possibly negative effects of exposure to virtual systems, it offers some potentially enlightening commentary.

The action of *Caprica* occurs some 58 years before the events of *Battlestar Galactica*. As a prequel, part of its purpose is to fill in the backstory – referred to in its parent series – of the invention and development of the Cylons. The overall series trajectory is towards the Cylon War, the first time the 'Cylons rebelled', and on to the cataclysmic events of the Cylon attack on the Twelve Colonies and the exodus and struggle of the surviving humans. Yet in other respects, this series operates independently as an interconnected political/family drama focusing on the Graystones and the Adamas. The narrative's major incident, which occurs in the pilot episode and resonates throughout the rest of the series, is the suicide bombing of a commuter train by the monotheistic Soldiers of the One (STO) (the society in *Caprica*, like that of *Battlestar Galactica*, is polytheistic). Amongst the casualties are Daniel and Amanda Graystone's daughter Zoe, and Joseph Adama's wife Shannon and daughter Tamara. For the remainder of the series, the narrative divides into three main plot strands that follow Daniel Graystone's attempts to create cybernetic 'life' in the form of robot soldiers (these 'Cybernetic Lifeform Node' are the beings we know from *Battlestar Galactica* as Cylons), Zoe and Tamara's avatar afterlives in

'Between Life and Death': Embodiment and Virtuality in *Caprica*

a virtual world (V-world), and STO priest Clarice Willow's bid for power which culminates in her aim to create a virtual religious paradise for monotheism. When Tamara's grandmother describes her as 'caught between life and death' ('Gravedancing' 1.5) she voices a common thread that runs through each one of these plot strands, and applies equally to the Cylons, the virtual avatars and Clarice's constructed afterlife.

Caprica's storylines follow the development of new technologies that have the potential to create cyborgs or to enable humans to approach a cyborg identity. In this respect, *Caprica*'s cyborgs are similar to the cyborgs I discuss in Chapters 5 and 7 with my analyses of *Bionic Woman* and *Dollhouse*. Besides its treatment of the invention of the Cylons, the series examines the cyborg connections that humans form with aspects of the virtual. In relation to each kind of cyborg, we see a breakdown of boundaries between the machinic/technological and the organic, and between physical and virtual worlds. The society presented in the series is shown at the point at which the boundary between the human and the technological begins to blur, where humans begin to move towards posthuman identities. I have mentioned that this narrative connects with cyberpunk and other cyborg fictions in which 'the posthuman comes to embody a state of transcendence of the "real world" through virtual technologies' (Toffoletti 2007: 11). The series follows several different characters who create avatars to engage with virtual spaces, and whose engagement with virtuality suggests a transition towards 'the posthuman', although as in cyberpunk fiction, such individuals do not 'necessarily want to leave the body behind'; rather, 'the posthuman operates as a site of ambiguity, as a transitional space where old ways of thinking about the self and the Other, the body and technology, reality and illusion, can't be sustained' (Toffoletti 2007: 13, 14).

In the world of *Caprica*, people are becoming cyborg simply by moving between physical and virtual worlds. Having created the holoband technology that allows access to V-world, Daniel attempts to create cyborg bodies in the physical world. His daughter Zoe's creation of an independent virtual avatar, an alternate self, has resonating effects in the series. The Zoe avatar becomes a key player in the drive to cross between the virtual and the embodied worlds and to create a form of sentient cyborg embodiment. The treatment of avatar-Zoe's character, together with the prequel's setting on a technologically advanced world, allows for some close exploration of cyborg technologies and virtual reality. These 'worlds which overlap, and which are simultaneously digital and non-digital' (Green 1997: 63) are also embodied and disembodied, as we move between the physical world, where cyborgs are created, and the virtual world, where embodiment is maintained through avatars. Zoe's presence as virtual self and as cyborg foregrounds debates about the nature of consciousness, identity, embodiment and the positive possibilities of the cyborg body. Her representation assists the narrative development, making it possible for the view of cyborgs/Cylons as enemy and as other to develop into more complex considerations of cyborg individuality and freedom.

Because *Caprica*, as a prequel to *Battlestar Galactica*, never operates independently, but must fit its storylines into the already established mythology of the rebooted series, there is a sense in which its audience already knows how the series ends. In effect, *Caprica* ends where *Battlestar Galactica* begins, with the Cylon attack and destruction of the Twelve Colonies. So, any storyline that features the process of creating Cylons draws attention to the outcome of this technological development. This is picked up in publicity images, both in network advertising and in other examples such as the DVD packaging, which focus on Alessandra Torresani as the avatar Zoe, semi-naked but covered by her long, black hair, holding up a red apple with a bite taken out of it.[1] The clear references here to ideas of original sin, the Garden of Eden, Eve and the tree of knowledge situate Zoe's and Daniel's technological ambitions as points that should 'be considered significant on a biblical scale' (Thrall 2015: 177). These images also forge a further connection with cyberpunk fiction, whose writers often imagine human contact with cyborg technologies, and especially with virtuality, in these terms. Gibson's character Case calls his exclusion from virtual space 'the Fall' (1993: 12) while Cadigan's characters comment that, 'Every technology has its original sin' (1991: 435). In *Caprica*, Zoe the avatar and Original Zoe figure as both Eve and serpent. Original Zoe unlocks the potential of virtual avatars and promotes her technological aspirations for a virtual heaven. Avatar Zoe makes and remakes her virtual and corporeal bodies, becoming cyborg both in V-world as an avatar and in the corporeal world in the body of the U-87 Cylon prototype. And avatar Zoe becomes a V-world 'God' with powers of creation and destruction. *Caprica*'s publicity materials underline the dangerous boundary-crossing in the narrative's technological discoveries about cyborgs and virtual systems.

Virtual Space and Cyborg Identity

Avatar Zoe has a complex existence in the aftermath of the bomb that kills the original Zoe Graystone ('Pilot Part 1' 1.1). Original Zoe designed her avatar to be both a backup copy, and an independent identity that can learn from experience. After Original Zoe's death, her avatar continues to exist in virtual space – V-world – in the form of an embodied individual with Original Zoe's thoughts, memories, and young, female body. When Daniel discovers the avatar, he treats it as a manufactured copy, a simulation of Original Zoe, not an individual in its own right; 'you're just an imitation,' he insists ('Pilot Part 2' 1.2). It becomes very evident, however, that avatar Zoe does develop an individual identity that is entirely distinct from Original Zoe's. Viewers distinguish the avatar from the human Zoe with the designation 'Zoe-A', something I will follow in this chapter. Not only does this name clarify which Zoe is which, it also emphasizes the continued artificiality – the virtuality – of Zoe-A's existence after Original Zoe's death.

The narrative that follows Zoe-A allows us to reconsider the status of the Cylons as antagonistic enemy figures. Although Zoe-A occasionally occupies a Cylon body, she is not an adversary or enemy, but is positioned as a hero, an individual on a quest for knowledge and self-realization. Where the *Battlestar Galactica* Cylons tend to be placed primarily as 'other' – although they question, trouble and complicate this definition in various ways – Zoe-A as cyborg takes a primary place, continually asserting her own authenticity and even her humanity. Indeed, in many respects Original Zoe serves as an adversary figure or villain in this narrative. Original Zoe is certainly not a particularly attractive character. She is arrogant, over-confident, cruel, and demonstrates hubris in her creation of the Zoe-A avatar and sociopathic tendencies in her investment in Clarice Willow's Apotheosis plan to create a virtual heaven ('Unvanquished' 1.11). In contrast, Zoe-A develops into a distinct and far more sympathetic character. As she becomes aware of her difference from Original Zoe, and asserts that difference, she becomes a more powerful individual within the physical and virtual worlds depicted in *Caprica*.

The presence of a distinctive virtual world in this narrative allows for some interesting explorations of virtual identities and environments. Cyberpunk and other science fiction narratives, and scholarly assessments of real-world cyberculture, often turn to virtuality's potential for *escape*. Virtuality is thought of as a space that allows the visitor or user to overturn or evade conventional boundaries, especially those confining aspects of gender, sexuality and race (Robins 1995: 135–6).[2] But in studies of early forms of interaction on the Internet, it was quickly apparent that '[g]ender is not erased in the virtual world […] but intensified discursively' (Hall 1996: 148). While individuals may carry out 'computer cross-dressing' on the Internet, 'gendered modes of communication themselves have remained relatively stable' (Stone 1991: 84). This means that gender performance in virtual space does not necessarily escape male-female binaries, and those binaries can be reinforced instead of relaxed. The possibilities for overthrowing boundaries are – as we have seen in relation to cyborgs in *Doctor Who* and *Star Trek: Voyager* as well as *Battlestar Galactica* – frequently complicated by the gendered presentation of cyborg characters, especially by those gendered as female. Any chances to trouble boundaries are just as frequently refused or shut down by narrative constructs that reinscribe certain characters, like Seven of Nine, in conventionally female (as well as human) terms. *Caprica* gives a complex presentation of virtual transcendence and cyborg subjectivity, offering the potential for blurred boundaries that may include gender, and certainly encompass virtual and corporeal identities. In many ways, Zoe-A does not escape gender boundaries, either as an avatar or as a metal-bodied cyborg. Yet at times she does offer the possibility of both virtual transformation and cyborg empowerment.

A Cyborg Dances: Zoe-A as Cylon/Cyborg

Zoe-A's connection with the U-87 Cylon prototype provides a point of contrast with other means of viewing the Cylon Centurions. In *Battlestar Galactica*, the metal Centurions are part of the Cylon 'race', but they are very rarely differentiated or accorded the status of individuals, unlike the humanoid Cylons who – as we have seen in Chapter 3 – do possess very definite individual personalities. Although the Centurions' positioning within Cylon hierarchy is occasionally challenged, this Cylon type is far more likely to be viewed by humans as an object of fear and terror, and by other Cylons simply as a tool (see my discussions on the notion of Centurion as 'toaster' and as slave in Chapter 3). In *Caprica*, Zoe-A's connection with the U-87 Cylon works to undermine the picture of the Centurion established through four seasons of *Battlestar Galactica*. Daniel Graystone attempts to maintain the status of the U-87 and other Cylon prototypes as 'tools', refusing any possibility that one or more might possess individuality or sentience. The prototypes follow the pattern established in the previous series: these Centurion-type Cylons provide muscle and might, and are used most notably as assassins (by Sam Adama, 'False Labor' 1.14) or military force (by Daniel Graystone, 'Apotheosis' 1.19). Zoe-A's involvement in their development does work to change viewer perception, which, in turn, may cause viewers to reinterpret aspects of *Battlestar Galactica*'s metal Cylons.

Strictly speaking, the virtual Zoe-A in the Cylon body is not a cyborg. The prototype Cylon body is a robot body; it is entirely mechanical. Zoe-A is a virtual construct; she does not possess an organic body (though she is represented *as* embodied within V-world). However, in terms of Zoe-A's visual representation on-screen, I classify her as a cyborg character in that she displays a self constructed from the virtual and the physical. The visual depiction of Zoe-A's interface with the prototype Cylon calls on the display of an organic (human) body as well as that of a metal (robot) body, as sequences cut between Zoe-A and the U-87 Cylon. I suggest that these sequences go further than 'troubling the viewer's perception' (Dell 2013: 138); they emphasize Zoe-A's embodied identity – which exists, even though she is a virtual creation – and reinforce aspects of her humanity (Kapica 2014: 624). Indeed, because viewers see the U-87 Cylon *as* Zoe-A for a considerable amount of screen time, this makes us more likely to see Zoe as human no matter whether she is represented as organically human, as a virtual self, or as cyborg.

In the sequences showing Zoe-A's intelligence inhabiting the U-87, directing and editing decisions work to:

cleverly [splice] images of the U-87 and Alessandra Torresani, inviting the television viewer to conflate the machine with the teenage, female Avatar Zoe. This juxtaposition underscores the already blurred lines between human and machine, layering visual representations in a way that serves a practical purpose (to remind us that Avatar Zoe is in control of the machine) and a thematic purpose (personification of – humanization of the machine). (Kapica 2014: 623–4)

Cutting between the imposing, tall and square, Cylon body, and Torresani's slight, slim female body creates a tremendous visual contrast, played on throughout the series in the framing of scenes and shots featuring the U-87 Cylon. In these sequences, Zoe-A is shown as embodied: a young woman, stylishly dressed in tailored clothes, often in monochrome grey or silver as a means of representing the metallic Cylon chassis. Yet the body depicted on screen is a paradox. In diegetic terms, Zoe-A has a virtual body that only exists in the V-world: the physical, concrete, organic human body that was the model for Zoe-A, Original Zoe's body, has been destroyed in the bomb blast. The interface with the Cylon body is Zoe-A's only experience of concrete embodiment and the only way in which she can interact with the physical world. With the Cylon body, Zoe-A can speak, she can make a telephone call; she can stand, walk and manipulate objects. Zoe-A animates the Cylon in a way that, for all his efforts and intelligence, Daniel Graystone cannot duplicate in other robot bodies ('The Imperfections of Memory' 1.8). Zoe-A personalizes the Cylon, creating an individual identity for this particular cyborg body. The visual effect that doubles between Torresani's image and the CGI metal body makes the U-87 Cylon an individual for the viewer too.

In her interface with the U-87, Zoe-A has the potential to demonstrate a breakdown of gender boundaries, especially in the visual contrasts of her virtual avatar-self and her concrete metal cyborg-self. These highlight tensions in the presentation of cyborgs that frequently struggle to escape from gendered representation. We see the Cylon Centurions of *Battlestar Galactica* presented as tall and hard-bodied, coded as masculine cyborgs, while the humanoid models are literally feminized in the bodies of Boomer, Athena and Caprica Six. In *Caprica*, while Zoe-A animates the body of the

U-87 she is *both* feminized and masculinized. As the U-87, she asks her friend Lacy anxiously, 'Do I look male to you?' – and after some hesitation, Lacy acknowledges the masculine coding of the Cylon, answering, 'Yeah' ('Rebirth' 1.3). However, Zoe-A as U-87 is subject to the feminizing gaze of the male technicians Drew and Philo who interact with her/it. The narrative contrasts 'negative, lascivious connotations' of speech and behaviour initiated by Drew (Kapica 2014: 624) with Philo's rather more positive interactions with the metal body he calls 'she'. While Philo's attitude may tend to appear more sympathetic, both attitudes result in feminizing the U-87 Cylon (Kapica 2014: 624; Thrall 2015: 178), and furthermore the visual cues offered to the viewer feminize the metal-bodied cyborg by doubling it with the body of Zoe-A/Torresani. Figure 8 shows this doubling effect: the camera does not show the U-87's cyborg body, but Zoe-A's virtual embodiment. The narrative presentation of Drew's and Philo's reactions to the U-87 Cylon, together with the visual representation of Zoe-A as the Cylon frame 'the exploitation of the robot body by Daniel and two other male scientists as an exploitation of the female body by men' (Wimmler 2015: 131). Visually depicting the Cylon as Zoe-A/Torresani encourages the viewer to

Figure 8: The U-87 Cylon prototype represented as Zoe-A (Alessandra Torresani), *Caprica*

identify instances such as 'Drew's leer and comment ("great piece of engineering") as misogynistic' and so to 'interpellate the U-87 as female within a patriarchal power structure' (Kapica 2014: 624). This process is extended in Zoe-A's interactions with Daniel while she occupies the U-87 body; Zoe-A is situated as experimental subject in relation to her 'father as scientific master' (Thrall 2015: 187).

In some respects, Philo's sympathetic attitude towards the U-87 Cylon acts as a bridge between virtual and corporeal worlds and between the metal machine and its human consciousness, the identity of Zoe-A. Philo speaks to the U-87 as though it is another person, not as though it is a tool to be commanded. In 'End of Line', for instance, he looks up into its metal face, seemingly making eye contact with its red eye-piece, while he says, 'We'll take care of you' in a solicitous tone. He opposes Daniel – his superior – in the same episode when he is told to 'burn off' the anomalies in the U-87's chip, arguing that by doing this they will destroy 'everything that makes this prototype distinctive'. He does not know that Zoe-A's identity animates this Cylon, yet he recognizes its individuality. Daniel's attitude towards the U-87, and to Cylons in general, contrasts with Philo's. Daniel refuses to acknowledge the possibility of sentience or individuality for any of his Cylon creations. These entities are 'real' to him as artificial bodies that can be commanded and sold: 'It is a robot [...] it is not a pet and it's definitely not a person' ('End of Line' 1.10). While Zoe-A can see that using a 'generative model' to create Cylons would make them 'unique, uncopyable' ('Imperfections of Memory'), Daniel sees them precisely as interchangeable and identical units that 'won't need to be paid. [A Cylon] won't retire or get sick. It won't have rights, or objections, or complaints' ('There is Another Sky' 1.6). Daniel's concept of the Cylons may be logical, but because viewers become used to the sympathetic cyborg embodiment and individuality of Zoe-A as the U-87, his attitude appears unimaginative, cold and unfeeling, and his ideas about Cylons as tools recalls the language of slavery (Thrall 2015: 170). His positioning of Cylons as slaves foreshadows the war that fans of both shows know is about to come. Nevertheless, Philo continues to make connections between virtual and corporeal and between avatar and robot, helping to create Zoe-A's cyborg identity.

In a key scene that works to cement Zoe-A's representation as a humanized machine, Philo dances with the U-87 Cylon ('Reins of a Waterfall' 1.4).

This visual representation, which embodies Zoe-A as dancer, is especially resonant for explorations of cyborg embodiment. Dance liberates Zoe-A's range of movement, and allows her physical expression in the body of the U-87. As Margaret R. Quinlan and Benjamin R. Bates note, 'dancing bodies simultaneously produce and are produced by' dance; dance 'is both a personal expression of being and a public performance' (2008: 66). Further, 'dance allows the dancer to perform the self': to express and to communicate aspects of the self (Quinlan and Bates 2008: 67). In the Zoe-A/U-87 dance sequence, such aspects of 'personal expression', performance and communication are evident, as well as possibilities for embodied freedom and connection with the corporeal world through the physical movement of dancing.

Embodied as the U-87 prototype, Zoe-A is restricted partly by the range of movement possible for a tall and solid metal body, and partly by the command structure in the Cylon's programming. The U-87 is not (or should not be) able to move unless it is commanded to do so; Zoe-A is able to move independently, but must conceal this ability in order to remain hidden within the U-87. The 'diagnostic tests' that Philo carries out allow Zoe-A to follow a standard movement sequence, but by adding music to the test sequence, and then allowing the Cylon specific movements, Philo begins to achieve his aim to 'make you dance'. We can view this as experimental silliness: making such a lumbering and large metal body dance is potentially comical, ridiculous or 'embarrassing' (Kapica 2014: 625). It could be seen as enacting Philo's (or any human's) power over Zoe-A as cyborg: the male technician is able to 'make' the female-coded cyborg move as he wishes. But the scene does not play this way. Instead of focusing on the metal Cylon body, the camera lingers on Zoe-A's virtual body, present through her technological interface with the U-87. There are references to the metal cyborg body in Zoe-A's high-heeled shoes that give her feet the solid appearance of the Cylon's metal appendages, and her grey dress with metallic glints in the fabric. Her face shows enjoyment and happiness – things that the Cylon face cannot display – and her arm movements in particular are sinuous and graceful, contrasting with Cylon movement which is often ponderous and deliberate (see also Thrall 2015: 189). By focusing on Zoe-A's (fully-clothed) body the scene foregrounds pleasure in free movement and emphasizes possibilities for connections between human and virtually-embodied individuals, especially as Philo, too, seems to derive enjoyment from the dance.

In contrast to Philo, Daniel's behaviour towards the U-87 Cylon, even when he suspects that Zoe-A has been downloaded into the robot body, is problematic. After attempting to coax and to surprise her into revealing herself ('Imperfections of Memory', 'Ghosts in the Machine' 1.9) he tries emotional and dangerous triggers to force Zoe-A to confirm her 'true' identity. However, Daniel's attitude is also complex and contradictory. After he first rejects Zoe-A's avatar identity as fake, he comes to embrace the concept that Zoe-A does have a valid, individual virtual identity. Meanwhile, Zoe-A's determination to remain hidden within the U-87, something that she maintains through the first eight episodes of the series,[3] brings her closer to a cyborg identity. 'I have to turn me off. Just be the robot,' she declares, while Lacy asks perceptively, 'Can you even do that any more?' ('Ghosts in the Machine'). Here Lacy appears to recognize that Zoe-A's interface with the Cylon body is more than an intelligence making use of a tool. Zoe-A's identity and personality become entangled within the metal body, and this is obvious to the viewer in the visual cues and doubling effects in all of the scenes featuring Zoe-A as the U-87.

Making a Place in Virtual Space: Life and Death in V-World

A parallel narrative strand in *Caprica* takes place in V-world, a virtual world accessible through the 'holobands' developed by Daniel's company. Entry into V-world gives a user access to a range of different scenarios, from the 'V-Club' raves, sex rooms and spaces that permit violence, murder and human sacrifice, to 'New Cap City', a duplicate Caprica City transformed into a 1940s-style *noir* world of intrigue and crime ('There is Another Sky'). Scenes or sequences that take place in V-world are – for the most part – clearly signaled to the viewer through the use of a sting: a pulse of sound and a visual of red computer code undulating on a dark background, positioned before the V-World scenes. Scenes that take place in the *noir* New Cap City feature strongly monochrome visuals and striking accents of deep colour, especially purples and reds. The V-world storylines dramatize the interaction between apparently embodied virtual individuals and their

'Between Life and Death': Embodiment and Virtuality in *Caprica*

immersion in created, fantasy landscapes in a digital environment. These storylines show that 'the process of meaning-making [in virtual space] is embedded in corporeal interaction between human bodies and computer hardware and software' (Green 1997: 63), and reveal that potential cyborg embodiment can be boundary-crossing and transformative, or dangerous and addictive.

The popularity of *Caprica*'s V-world, and its addictive potential, parallels our own discussions of the ways people choose to engage with any kind of online, virtual role-play (such as in gaming, Second Life, or aspects of social media). Just as we debate the effects of simulated violence in computer role-playing games, so the characters of *Caprica* show a variety of responses to the possibilities of V-world. For some – particularly teenagers – it is a fantasy world that allows them to explore forbidden behaviours; Zoe-A and her friends have experimented in V-Club, 'where what are still by definition children play "adult" games of debauchery, murder, and human sacrifice' (Thrall 2015: 176). The game-world of New Cap City allows its players the chance to 'be something' by winning virtual wealth and status ('There is Another Sky'). Equally, players can lose everything, including access to the game space, if they are virtually 'killed'. New Cap City's game-world is enticing and addictive, but it is also mysterious. Its rules are unwritten (and possibly nonexistent): 'finding out the object of the game *is* the object of the game' ('There is Another Sky'). These V-world game-spaces highlight problematic aspects of virtuality. In general, V-world is lawless, criticized by Amanda Graystone as a 'moral vacuum' ('Gravedancing' 1.5) and by Clarice Willow and the STO in similar ways. Zoe-A voices disquiet about 'the way people see this place [V-world] as an excuse to cut corners or [...] do things they know are wrong but just because they're in here, they're not wrong any more' ('Imperfections of Memory'). Tamara rejects the idea that only V-world allows people to 'be something', telling her guide Heracles, 'Maybe if you weren't in here playing this game you could be something out there too' ('There is Another Sky'). These examples show that V-world affects individuals in real and lasting ways, and *Caprica* dramatizes the idea that corporeal selves can be corrupted through their continued engagement with the virtual space.

This is especially evident in the storyline following Joseph Adama's search for his daughter's avatar. Joseph's continued immersion in V-world constitutes an escape from the corporeal world – in which his wife and daughter have died – into a virtual version in which at least an avatar Tamara survives. Initially, Joseph's reactions are presented sympathetically, and as a point of contrast with Daniel's more cynical manipulations of cybernetics and virtuality, but as Joseph extends his time spent as an avatar in V-world, takes virtual 'amps' to pump up his avatar's abilities and neglects his corporeal body's needs (refusing food, for example), characters' – and viewers' – sympathies diminish ('End of Line'). Evelyn (who, disguised as the avatar Emmanuelle, has been Joseph's guide in V-world) and Tamara demonstrate their rejection of V-world and its game spaces. 'Emmanuelle' pleads with Tamara to help Joseph, recounting his withdrawal from the physical world: 'He missed his own son's ink day [a coming-of-age ceremony in which the young person receives his first tattoo]. He's using amp. He's lost.' Paradoxically, Tamara the avatar insists on the negative aspects of V-world. She tells Joseph, 'This place is bad for you. [...] You're killing yourself with that stuff. [...] You're wasting your life. I don't want you watching me, because if that's all you do, that's all you'll ever do' ('End of Line'). Shooting Joseph's avatar, and 'killing' him in V-world, forcibly returns him to the corporeal world, where he will have to deal with his grief, and rebuild his connections with others. Tamara's actions resonate with her earlier comment to Heracles, and tell Joseph that he can be 'something out there too', away from the temptations of V-world.

V-world does offer transformative possibilities as well as the possibility of corruption or of virtual annihilation, although these possibilities do not occupy a central place in the series narrative. In order to interact in V-world, individuals must create avatars, virtual versions of themselves. These virtual selves match contemporary findings on gendered interaction in virtual spaces, where gender distinctions and boundaries tend to be maintained (Hall 1996: 148) or at least to retain 'traditional binary conventions' (Roberts and Parks 2001: 265). The participants in V-world enter that world as virtually-embodied entities, and though they may change their appearance, as Evelyn does in her disguise as 'Emmanuelle', V-world avatars seem to retain the gender of their physical originals. Those interacting in V-world, especially those who find their way into New Cap City, become invested in the development of their virtual selves, and create a persona that is distinct from their physical self. This is even the case for those who are supposed to profess a rejection of V-world. Clarice Willow's husbands Nestor and Olaf are shown as keen players of the New Cap City game; Olaf has developed his avatar for five years, which suggests that the avatar's death at Zoe-A's hands is a potentially traumatic event ('Dirteaters' 1.16). These examples are limited, but they do at least suggest that a participant could decide to create a different sort of avatar, one that allowed the user to challenge established boundaries of gender and other embodied conventions.

Zoe-A and Tamara do emphatically challenge boundaries in V-world. Within this virtual world, their avatars occupy a unique place. Both personalities exist only as avatars, as copies or simulations of their corporeal selves. In this respect, they follow the mode of simulation envisioned by Walter Benjamin or Jean Baudrillard: as avatars whose embodied selves have died, they are copies with no original, and this accentuates their distance from the physical world and their entry to the hyperreal V-world. During the series, V-world itself becomes 'a space of transition, from image to a new reality' (Dell 2013: 140); that space, and Zoe-A and Tamara, trouble the boundaries between the corporeal and the virtual and between life and death.

Zoe-A and Tamara maintain certain connections to the corporeal world, even though they are pure avatars. Their separation from the physical world – the deaths of the embodied Zoe and Tamara – is expressed in strongly corporeal terms. Zoe-A's bloody face and arms are a visual reference to Original Zoe's violent death in the bombing, and Tamara's panicky reaction to her absent heartbeat further stresses continued physical connections ('Pilot Part 2'). As they develop as virtually-embodied individuals, both avatars retain strong connections to versions of the corporeal. Each keeps her respective embodied appearance, so that they continue to look the way their original bodies looked when alive (and we can note that their parents are always able to recognize them in V-world). They conform to some of the rules of the virtual space, such as its versions of gravity and cause and effect – they do not fly, for example, as characters in *The Matrix* do when they manipulate their virtual world. They can be wounded and bleed, something we see when Tamara is shot ('There Is Another Sky') and Zoe-A is beaten ('Things We Lock Away' 1.13). However, their status as copies without an original allows them immortality and other special powers within V-world. Their adopted roles as 'Avenging Angels' marks the virtual world as they kill other avatars, throwing them out of V-world and continuing to realize Tamara's words: 'If you weren't in here, you could be somebody out there'. In turn their new vigilante identity marks the corporeal world where 'T-shirts and signs with images of them as Avenging Angels appear' (Dell 2013: 140) and people enter V-world especially to seek them out and engage them in combat, so further breaching the boundaries between the physical and the virtual ('Dirteaters').

The process of marking the virtual space goes further when Zoe-A and Tamara manipulate aspects of virtuality. Tamara 'draws' her flower symbol on walls and pavements ('Ghosts in the Machine'), and Zoe-A alters the computer code of V-world to create different landscapes ('The Heavens Will Rise' 1.17). Their creation of different, distinct, and sometimes hidden or secret virtual spaces, such as Zoe-A's password-protected secret room located within the V-Club, challenges the conventions, rules and limitations of virtual space. From the pilot episode, the narrative clearly frames Zoe-A as a gifted individual with a perceptive relationship to technology. We see that her interaction with the U-87 Cylon transforms that metal body into an independent and intelligent cyborg body with unique capabilities. Her interaction with virtual spaces in her avatar body transforms those spaces too. In a 'date' with Philo that takes place (for obvious reasons) in V-world, the two sit on a beach looking onto water and a rocky, tree-lined cove. It is a superficially beautiful space but, as Zoe-A comments, it is 'fakey-fakey. That tree over there [is] identical to this tree' ('Imperfections of Memory'). Zoe-A underlines the point that, if programmers adhere to strict, linear rules of virtual-reality creation, the result is a landscape that does not appear to be convincingly 'real' because it does not allow for enough diversity.

Zoe-A's power over V-world – and over its spaces created out of computer code – is in her ability to bring 'reality' to the virtual. In her creations of virtual spaces, she demonstrates interaction between her corporeal cyborg embodiment and her 'embodiment in virtual locations; that is, in worlds which overlap, and which are simultaneously digital and non-digital' (Green 1997: 63). Zoe-A re-forms the high-rise buildings and neon signs of New Cap City into a mountain fortress with forests and fantasy creatures ('The Heavens Will Rise', 'Here Be Dragons' 1.18). Unlike the 'fakey-fakey' virtual beach and forest, Zoe-A's landscape creations follow her idea that 'living systems use generative algorithms' to create in V-world 'an infinite variety of tree-like trees' ('Imperfections of Memory'). Entering into Zoe-A's landscape, Daniel marvels, 'Look at these leaves. Each one is different. And this light. It's all so incredibly real. And I don't have the foggiest idea how she did it. […] It's one thing to write code, but what Zoe's done here is… Well, it's close to what the gods did in the old creation myths' ('Here Be Dragons'). Indeed, within V-world Zoe-A is 'God' with powers of creation and destruction over avatars and virtual spaces ('Dirteaters', 'Apotheosis').

How to Live a Virtual Life: Apotheosis and Grace

The exploration of virtual environments in *Caprica* shows the many ways individuals seek escape from the physical world: through fantasy role-playing, seeking experiences that are forbidden in the corporeal world (like murder or human sacrifice), or by attempting to immerse themselves in the virtual realm, valuing the virtual above the corporeal. These examples show how corporeal selves can approach a cyborg existence through virtual experiences in an avatar body. V-world also holds the promise that corporeal death can be overcome, as evidenced by the continued existence of Tamara and Zoe-A after their physical bodies have died. Daniel's 'Grace' programme and Clarice's 'Apotheosis' plan aim to overcome death by creating hyperreal environments. With 'Grace', Daniel plans to replicate Zoe-A's and Tamara's continuing existence in V-world by creating avatars of people who have died. Using similar principles, Clarice intends to create a virtual world in which avatars can be 'resurrected' after the deaths of their physical bodies ('Unvanquished'). Daniel's Grace programme plays on human frailty and offers to overturn the inevitability of death, once again breaking through boundaries: 'Imagine never having to say good-bye to your loved ones again. Imagine a future without loss, brought to you today' ('False Labor'). Clarice describes her virtual vision in similar, though more religiously inflected terms: 'Imagine a world in which death can be conquered, life everlasting in a virtual heaven that we have built' ('End of Line'). Clarice's plan does more than 'remove the need for faith' in an afterlife. While 'apotheosis' suggests that we will see a transformation of the mortal into the divine, this particular plan threatens to give reality the status of a virtual world, to make the physical world into meaningless hyper-reality: 'The real world will turn into a game like New Cap City. People will kill, rape, destroy. They'll be forgiven and blessed, and go to heaven anyway!' ('Apotheosis'). Grace and Apotheosis push at the limits of virtuality, collapsing the boundaries between life and death and between corporeal and virtual. In both cases, the promise of life after death is available only to the worthy: only those who have paid for Grace will return as avatars; only those who have pledged devotion to the One True God will be resurrected.

Grace and Apotheosis depend on a virtual reality that is indistinguishable from the physical world. The difficulties associated with this are apparent in the storyline that follows Daniel's attempt to create a stable, independent and individual avatar, duplicating Zoe's achievement with Zoe-A. Daniel's interaction with an avatar version of Amanda Graystone shows how far he is from making the virtual seem 'real'. Avatar-Amanda is unable to maintain independent thought, and instead she loops back to a basic programme that is designed to please and seduce, and speaks in quotations from corporeal Amanda's diary. The scenes between Daniel and avatar-Amanda are complicated from a viewer's point of view because the usual sting heralding the appearance of a V-world sequence does not appear; Daniel's interactions with avatar Amanda flow into the scenes that take place in the physical world. This makes it difficult for the viewer to tell whether a scene exists corporeally or in V-world, and this tension encourages the viewer to watch closely for clues as to Amanda's status in these scenes. The STO faithful likewise encounter problems in creating their virtual space; Clarice criticizes early designs for being 'too traditional' and therefore falling short of her vision of a virtual location that must 'glorify God' ('Dirteaters'). And of course, Clarice's plan is predicated on the destruction of the corporeal body as well as on a privileging of virtual space, something that contrasts with the STO's attitude towards the existing V-world, which they consider to be corrupt and immoral. According to the plan, a new kind of V-world will exist so that 'scanned avatars of our martyrs will be uploaded into V-world heaven' ('The Heavens Will Rise'). Clarice's positive language obscures the fact that 'a lot of good people are going to die' ('The Heavens Will Rise'). Notably, Clarice avoids martyrdom for herself, although she has an avatar-body that can and does access her created 'heaven'.[4]

Daniel's attempt to overthrow death itself with the Grace programme fails because he cannot copy what Zoe achieved with Zoe-A. He is unable to create an independent avatar with the ability to learn and develop as an individual. Zoe-A, however, is very clearly positioned as one who has the potential to do absolutely anything within V-world, and who has the ability to cross over into the physical world, too. This potential is signalled very early in the series. In 'Rebirth', Zoe-A, in the body of the U-87 Cylon, sits with Lacy in Original Zoe's bedroom. Incongruously interacting with a young girl's private domain in the solid metal cyborg body, Zoe-A attempts to voice her confusion: 'I'm Zoe, and the avatar, and the robot.' Lacy helps her find the right descriptive word, 'a trinity – three faces in one thing.' By the time of the events of the series finale, Zoe-A is able to bring her three faces together to defeat Clarice Willow in the corporeal world and in the V-world 'heaven'. Zoe-A animates the damaged U-87, and so can physically attack Clarice and the other STO terrorists, and defend her parents. And her command over V-world's code, the ability that allows her to create her own virtual spaces, enables her to destroy Clarice's virtual Apotheosis. Here, Zoe-A's manipulation of virtuality is presented visually, as a battle fought by bodies in a landscape. Zoe-A's and Clarice's avatars face each other in the artificial heaven, which is represented as a pillared temple in a garden. While Clarice protests that Apotheosis 'is God's will', Zoe-A declares, 'I *am* God', voicing her complete command over all aspects of virtuality in V-world, as well as her own attainment of apotheosis. In her fights with Clarice in the physical world as the U-87 and in V-world as a god-self, '[t]he Cylon is Zoe, Zoe is the Cylon and the avatar, traversing the certainty of pre-defined borders and existing simultaneously' inside and outside V-world (Dell 2013: 141). As avatar *and* robot, Zoe-A is the boundary-crossing cyborg who moves between embodiment and virtuality and across life and death, and finally re-enters the physical world in a new corporeal cyborg body.

'The Shape of Things to Come': Cyborgs, Corporeality, Virtuality

The final scenes of *Caprica* include several moments that once more admit possibilities for the transgression or breaking down of boundaries that have divided the physical and the virtual. These include new perspectives on the Cylons' cyborg embodiment, and on the possibilities of virtuality. A new and more positive vision of the Cylons is seen to develop after the Cylon 'marine troop' prevent the STO suicide bombers from destroying the Atlas Arena in the middle of a Pyramid game ('Apotheosis'). This action by Cylons causes a turning point in human attitudes, which will make it possible for Cylon bodies to be integrated into the everyday life of the Twelve Colonies.[5] The arena battle shows the Cylons' augmented cyborg capacity: they have sensors that allow them to detect explosives and thus find the bombers, and their targeting functions enable them to shoot each bomber, without causing harm to other humans. At the end of the battle, the Cylon troop throw their own bodies upon the final bomber as he detonates his explosives, smothering the blast and destroying their own metal bodies in the process. In the coda to the concluding episode,[6] we are shown a brief glimpse of a statue that commemorates the Cylon attack force, according these metal bodies an honour that is given to humans of particular stature or who have carried out especially impressive or heroic tasks. It would appear that these Cylons have worked to 'protect' humans, as Daniel suggests ('Apotheosis'). But this explanation masks some troublesome points. In their actions against the STO bombers, these Cylons can only do what Daniel tells them to do, so that in their work of 'protecting us' they are literally only following orders. And – at least on the face of it – Daniel still rejects the notion that Cylons might be individuals, telling a television interviewer: 'I think people are smart enough to realize that as useful as they are, Cylons are tools – nothing more – and to forget that, to blur the distinction between man and machine and attribute human qualities, is folly' ('Apotheosis').

However, these distinctions do continue to blur in both physical and virtual worlds. Having demonstrated her mastery over V-world, Zoe-A remains within a small section that Daniel has created, a space he describes as 'an exact replica of the home you grew up in, with every creature comfort at your fingertips' ('Here Be Dragons'). Daniel's description itself is filled with contradiction; does a virtual body need a 'home' or 'creature comforts'? Daniel privileges Zoe-A's cyborg embodiment over that of other Cylons. In the coda, Daniel's television interview is intercut with a static scene of Amanda and Zoe-A in the virtual home. While Daniel insists

'Between Life and Death': Embodiment and Virtuality in *Caprica*

publicly that 'Cylons are tools – nothing more', in the private space we see Amanda stroking Zoe-A's arm as they cuddle together on the sofa. Daniel's words may well be an 'attempt to put back boundaries' between the corporeal and the virtual (Dell 2013: 140), but in another sense, his attitude in the corporeal world is the opposite of his attitude in the virtual world. He responds to Zoe-A as his daughter, not as a copy of her. He values her special abilities with coding and with the creation of avatars – Zoe-A and Daniel work together to make her another corporeal body. It appears that, for Daniel, neither corporeality nor virtuality are so easily classified and categorized. By the end of the series Daniel's insistence that 'as useful as they are', Cylons are 'tools, nothing more' ('Apotheosis') looks like a public 'attempt to re-draw the boundaries he disrupted' (Dell 2013: 142), but in private he continues to disrupt those boundaries as he works with Zoe-A to create a more human-like artificial body. Their success is one of the last moments of the coda, where we see Daniel and Amanda welcome Zoe-A back into a physical body in the corporeal world.

It is evident from *Caprica*'s coda that Cylons, too, continue to blur the boundaries between the virtual and the physical. They are shown to have access to virtual space; they appear in a virtual church where Clarice Willow preaches to them. Clarice's question 'Are you alive?' links *Caprica* to its parent series, and indeed loops back to the opening scenes of that series where a Six model asked the Twelve Colonies' representative the same question (*Battlestar Galactica* 'Pilot'). Clarice's sermon contrasts directly with Daniel's interview statements. Where Daniel calls the Cylons 'tools', Clarice recognizes Cylon individuality and personhood as she answers her own question: 'The simple answer might be you are alive because you can ask that question. You have the right to think and feel and yearn to be more because you are not just humanity's children, you are God's children […], equal living beings with the same rights as those who made you.' With the appearance of the aural and visual sting just beforehand, these scenes are clearly signaled as taking place in V-world, and this is cemented by Zoe-A's appearance in one of the virtual pews. The virtual space, visualized as a stone cathedral, follows Clarice's earlier description for her imagined virtual heaven with 'soaring arches and stained glass windows and statues built into the walls' ('Dirteaters'). The admittance of Cylons to V-world once again links *Caprica* to *Battlestar Galactica*. In the parent series, Cylons have the ability to 'visualize', to create virtual spaces and share them with others, as Boomer does with Tyrol in 'Someone to Watch Over Me' (4.17). Putting Cylons into V-world carries with it the implication that Cylons have the potential to create personalized virtual spaces as Zoe-A does, so offers an explanation for the Cylon ability to visualize. Visualization comes into play in ideas envisioned for a second season of *Caprica*, where a storyline would have followed connections between Zoe-A and the Cylon Final Five:

> The idea was that Zoe would eventually have run into a V-World that's a sleepy little earth-like fishing village. A man is fishing at the end of a long pier and it turns out to be Aaron Douglas [Tyrol]. The Final Five keep their brains active on their long journey to the 12 worlds by using their own V-World programs. They fish together for a while. Tyrol is very interested when she explains who she is and what her family is trying to accomplish. He gives her the gift of a fishing lure. When Zoe returns, the lure turns out to be code that gives them the piece they've been missing and Zoe gets a goo-bath [and a corporeal body]. (Murphy 2013)

This account of further connections between *Caprica* and *Battlestar Galactica* also links virtual and corporeal cyborgs, as Zoe-A's virtual self discovers a key piece of information that will allow her a physical self once more.

The final sequence of the series, its coda, dovetails with *Battlestar Galactica*'s four seasons in its hints about Cylons in virtual space. It loops back to the beginning of *Caprica*'s narrative with Daniel's drive to construct the metal-bodied Cylons, and it looks forward to the events of *Battlestar Galactica* in the appearance of Zoe-A's physical body using exactly the same visual representation as the Cylon resurrection tanks. Kevin Murphy's ideas for a possible Season 2 of *Caprica* had Zoe-A as an undercover cyborg:

> We would have learned that [law enforcement agent] Jordan Duram […] is Zoe's commanding officer. He figures out her secret and helps her keep quiet in return for her assistance on sensitive black-ops missions. (Murphy 2013)

The idea of a prototype female cyborg character who must hide her true identity and work with a quasi-government agency on secret missions sounds very similar to the subject of my next chapter, the rebooted *Bionic Woman*. With intertextual connections to the world of *Caprica* and *Battlestar Galactica* in its showrunner (David Eick) and casting (Katee Sackhoff as cyborg Sarah), *Bionic Woman* presents contested versions of cyborg embodiment as both liberatory and restricting, and follows another development of new technologies with the potential to transform embodied presence in the physical world.

5

The Cyborg as Action Hero: *Bionic Woman*

The cyborgs examined in this and the following two chapters (*Terminator: The Sarah Connor Chronicles* and *Dollhouse*) illustrate examples of the female action hero and the related visual representation of female characters within a superhero narrative. The reimagined *Bionic Woman* has a clear connection to other twenty-first-century cyborg television: its executive producer, David Eick, had the same role on the rebooted *Battlestar Galactica* and on *Caprica*. It seems evident that much of the impetus behind *Bionic Woman*'s reimagining was the success of *Battlestar Galactica* and especially viewer interest in its cyborg characters Six, Boomer and Athena. The new series follows the general structure of the original *Bionic Woman* (1976–8): a young woman is mortally injured and in order to save her life is given robotic ('bionic') implants in both legs, one arm, one eye and one ear. Having become cyborg, the 'bionic woman' is recruited as an agent for a mysterious quasi-governmental organization (in the original series, the Office of Scientific Intelligence [OSI]; in the reboot, the Berkut Group). The 2007 Jaime Sommers is given a different back-story; in the original series she is a professional tennis player and – possibly more crucially – the girlfriend of bionic Steve Austin, the 'six million dollar man'. In the reimagined show, Jaime is a college dropout supporting her teenage sister Becca by working as a bartender. The show situates the central character in a maternal role/relationship within a family unit, and frequently downplays the extent of her physical abilities. This suggests that Jaime's cyborg character is made more acceptable to a general audience through the emphasis on family connections and other links to a 'normally' embodied self.

The 2007 *Bionic Woman* presents the cyborg as protagonist and as adversary, introduces themes of power and control, and places its central characters in conflict with aspects of their own embodiment, with storylines that frame them as subjugated and as disabled by their cyborg augmentations. *Bionic Woman* shows the female action hero in different guises, with both central character Jaime and adversary Sarah – the 'first bionic woman' – filling this role. Additionally, Jaime is represented as a cyborg/human hybrid, something that encourages connections with other television narratives that present various versions of the female action hero, such as *Buffy the Vampire Slayer, Alias* and *Dark Angel*. Jaime and Sarah are situated in the narrative in potentially complex relationships with Will and Anthony Anthros, the inventors of the bionic technology. They are also involved with individuals who work for the Berkut Group, 'a private, clandestine group dedicated to stopping rogue organizations from ending civilization as we know it' ('Paradise Lost' 1.2), including its leader Jonas, and agents Ruth, Jae and Antonio.

Looking at the 1970s *Bionic Woman* series illuminates the way Jaime's character is positioned in the 2007 version. The original series, and its contemporaries, like *Charlie's Angels* (1976–81) and *Wonder Woman* (1975–9), that featured other versions of the female action hero, offer a complicated perspective on the presentation of female characters. All these series 'featur[ed] attractive women in title roles that negotiated liberal feminism and antifeminism' (Jenkins 2011: 102) but continued to present these female characters 'in comic book settings that could never be mistaken for reality' (Douglas 1995: 218). *Charlie's Angels* is a typical example, with its recurring 'missions set in health spas, massage parlours and Las Vegas nightclubs' which 'ensured the sexual spectacle of the Angels […] appearing either scantily clad or in a variety of sexually provocative costumes' (Gough-Yates 2001: 89). In *The Bionic Woman* too, 'Jaime goes undercover as a nun, a stewardess, a beauty pageant contestant, and a professional wrestler – to save the world!' (Oler 2008: 38). These assumed identities give 1970s Jaime the chance to oppose sexual stereotyping; Tricia Jenkins notes that such opposition is present in

'Bionic Beauty' (1.7), an episode in which Jaime goes undercover at a beauty pageant (2011: 111, note 5). However, the series is, as Anna Gough-Yates asserts of *Charlie's Angels*, 'a deeply contradictory text' (2001: 90); although it promised a certain degree of freedom for its female character, '[d]espite her ass-kicking abilities, the bionic woman was confined to fighting for justice in hyperfeminine spaces' (Oler 2008: 38).

As for the depiction of Jaime's cyborg embodiment in the original series, this too is treated in contradictory ways. As Tricia Jenkins notes, the writers and producers were concerned to follow a 'non super-hero approach' with regard to Jaime's character (Philip de Guere, in Jenkins 2011: 105), making sure that she was not aggressive or 'threatening'; 'she never actually slugged anyone' (Kenneth Johnson, in Jenkins 2011: 106). 1970s Jaime fights verbally as much as physically, something we can see in episodes like 'Kill Oscar Part 3' (2.6) or 'On the Run' (3.22) where her reasoning appeals to the (male) adversaries of each episode. For the 2007 reboot, the key question is (as producer David Eick describes it) 'not so much Can a woman do what a man can do? It's if the answer's yes, what does that mean?' (in Quinlan and Bates 2009: 51). Eick's comment appears to point to possibilities that will allow the depiction of the new bionic woman to move beyond the 'feminine' stereotyping of its original. However, the reboot still reflects some similar contradictions; the series offered 'hopes that a technologically enhanced woman could be a true feminist superhero. And, indeed, technology does level the playing field for Jaime Sommers, but it does not liberate her – much to the disappointment of many feminist fans' (Oler 2008: 39). The bionic women are given power, but it is frequently revealed to be conditional and dependent on others, especially on male characters. This aspect of the 1970s series (in which Jaime depends on Oscar and Rudy) is paralleled in the 2007 series (in which Jaime and Sarah depend, in various ways, on Will and Anthony Anthros and their work with the bionic technology, and on Jonas and Jae of the Berkut Group).

In other respects, the 2007 *Bionic Woman* does present female characters who demonstrate their physical power as superheroes. The rebooted, twenty-first-century bionic women do not appear to be constrained in quite the same way as 1970s Jaime with her non-superhero superpowers that did not allow her to hit anybody. 2007's Jaime and Sarah can engage in physical action, a feature we see in other television narratives that depict female superheroes or female action heroes, such as *Buffy the Vampire Slayer, Dark Angel, Alias* and *Heroes*. *Bionic Woman* follows the general pattern of twenty-first-century female action heroes who wield strength and power, but whose abilities are portrayed in contradictory ways. In such narratives, the female superhero frequently struggles to use or control her superpowers, is directed by hierarchical organizations or (male) superiors, and has difficulties with relationships and family connections. All these factors complicate the female superhero's potential as a strong and independent character, and this is certainly true of the presentations of Jaime and Sarah in this series.

Such complications extend to the female superhero's physicality on the television screen. Such a character 'not only assumes the central role but destroys conventional ideas of the female body as passive, as to be looked at […]. The female hero *takes up space*' (Heinecken 2003: 4, emphasis in original). These characters are positioned against traditional versions of femininity which 'urge women to make their bodies small and to take up less space' (Heinecken 2003: 3). Paradoxically, however, the female superhero of television is often portrayed by small and slight actors who do 'take up less space' but are nevertheless physically powerful within the narrative. The casting of the 2007 *Bionic Woman* offers *two* potentially strong and active female characters with powers that come from their cyborg embodiment, and neither follows the pattern of the petite, supernaturally powered female action hero. Both Michelle Ryan as Jaime Sommers and Katee Sackhoff as Sarah Corvus are taller, broader and 'take up [more] space' than do female action heroes in other television narratives. Ryan and Sackhoff's physical appearance do contribute to a sense of power and strength that is appropriate for characters with bionic enhancements. In fight scenes, they are matched for height, and contrary to the 1970s series in which Jaime 'never actually slugged anyone', in the rebooted series physical violence is not only allowed but is featured in highly dramatic set-piece scenes like the fight between Sarah and Jaime at the end of the pilot episode.

These characters are written as active, intelligent and complex individuals. With the casting of Katee Sackhoff as Sarah Corvus, the series makes use of elements of 'intertextuality of casting' (Bussolini 2013), which gives a further dimension to its status as a narrative of cyborg embodiment. Sackhoff's involvement creates two possible ways to view *Bionic Woman* as a series: in one way it is a reboot, a 'reimagining' of the original 1970s series; in another, it shares certain themes and concepts with a completely different series. Including Sackhoff in a television series produced by David Eick creates connections with the successful *Battlestar Galactica*, and fans of that series might reasonably expect that they would find in *Bionic Woman* a similarly gritty 'reimagining' of the original version.

There is a clear difference in tone between the 1970s and 2007 *Bionic Woman*, and a sense of this difference is immediately apparent in their title sequences. The original *Bionic Woman* begins with computerized text on a black background which summarizes the story of Jaime's injury and replacement bionics. Upbeat string music accompanies shots of Jaime learning to use her bionic ear and arm, and running and jumping with her new bionic limbs. Stills show Jaime smiling and laughing with her colleagues Oscar Goldman and Rudy Wells, implying that her new bionic embodiment has also given her a happy and fulfilling lifestyle. In contrast, the 2007 titles are very short, reflecting a trend in contemporary television for minimal or non-existent title sequences. The *Bionic Woman* titles incorporate fast cuts between shots of Jaime's work at the bar, her accident and recuperation, with short clips, taken from the pilot episode, of Jaime's fights with Sarah and escape from the research facility where she was fitted with her bionics. Intercut with these scenes is the silhouetted image of a woman hitting her fists against frosted glass before breaking through it, and the credits end on an image of Jaime running away from the camera, all filmed against dark backgrounds. These signal the very different tone of the twenty-first-century version. The faceless woman behind the glass could be read as Jaime, Sarah or any number of other nameless future bionic women; the dark settings and scenes of violence and flight set up the series' engagement with issues of power and control. Although Jaime and Sarah are given physical powers that amount to superhuman abilities, very often they are shown as *not* in control over their own bodies, work, relationships or future.

The Bionic Body and Cyborg Physicality

> Yeah, don't even get me started on how objectifying this whole 'bionic woman' thing is. (Sarah Corvus, 'Sisterhood' 1.4)

Compared with the cyborgs I analyse in other chapters, Jaime's version of cyborg embodiment connects with characters like Seven of Nine, Oswin in *Doctor Who*'s 'Asylum of the Daleks', or Nina Sharp in *Fringe*, those who have lived as entirely organic bodies before they were made cyborg. Nina's portrayal parallels Jaime's in the visual presentation of their cyborg embodiment, especially in the way their bodies are represented most consistently within the narrative as apparently wholly organic (see Chapter 8 for a discussion of Nina as cyborg). We rarely see evidence of the technological aspects of Jaime's bionic arm or legs, except in hints or brief glimpses, and these are usually at times of injury or malfunction, when Jaime tends to be represented as detached or alienated from her own body. This is clear from a small example: when she breaks her toe, she hears the technician Nathan describe it as 'my toe' and Jonas announce that she owes him $27,269.31 for a new one – quite a price when we recall that the whole of Steve Austin's bionics cost six million dollars ('Faceoff' 1.4). This part of her body becomes a technological item that can be replaced, and that does not even belong to her. By extension, this is true of any part of her body that has been augmented with bionics, and since her augmentations include nanomachines called 'anthrocytes' teeming through her blood, we might read her entire body, including its blood and tissue, as cyborg and therefore under the ownership of the Berkut Group.

As its title suggests, *Bionic Woman* makes the cyborg its central character. Jaime is not positioned as a supporting character, to be viewed through the eyes of the main human characters and judged by their standards (as in the depictions of most of the cyborg characters in *Doctor Who*, *Voyager*, *Battlestar Galactica* or *Terminator: The Sarah Connor Chronicles*), but the focus of the action. The episodes revolve around Jaime's efforts to balance her home and family life with her sister with her separate identity as the crime-fighting 'bionic woman'. Jaime is the point of contrast for Sarah, 'the first bionic woman', who is often situated as her double or mirror-image. Through Sarah, the narrative questions the presumed advantages of cyborg identity and attempts to deal with some of the complications inherent in machinic embodiment. Both Jaime and Sarah are already liminal or hybrid characters, chiming with their cyborg embodiment; Anne Balsamo points out that 'cyborgs are hybrid entities that are neither wholly technological nor completely organic' (1995: 11). I define Jaime as hybrid in other ways too, which allows comparison across different fantasy/science fiction television narratives.

We see versions of the female action hero as hybrid in characters like Buffy in *Buffy the Vampire Slayer*, Sydney in *Alias*, Max in *Dark Angel*, and Olivia in *Fringe*. These characters possess special abilities or powers, ranging through Sydney's skills with spycraft and Buffy's demonic slaying powers to Max's genetically-modified and Olivia's drug-modified capabilities (and see Chapter 8 for more on Olivia's character). Hybridity is part of all these characters' embodiment: like Buffy or Max, Jaime appears to be an ordinary young woman, but has superhuman capabilities and strength, which transcend the usual boundaries of organic/human physicality. Similarly, these characters demonstrate hybridity as they negotiate a range of different roles, for example, daughter, student, CIA agent, surrogate parent, bike courier or love interest.[1] For Jaime, as for many such characters, tension is generated through the inappropriate collision of different roles at different times, and through the need to keep her physical hybridity – her cyborg embodiment, which she cannot alter – a secret. There are similar storylines in *Buffy* and *Alias*, for example, where Buffy's status as vampire slayer, or Sydney's as CIA agent, must be concealed, even from family and friends.

Many of these hybrid female action heroes create or choose their own, often unconventional family structures and relationships. Situating a physically powerful female hero within a family structure does essentialize the character in some respects, returning her to a framework in which she is nurturer or nurtured, for example. But such relationships allow the characters to be humanized, too, giving the viewer a point of connection with them. This aspect of *Bionic Woman* is especially notable in the contrast between Jaime's family dynamic and Sarah's. Jaime's surrogate-parent role is emphasized from early in the series, and we might view her struggles with her sister as a means of humanizing this bionic woman through her family bonds.[2]

Jaime's family circumstances help to code her in other ways. As Lorna Jowett argues, science fiction television can illuminate difference, especially regarding race and class. In *Dark Angel*'s post-apocalyptic world these aspects coalesce around the character of Max (Jessica Alba) who is a woman of colour, working class *and* a genetically engineered hybrid (Jowett 2005). At the start of the series, *Bionic Woman* shows Jaime as a college dropout earning a living from bartending. Yet despite her far from lucrative employment (at least until after she becomes a cyborg and begins to accept assignments from Berkut) she is positioned as middle class through her surroundings – a spacious apartment, with trendy exposed brick walls – and her appearance – costuming in understated, classic clothes and subtle makeup. The narrative emphasizes her intelligence and academic credentials, and these are used as a sign of her special potential as well as her devotion to family: 'I was accepted to Harvard! And I am not at Harvard because I am raising my sister!' ('Paradise Lost' 1.2). In contrast, Sarah Corvus is presented in an implied working-class, blue-collar context. Sarah does not have a stable home life; she had a sister, but is implicated in the car crash that killed her; Sarah is on the run from the Berkut Group, and her living space is a run-down, cheap motel room ('Pilot' 1.1, 'Sisterhood').[3]

These differences appear designed to highlight Jaime's close family connections and Sarah's isolation. Yet Jaime is still isolated. She cannot tell anyone close to her about the key facts of her hybrid identity, in case she exposes them to danger. Will, her former boyfriend and one of the inventors of the bionics, was evaluating her for unknown purposes, and seems to have been planning to turn her into a cyborg all along. The technology that gives Jaime her new abilities could have serious consequences for her: her bionics might fail as Sarah's are failing ('Sisterhood') or she could be kidnapped and 'stripped for parts' ('Do Not Disturb' 1.8). Jaime does not develop a 'chosen family' with Jonas and the others from Berkut, partly because, with just eight episodes, the series does not have the time to explore those kinds of developing relationships, and partly because Jaime's relationships with Berkut are marked by issues of power and control. Sarah, the one individual who is like her, is at best untrustworthy and at worst likely to kill her. Jaime's cyborg embodiment, far from allowing her boundary-crossing freedoms, appears constrained and contained by the demands of her family relationships and by the power structures of the Berkut Group that effectively owns her.

'I'm losing control again': Sarah Corvus, the First Bionic Woman

Where Jaime's character seems to represent a version of the 'fantasy of liberation' others have noted with regard to the 1970s original and to other female action hero series like *Charlie's Angels* (White 2006: 172), Sarah's offers a more complex representation of cyborg embodiment. Sarah is the first bionic woman to appear in the narrative, and she is immediately situated as violent and dangerous. In the first moments of the pilot episode, she is discovered in the middle of a violent bloodbath in the Berkut Group's Wolf Creek Research Facility; her blonde hair and white hospital gown are covered in blood, and she stammers, 'I didn't want to…I'm out of control…' before she is shot. This choice of opening scene signals a dark and ominous story, setting the scene for a potentially dark reboot of the original *Bionic Woman* series. That 'the first bionic woman' is shown as an out-of-control murderer immediately creates unease for the viewer and demonstrates the destructive tendencies of this cutting-edge and secret technology. The way Sarah's character is set up ensures that, when Jaime in turn is fitted with her bionic limbs and senses, the viewer is more inclined to look on them apprehensively, awaiting a similar outburst of bloody violence which Jaime, too, will be unable to control. As the series progresses, what is emphasized for both Jaime and Sarah is not so much the possibilities offered by adapting to and enjoying the additional powers of the bionics, but the negative consequences of this kind of cyborg embodiment, especially the likelihood that, sooner or later, their augmentations will malfunction.

We can read Sarah as a dark double for Jaime, and their confrontations echo (and develop) the original series' episodes that feature a literal double. Lisa Galloway is recruited by surgeon James Courtney to infiltrate the OSI. With plastic surgery that makes her physically identical to Jaime ('Mirror Image' 1.13), she attempts to masquerade as Jaime and to replace her ('Deadly Ringer 1 and 2' 2.15/16). As Lisa does not have Jaime's bionic abilities, she uses an experimental drug to duplicate her strength, which causes physical degeneration. Lisa manages to play Jaime well enough to infiltrate her workplace, where she chats and jokes with Oscar and Rudy, and even to play the part for Jaime's mother. The reboot features Sarah in similar ways, especially when she charms her way into Jaime's and Becca's apartment and assumes the role of new neighbour ('Sisterhood'), in a sequence that appears to allude to the female stalker narrative of *Single White Female*. Sarah's role-playing has already featured in the pilot episode, when she appears in the bar where Jaime works. In that scene she is costumed as a *film noir* femme fatale, with black clothes, blonde hair, scarlet lips and a cigarette, and she very obviously acts out a role that is specifically designed to attract Jaime's attention. Indeed, in interview Sackhoff describes Sarah explicitly as a 'dangerous [...] femme fatale' and parallels the character with a counterpart in *Battlestar Galactica*: not Starbuck, the role of Sackhoff played, but Six (Weintraub 2007). The kind of performance we see Sarah give in the pilot episode suggests that her cyborg embodiment encompasses some aspects of the hyperfeminine cyborg that is evident in the female cyborg characters of *Battlestar Galactica* (see Chapter 3).

Sarah's complex identification with her bionic augmentations and her struggle to create a whole body out of the competing components that make up her embodiment are compelling storylines, and although Jaime's character faces similar struggles, her conflict with her new embodiment is consistently downplayed. Tammy Oler's comment that, 'Sarah is a magnetic villain/mentor, a vision of hysterical, out-of-control female power who alternately desires and loathes her male creators' (2008: 38) highlights some of the complexities that surround this character. The 'out-of-control [...] power' that Sarah exhibits is something Jaime has the potential for, while describing Sarah as 'hysterical' places her in the all-too-familiar category of monstrous female. I suggest that Sarah's character is compelling because she is able to articulate the troubling and frightening possibilities of cyborg embodiment, in ways that Jaime, positioned in the narrative as female hero, cannot (or is not allowed to) do.

In such a brief narrative, Sarah's complex character cannot approach any sort of resolution, but the writers jettison Sarah part way through the series as though her situation is quite simply unresolvable ('Faceoff'). I see the treatment of Sarah's story as indicative of some of the tensions around the treatment of the female action hero/superhero in contemporary television narratives. As previously noted, these female characters' potential for augmented strength and power tends to be contained through narratives that humanize them through their relationships. Sarah has no such relationships and her narrative status is confused: is she a mentor or a villain, a sympathetic cyborg or a monster? Jaime's story is not resolved, either, but as we can see from critical comments on the early episodes, Sarah's character gives the series something that is not provided by Jaime's alone. Several critics note the compelling effect of Sarah's character and Sackhoff's performance, regretting that Sarah is not the lead character

(McNamara 2008), and viewing her as 'infinitely more likeable as an antiheroine' (Goodman 2007). In some respects, the watchable elements in Sarah's character follow the pattern of the interesting villain, or the alluring femme fatale. In others, it is the very instability of Sarah's character that makes her interesting: she is more unpredictable than Jaime, and thus potentially more dangerous as well as more likely to achieve a form of cyborg boundary-crossing.

Of the two bionic women, Sarah more often describes what has happened to her body as a positive outcome, despite her knowledge of its difficulties and flaws. In one conversation with Jaime, she describes her apparent death in the pilot episode as another stage in her cyborg transformation. She was already cyborg when she lost control of her embodiment ('Pilot'), but her loss of control and physical death brings her a new, still more super-powered body:

SARAH: Jae shot me. And as far as the world was concerned I was dead, but Will revived me surgically.
JAIME: He raised you from the dead? [...]
SARAH: ...whatever he did changed something in me. It's like my emotions were gone with it. I felt like a pure machine, like I could do anything and I loved it. ('Sisterhood')

Jaime's turn of phrase has Sarah resurrected into a new life in a body that becomes 'pure machine'. In her encounter with Jaime in the pilot episode, Sarah presents and displays this body, and explains its superior functions, in a knowing and even tongue-in-cheek manner; for example she undercuts her dramatic announcement, 'I'm [...] the *first* bionic woman' with an ironic, 'Ta-dah!' Her description of her 'pure machine' embodiment is delivered in an intense tone, with her concentrated gaze fixed on Jaime while she explains her feelings about her own bionic body.

At times even the series writers appear undecided as to Sarah's motivations. Sarah seeks Jaime out deliberately, manages to be nearby when Jaime's bionic eye and ear activate, reassures and advises her, actions that do suggest a mentoring role for Sarah ('Pilot'). The fight between the two bionic women at the end of the pilot episode looks like a battle of enemies, but at the same time, by forcing Jaime into a physical confrontation and goading her – 'you're gonna have to do better than that' – Sarah draws out

Jaime's bionic abilities and helps her to improve her strength and skill. In terms of gender role and performance, Sarah appears as much less conventional than Jaime, who seems to yearn for the roles of wife and mother, as well as for her pre-cyborg embodiment. Sarah plays with gender identity, dressing deliberately as femme fatale, for example, while Jaime recommends the notorious *The Rules* dating guidebook to her sister, forbids Becca to telephone a boy she is interested in, and spends much of one episode's covert operation flirting with her CIA counterpart, as well as hiding her special powers from him ('The List' 1.6). Such instances place Sarah in a more complex position than Jaime, and invite readings of her as a potential 'radical border crosser' in the mode of Haraway's cyborg (Kafer 2013: 103).

Contrasting with her possible role as mentor to Jaime, Sarah is presented as dark, flawed and disturbed. Her attitude towards her own body and her bionics is a more complex one than her 'pure machine' speech might suggest. It is in some ways reminiscent of the writings of posthuman enthusiasts like Arthur and Marilouise Kroker, Hans Moravec or Marvin Minsky, who celebrate the potential for the body to be discarded and 'reborn in its technofied forms' (Kroker and Kroker 1988: 21–2). Although Sarah does not necessarily exhibit a wish to leave her body behind, she does privilege her bionic components over her organic flesh. Fitted with bionic legs and arms, and one eye, she announces that 'I did the other [eye] myself. Part of my chest too. I'm cutting away all the parts that are weak' ('Pilot'). That statement figures her organic self as 'weak' and lesser, her technological altered self as strong. But the technology cannot fulfill her – apparent – aim of transcending the flesh. Her bionics, which are early, experimental versions of Jaime's augmentations, are beginning to fail, and so threaten her life. Sarah herself recognizes this at the end of her conversation with Jaime; after she has described the strength and power she felt when Will resurrected her from death, she says, 'I'm losing control again. Whatever Will did to save me was temporary' ('Sisterhood'). Sarah's dream of transcendent strength and power through her cyborg embodiment is an illusion. Still, although she disavows the bionic components that have 'turned me into this thing' ('Sisterhood'), Sarah is trying to save her cyborg body from rejecting the bionics. In this, she attempts not only to stay alive but to hold on to her hybrid, cyborg self.

'Fifty million dollars' worth of my property': Power and Control

As is evident with the storylines that follow Sarah's character, the 'first bionic woman' is far from in control of her own body and her augmented abilities. This is true of Jaime, too. Sarah engineers the crash that injures Jaime and is the catalyst for her transformation into a cyborg; however, there are strong suggestions that Will was already preparing Jaime for a transition into a bionic body. While in the pilot episode Will's use of the bionics as replacements for Jaime's damaged limbs is played as a desperate attempt to save his fiancée (it is evident from other characters' behaviour that he is circumventing normal procedure within the Wolf Creek Research Facility), as the series continues his motivation is reconsidered with far more dubious overtones. Jaime and Will have been dating for 'five months and 14 days' and when Jaime announces her pregnancy, Will immediately proposes marriage, something that seems to suggest that he is committed to a continuing romantic relationship. After the crash, Jaime's injury, miscarriage, and reconstruction with the bionics, and Will's assassination at the end of the pilot episode, Jaime finds that Will has been keeping a file on her 'this thick!' containing personal records, photographs, and intelligence tests, which suggest ulterior motives for his apparent devotion to her ('Paradise Lost'). There are implications, voiced by Sarah, that Will was preparing Jaime for cyborg transformation: 'How do you know you weren't being primed anyway? [...] Will studied you like a lab rat. [...] There was never any reality to any moment you ever thought you shared with him' ('Sisterhood'). Jaime's discovery that Will was working outside the Berkut Group ('Faceoff') makes it much more likely that Sarah is correct, and Jaime figured as a potential test subject, not a romantic interest, all along.

Jaime's lack of control is dramatized in various ways. Her lack of agency is most obviously present in Will's decision to 'heal' her by incorporating the bionic parts and anthrocytes into her body without her consent. In hospital in the Wolf Creek Research Facility, she attempts to assert her agency over her own body, screaming, 'Leave me alone!' and 'What have you done to me?', but her obvious terror is cancelled out by Will's swift explanation of the positive benefits of her new bionic parts, by the speedy reaction of the medical staff to sedate her when she screams at the sight of her new bionic legs, and by subsequent comments from Ruth and Jonas who confer: 'I think she's a good candidate', 'How long till she's combat ready?' All three disregard Jaime's own wishes, and focus instead on her potential as a resource for their organization.

The point that Jaime's and Sarah's cyborg bodies are created from technology developed by Will for the Berkut Group entangles their cyborg embodiment with the military-industrial complex. Theirs is a position Haraway notes in the 'Manifesto for Cyborgs' when she identifies the cyborg as 'the illegitimate offspring of militarism and patriarchal capitalism' (1985: 68). This reading potentially sets limits on the cyborg's abilities for boundary-crossing transcendence. A conversation with Will emphasizes the militaristic nature of Jaime's cyborg embodiment; he tells her, 'you're hardwired for highly specialized warfare'; Jaime accuses him in turn, 'You made me into a soldier' and I note that Sarah *was* a soldier when Berkut recruited her ('Pilot'). Jaime and Sarah share 'the same baseline programming' that governs their fighting strategy and abilities, and allows Sarah to predict Jaime's cyborg instincts in combat ('Sisterhood'). These factors give a sense of uniformity to their cyborg embodiment; their bionics cause them to behave in particular, predictable ways, and they are clearly programmed by their technological augmentations. Jaime loses control over her own embodiment once her bionics are activated. With her bionic augmentations she has abilities that are quite outside her own organic experience. She is able to overpower a man who attacks her with a knife, and can disarm and almost stab him with ease, protesting to Will shortly afterwards, 'I nearly killed a man!' Since Jaime has no training in any kind of combat, her movements and actions are controlled by her cybernetic hardwiring, which is part of her bionics.

Despite Will's assurance that 'you're still in control', there is clear evidence that this is not so, and that in addition to the control the bionics have over her own body, Jaime is bound by the organization that 'rescued' her: as he tells her, 'we're the only ones who can protect you' ('Pilot'). Sarah and Jaime are dependent on Will and on his father Anthony Anthros who invent, develop and control their bionics. While Will researches and grooms Jaime for transformation into a cyborg, Anthony promises Sarah a cure that will make use of Jaime's more up-to-date technology. Within the Berkut Group, Jonas controls access to the technology, and represents himself in a way that once again highlights Jaime's (and Sarah's) dependency on him. Jonas tells Jaime, 'Fifty million dollars' worth of my property is inside you, so I guess you could say I'm your landlord.' He stops short of saying that Jaime herself is his property, but the suggestion hovers in several conversations through the remainder of the series. The manner in which Jonas, representing Berkut, claims ownership of Jaime echoes the original *Bionic Woman*'s 'On the Run' (3.22) in which Jaime attempts to retire from the OSI. In that episode, US senators present the argument 'that Jaime's body represents a state secret and that she knows too much about bionics and the OSI to live outside of government surveillance and control' (Jenkins 2011: 101). 2007's *Bionic Woman* positions the Berkut Group as explicitly *not* part of the government, although it is occasionally aligned with its aims and works with the CIA in several episodes. In that respect, the soldier-like aspects of Sarah's and Jaime's cyborg embodiment is distanced from official military organizations, and enmeshed with more clandestine – possibly even illegal – operations.

These bionic bodies are always under surveillance; in fact, the cyborg body itself becomes a surveillance device. In 'Sisterhood', Jaime discovers that she has been implanted with a GPS tracker, and when she challenges Jonas, he reveals that 'we're also streaming video from your head [...] it's grafted onto your cerebral cortex'. The camera and tracking devices implanted in Jaime's body, and monitored by Berkut's technicians and by Jonas, position her cyborg body as one that is constantly watched and controlled, specifically by male technicians who we see seated in front of a bank of computers, monitoring Jaime's movements. Later in the same episode it is Sarah, once more, who warns Jaime about the intrusive gaze of Berkut's surveillance technology: 'those Berkut guys look at you in the shower! Don't even get me started on how objectifying this whole bionic woman thing is'. Jaime has already acknowledged 'it's a little pervy' in her argument with Jonas, but her claims to 'privacy' and 'dignity' seem irrelevant; it is clear that for Jonas, her cyborg body belongs to the Berkut Group. Jonas emphasizes what Jaime would lose along with the surveillance equipment in her brain: 'We could take it out, but you wouldn't be able to move the left of your body.' Not only do such exchanges demonstrate the extent of Jaime's dependency on Berkut, but they also further emphasize her lack of control over any aspect of her own body.

There are ways in which Jaime's organic, human body can surpass her hardwiring. Jae assures her that although 'part of your programming includes artificial intelligence', if she is reliant on that programming to guide her movements, her fighting style will be 'too predictable' ('Sisterhood'). In this instance, Jaime's fighting is too machine-like. Instead, Jae tells her to 'circumvent the programme'. The act of 'hack[ing] into myself' makes Jaime more unpredictable, more 'human', and thus a more effective fighter and strategist. In a parallel scene, Sarah encourages her to take control of her tracker and turn it off. 'They don't want you to know how powerful you are. [...] Visualize the tracker. Disable it with your thoughts.' Antonio wants to find 'the animal' in Jaime, particularly in her fighting style, which further suggests that a combination of machine technology and organic instinct would produce the most effective fighter/agent ('Sisterhood'). The message to allow her human, organic side to surface at moments when her bionic technology appears to be controlling her comes through friend and potential-enemy characters. Both Jae and Sarah teach Jaime that she can change her programming and can adjust her bionics to suit herself, and that, by doing so, and allowing her human embodiment presence, she can become a more effective bionic person.

Bionics, Prostheses and Disability

In examples such as these, we can see the potential for a positive representation of Jaime's embodiment, in particular the opportunities Jaime has to combine human and machine embodiment to create an effective cyborg. Jaime appears to be empowered by the knowledge she gains about her cyborg embodiment, as she discovers the ability to hack into herself, change her programming, and prioritize her organic self to achieve control. We might see Sarah's 'pure machine' embodiment as empowering in certain ways, too. However, we can view these bodies differently, and less positively, as comprehensively subjugated by their technological components. If we are to accept Sarah's testimony, it is possible for the bionic components to take control of a body, causing a person to behave without volition, even to the extent that s/he will attack and kill ('Pilot'). There is evidence that Sarah's body is 'out of control', or unable to function, in other ways. We see how bionics may lessen a person's embodied control in a scene in Sarah's dingy motel room. She attempts to eat cold baked beans from a tin, but her hand is shaking so much that she cannot get a spoon to her mouth ('Sisterhood'). The narrative of *Bionic Woman* shows Jaime and Sarah positively as bodies that are restored, revived or resurrected through technology, and, more negatively, demonstrates the ways in which those bodies lack control, agency and functionality. The series nevertheless stops short of investigating Jaime and Sarah as disabled bodies. Looking at them in this way adds a further dimension to the versions of cyborg embodiment that this series explores.

'Cyborg theory has traditionally assumed a fully functioning human and a fully functioning machine' (Quinlan and Bates 2009: 51), but with Jaime and Sarah, we see neither. Sarah and Jaime are disabled women. Without her bionic augmentations, Jaime would be classified as paraplegic, and Sarah, who has bionic legs and arms, as quadriplegic. Both women have lost sense abilities (their sight, their hearing). As I mentioned at the beginning of this chapter, Sarah and Jaime exist as completely organic bodies before they are injured and are transformed through their bionics. The focus on Jaime in and immediately after the car crash illustrates the point that 'anyone can become disabled at any time' which 'makes disability more fluid, and perhaps more threatening, to those who identify themselves as normates' (Thomson 1997: 14). Further, both characters enact 'disabled' bodies that 'can […] seem dangerous because they are perceived as out of control […] looking and acting unpredictable' (Thomson 1997: 37).

The sudden crash that injures Jaime transforms her body even before her bionic augmentations are in place. Without her legs and arm hers is no longer a body perceived as 'normal' or 'whole'; additionally, the crash causes her to miscarry, so that hers is no longer a pregnant body. Margaret M. Quinlan and Benjamin R. Bates' study of viewer perceptions of disability on the show reveal that many view Jaime's cyborg embodiment as a cure for her disability, something that should afford her positive feelings since her 'prostheses are seen as relieving disability' (2009: 55). With this interpretation, viewers struggle to accept the character's anger at her changed embodiment (Quinlan and Bates 2009: 52, 54). This is complicated by the character's visual representation, since from the display of her body in everyday scenarios and in action scenes it appears, not only that she is intact bodily, but also that she has enhanced powers and abilities available to her through her augmentation. If we examine the limits as well as the potential of the cyborg embodiment depicted in the series, it allows us to question whether 'cyborgs [are] really the vision of the future that would transcend the limits of "normalcy" and allow those with disabled bodies to be seen as part of the range of beings which inhabit society' (Meekosha 1999: 26). In this reading, Jaime and Sarah are represented as 'other' both as cyborgs and as disabled women.

The bionic replacements for Jaime and Sarah's lost limbs and senses may well be seen as advantages: these women have abilities that they did not have before they were disabled. But their bionic components are not always 'fully functioning'. The very technology that has saved Jaime and made Sarah powerful is the technology that seems likely to kill them as the anthrocytes in their blood degenerate and cannot prevent their organic bodies from rejecting their bionic parts. In Sarah's case, we see her cyborg body degenerating to a degree that threatens Sarah's continued survival. This future is also projected for Jaime – if a solution cannot be found, then she can look forward to a similar process of degeneration on her own body ('Sisterhood'). Their cyborg nature is only ever partly integrated into their organic bodies, and their bionics are never presented as wholly benign or stable. Jaime's comments about her cyborg augmentations show a tendency to view them either as separate from her body, as in references to 'the bionics', or as additions that make her body monstrous and appalling, as when Jaime calls herself 'a bionic freak' ('Paradise Lost'). Even Sarah occasionally reveals similar feelings, and describes the bionics as negatively transforming her, 'They've changed me, turned me into this…thing' ('Sisterhood').

In this narrative, the disability of the body is present in the failing bionics, while the body it(her)self is always or nearly always presented as whole, strong and beautiful. For the most part, Sarah and Jaime are represented as bodies that do not reveal their disability or their cyborg embodiment. Visually, they are depicted as complete and completely organic bodies. Their secret, hidden bionic parts reflect the ways in which prosthetics allow individuals to 'hide' disability: 'artificial limbs are ideally invisible in order to facilitate mimicry of nonamputees and passing as able-bodied' (Kurzman 2001: 379). We see Jaime's amputated stumps only briefly before her bionic legs are fitted. The disconnection in this narrative between the organic body and its technological augmentations matches the way medical terminology constructs a 'rigid and absolute' division 'between the body ("self") and the external world ("nonself")' with 'a conception of the nonself world as foreign and hostile'; for example, cancer cells 'threaten' (Martin 1997: 548). The scenes showing the car crash, Jaime's operations and recovery all work to breach the boundaries between 'self' and 'nonself' in addition to the other boundaries that a cyborg body tends to rupture.

The car crash fractures the pilot episode, breaking into Jaime's apparently happy life with a catastrophic and violent impact, as the crash erupts into the two-shot focused on Jaime and Will driving home after a romantic dinner and talking about potential names for their baby. The glaring lights of the truck that runs into them appear suddenly from the passenger side of the car and the front of the truck is only visible for a moment, together with a close-up of Jaime thrown sideways at the moment of impact, before the scene cuts to an exterior shot of the crushed car spinning out of control. The abrupt event and the change of pace from static conversation to violent impact and action mirror the way this character's cyborg embodiment impacts the organic body.

The operation scene is the only visual in the series that shows Jaime without legs: we can see clearly that the lower part of her legs have been amputated and they are thickly wrapped in bandages, so that they appear rigid and misshapen. The viewer is slightly distanced in this brief shot; we take up Jonas' and Ruth's viewpoint from a platform raised above the operating theatre, and behind a glass wall. The view of Jaime on the operating table cuts to Will in the process of reconstructing her legs and arm, and here Jaime's limbs are represented as computer graphics on screens, again a visual that distances us from the operation itself, and from the body operated upon.

The next time we see Jaime she is waking up to hear the news of her injuries. Will describes the 'molecular machines, anthrocytes' in her bloodstream positively, '[they're] healing you at an exponential rate…they're making you better'. However the visuals in the scene reject this interpretation. Jaime's eyes turn from Will to her own arm, and she throws back the covers to see her legs. Figure 9 shows Jaime's legs from her own viewpoint. Her limbs appear partly transparent, and the cybernetic skeleton shows through, glowing with the anthrocytes' activity (what Will has just

The Cyborg as Action Hero: *Bionic Woman*

Figure 9: Jaime's bionic legs with 'anthrocytes', 'Pilot', *Bionic Woman* (1.1)

described as a healing process). Jaime reacts in fear and horror, screaming hysterically, and fighting Will and the medical staff who rush to sedate her. The glimpse of her legs – an expensive special effects shot – follows the convention of depicting gory sights on television briefly or partially, and so implies that Jaime's legs are more shocking than they appear. The lighting in this scene, as well as its musical cues, shifts the viewer between the bright, clinical environment, where everything is highly visible, and a yellow-tinged viewpoint accompanied by unsettling percussive beats, moving us into Jaime's horrified perspective. This, too, shifts us between the inside and the outside of Jaime's body, and between the 'self' and 'non-self' aspects of her changed embodiment.

The ways in which disabled characters are portrayed in narrative are frequently used as shorthand for a character's behaviour or motivation. But as critics point out, such characters' 'disabilities surface to explain everything and nothing with respect to their portraits as embodied beings' (Mitchell and Snyder 2001: 224). On occasion this form of character motivation surfaces in *Bionic Woman*. Sarah's (potentially) villainous character is explained partly by her 'natural' state of being: Anthony Anthros taunts her, 'You had a history of sick behaviour even before you became a bionic candidate' ('Sisterhood'). In other points in the narrative, the effects of her bionic augmentation come into play, making her into a killing machine

('Pilot'). Many of Sarah's actions are motivated by her physical state; for example, she needs to convince Jaime that she is an ally because she needs information from Jaime's new bionic implants that could help to repair her older ones. For her character, far more than for Jaime's, the bionics are seen to affect her embodiment and her motivation very directly.

Examining Jaime and Sarah as disabled bodies as well as bionic bodies emphasizes the contested state of their cyborg embodiment. They can be seen as disabled, as hybrid, as soldiers, as pieces of military technology, as scientific experiments. The series itself can also be viewed as hybrid, full of opportunities to contest and question the positioning of bodies and individuals within governmental, military and medical contexts. Although as a narrative *Bionic Woman* has the potential to be a transformative text for cyborg embodiment, it reveals a tendency to turn away from the augmented female hero and to attempt a reinstatement of the non-augmented, organic body. The series retreats from its presentation of Jaime and Sarah as super-powered bionic bodies in the first four episodes – a presentation that in any case is undercut by Sarah's representation as damaged and flawed. In the latter four episodes, Jaime is more rarely seen to make use of her bionics in ways that can be interpreted as super-human. She is more consistently seen on screen as an apparently organic, whole, human body, and the narrative does not deal with the fact that her bionic augmentations are continuing to decay and destabilize. Quinlan and Bates critique this aspect of the narrative: '[the series] chooses to present information and images of gender, disabilities and cyborgs as discrete categories only' and does not show either Jaime or Sarah as 'a woman, an individual with a disability, and a cyborg at the same time' (2009: 55). The possibilities for any kind of cyborg embodiment that might transcend all such categories, or combine and utilize them in new ways, are never properly explored.

In Chapter 6, I turn to another narrative that explores oppositional and hybrid connections between organic and technological forms of embodiment. In most of the television texts I have examined so far, the female cyborg body has been predominant, encouraging discussions of the sexualized body, the femme fatale, and the female action hero. Some of these versions of the cyborg are present in *Terminator: The Sarah Connor Chronicles*, but the series offers other versions, and in particular includes some key examples of the male cyborg body. I consider differences between representations of masculine and feminine cyborgs, as well as connections between cinematic and televisual cyborg narratives, and look at ways in which this narrative – like others explored in this book – suggests possibilities for hybridity as a positive development for both organic and technological embodiment.

6

Us and Them: *Terminator: The Sarah Connor Chronicles*

Elsewhere in this book, I discuss television series that reboot older series, taking elements of the original shows and reworking them in ways that reflect contemporary preoccupations around technology, power relations, gender and society. We can see this in *Bionic Woman* (Chapter 5), *Doctor Who*'s Daleks and Cybermen storylines (Chapter 1), and *Battlestar Galactica*'s Cylon–human conflict (Chapter 3). My readings of the developing *Star Trek* series (Chapter 2) show other ways in which a television narrative might draw on an earlier one from the same franchise. In this chapter I look closely at a narrative that both reworks and refers to its cinematic origins in the *Terminator* film franchise, but does so through a televisual format. Its representation of cyborgs carries inflections of the versions seen on the cinema screen, and its narrative partly rests on viewer knowledge of the existing cinematic mythology. The transfer of that mythology to television allows the narrative to branch in a variety of ways, encompassing representations of male and female cyborgs, of 'muscular cyborgs' and cyborg action heroes/heroines, of family dynamics that admit cyborg individuals and help those individuals to develop their emotional intelligence. As with most of the narratives I examine in this book, *Terminator: The Sarah Connor Chronicles* presents a multifaceted view of technology and cyborg embodiment. Its cyborg bodies maintain aspects of the film franchise's technophobia, but at the same time offer new ways of interacting with technology that may break through the binaries of technophobia/technophilia.

'Come with me if you want to live': Cinematic Cyborgs Move to Television

Terminator: The Sarah Connor Chronicles (*TSCC*) picks up the film franchise story of Sarah Connor's ongoing battle with cyborgs sent from the future to kill her and her son, John. These cyborgs target John because, in the future, he will lead a human Resistance against sentient killer machines that develop from present-day technological inventions, primarily the Skynet military artificial intelligence that will initiate a nuclear apocalypse. The film franchise sets out a timeline of key dates in the battle between humans and Terminators, beginning in 1984 when a Terminator arrives from the future with a mission to kill Sarah Connor (*Terminator*), and continuing to 1995 when Sarah, John and a reprogrammed Terminator interfere in the development of Skynet and avert apocalypse (that should have happened on 29 August 1997; *Terminator 2: Judgment Day*). In the third film, *Terminator 3: Rise of the Machines*, Sarah dies of cancer some time in 1997 and July 2004 sees the apocalypse take place. *TSCC* continues from the events of *Terminator 2* and, as Lorrie Palmer notes, 'revise[s] the narrative timeline of the film series by eliding the events' (2012: 84) of *Terminator 3*. This 'conjoined relationship' of film franchise and television series (Palmer 2012: 84) makes it possible for *TSCC* to build on and to divert from the narrative and mythology established through the film franchise, creating appeal for existing fans of the films and for television viewers with an interest in science fiction action. Both film franchise and television narrative explore some similar themes: the family, the strong (female) fighter or female action hero, the physically powerful cyborg, the technological apocalypse. Following its 'alternate timeline' (Friedman, in Goldman 2007), the television series introduces new storylines and offers some fresh explorations of cyborg embodiment and the body of the female action hero. In creating parallel family groups which include cyborg beings, *TSCC* suggests some different ways in which humans might coexist with technology, and suggests, too, that technology might not always be deadly or apocalyptic. A major feature of the series is the 'continued ambiguity' of its cyborgs; they 'may threaten our destruction but they may also bring about our salvation' (Bennett 2014: 14, 15).

In its first episode, the television series cuts through the established timeline of the feature films by having Sarah, John and a protector Terminator jump forward in time, from 1999 to 2007, taking them near to the series air date ('Pilot' 1.1, first broadcast 13 Jan 2008).[1] As the *Terminator* feature films are filled with time-loop paradoxes and attempts to alter time, it is not surprising that the television series utilizes this aspect to its own advantage. Setting – or re-setting – the series in the present immediately re-draws its technological boundaries as well as its narrative ones. Characters are able to interact with the internet, with mobile telephones, and with other now-essential twenty-first-century technological devices. Further, once alternate timelines are established in the television series, the narrative becomes open to infinite possibilities. The television narrative is certainly not bound by, for example, the news of Sarah's death from cancer in *Terminator 3*, though this possibility is worked into *TSCC*'s ongoing story. And because of its serial format, the television series can 'engage and speculate more than thrill or titillate' (Myles 2012: 335). While it may include fewer set-piece action sequences, the television narrative allows all the characters, cyborgs and humans, time to develop as rounded and individual personalities. Most of its regular characters are part of the Connor family, or connected to it in some way; for example, Sarah and John are joined by John's uncle Derek Reese, who like his brother Kyle is sent into the past to protect John and ensure the future success of the Resistance.

Anticipating a fourth *Terminator* film, Angel Mateos-Aparicio questioned '[w]hether it will finally depict a female cyborg that helps the Connors against the mechanized threat' (2007: 273). *TSCC* offers two female cyborgs that – as it turns out – are both involved in helping the Connors. These cyborgs are major characters in their own right, with their own story arcs and character development. In a narrative in which killer, enemy cyborgs predominate, the storylines around the Terminators Cameron and Catherine Weaver allow for some reconsideration of the female cyborg's embodiment and representation. In some respects, these cyborgs do conform to the trope of the technological female body that is sexually alluring yet terrifying, that represents 'the threat of unleashed female sexuality' (Springer 1996: 114), and that complicates boundaries between technophobia and technophilia. Yet in other ways, these characters resist such typical representations and instead suggest new forms of female cyborg embodiment. For a character like Cameron, who appears as a slight teenage girl, cyborg embodiment and empowerment are significantly altered: the 'female cyborg [...] wields her ability to pass as a normal teenager to help carry out her mission of protection' (Palmer 2012: 89). That Cameron reveals her true role by speaking one of the film franchise's classic lines, 'Come with me if you want to live', to John Connor makes connections with characters in the first two films, and by doing so, suggests a certain authority for her character within the narrative. *TSCC*'s representation of versions of the female cyborg has an effect, in turn, on the representation of its key human female character, Sarah Connor.

Versions of Female (Cyborg) Embodiment

The casting choices for *TSCC* stimulated extensive comment, but it was Lena Headey's casting as Sarah Connor which caused a furore. It is evident that viewers expected a casting that would make an obvious connection between film and television series, with a '*muscular* action heroine' (Tasker 1993: 132, my emphasis) resembling Linda Hamilton's portrayal of Sarah Connor in the film franchise. In critiques of *TSCC*'s casting, Hamilton's physicality is referenced as an ideal for the Sarah Connor character, while Headey is seen as 'weedy' and 'feeble-looking' (Smith 2008). This shows a reversal of opinion. As Lorrie Palmer notes, Hamilton's portrayal previously attracted negative criticism (2012: 91); her muscled physicality was described as 'symbolic cross-dressing', for example (Brown 1996: 59). But in the debates around Headey's casting, '[Hamilton's] muscles, that used to be described as gender parody, as male drag, as a disavowal of femininity, as misogynistic and ultimately patriarchal, now seem to signify something else' (Palmer 2012: 91). In his defence of the casting choice, series writer/creator Josh Friedman describes Headey as 'obviously smaller and thinner, but she's tough. [...] The most important thing was finding an actress who embodied that spirit and who was believable in that role and not just some glammed up, Hollywood, actressy thing' (Goldman 2007). Headey observes that

> I'm playing a mother who is a single parent, bringing up a teenage son, who also happens to save the world – as a byline to her life. And the way I would play that is someone who's passionate and scared and angry and a mother, all these things. So I approach that just trying to be honest within the boundaries of her. (Powers 2009)

It is worth noting that Headey does not mention 'action' specifically, or refer to the physical demands of the role, but foregrounds mothering as a key component of her character. Her comments here focus on the realism of the character within the unfolding television narrative. It is true that Headey's Sarah Connor is not obviously muscled, but Palmer describes convincingly a process by which this slight, spare, wiry fighter could emerge as a result of the character's embattled circumstances (2012: 92).

The adverse comments from viewers highlight expectations that specifically relate to the interplay between the film franchise narrative and the aspects of that narrative that are transferred to a televisual format. It has been noted that, in the first film, Sarah is only a hero by virtue of her impending motherhood, and in the second she is almost excessively modelled on the hypermasculine action *hero*, 'erasing any of the feminine qualities she was still able to retain' (Dominguez 2005 par. 21). By contrast, 'the television characterization of Sarah Connor is not masculinized by excessive muscular display in order to play an active sf heroine' (Palmer 2012: 94). Sarah's characterization follows the depiction of other female action heroes on television, especially the tendency to cast small and slight actors in highly physical roles (in Chapter 5, I note that *Bionic Woman* counters this tendency in its casting of the female leads). Generally, a television viewer is 'accustomed to slightly-built, unapologetically feminine women taking over the job of butt kicking from the hypermuscular and excessively gendered stars of 1980s and 1990s cinema' (Palmer 2012: 84). So we can read Headey's version of Sarah as a version of the female action hero that 'renaturalizes and even reclaims the female warrior body from its big-screen excesses, its visible (and cultural) signifiers of muscles, and from the *T2* Sarah's truncated personal relationships' (Palmer 2012: 92).

Reimagining Sarah as a slight, spare fighter offers a new vision of a character who was so iconically rendered as a muscular heroine, and critically evaluated in terms of her conformity to male/masculine forms of embodied power (Jeffords 1993; Cornea 2007). The television Sarah's physical likeness to female cyborg characters in the same narrative offers the possibility that cyborg embodiment can also be reimagined, especially as all the cyborg characters in *TSCC* are likely to be compared and contrasted with the film franchise's original hypermasculine Terminator. As Friedman comments, the character of Cameron was written specifically for Summer Glau (Goldman 2007). This appears to indicate that a particular type of actor was required to play this Terminator, and that the intention was to present a completely different form of cyborg embodiment; Glau is 'the physical, visual and iconographic opposite of Arnold Schwarzenegger's weighty and slow-moving [cinematic] Terminator' (Palmer 2012: 88). As with Sarah's casting, the cyborgs Cameron and Season 2's Catherine Weaver follow the pattern of the slightly built female action heroes of television. Furthermore, casting Glau links this Terminator to her previous roles in other television series. Considering Glau in light of other roles, especially as River Tam in the cult science fiction series *Firefly* and its cinematic sequel *Serenity*, encourages a complementary view of her character in *TSCC* as complex, broadly sympathetic, but with undercurrents of menace and mystery; another example of 'intertextuality of casting' (Bussolini 2013).

Glau's casting complicates representations of the female cyborg which tend to follow the 'sf convention of presenting female sexuality as analogous to threatening, embodied technology', something that 'has increasingly been interrogated – and reconsidered – as it has passed from cinema to television' (Palmer 2012: 86–7). While we still see examples of sexualized – especially feminized – embodied technology in television series, these are far more likely to be ambiguous or ambivalent character portrayals that allow for cyborg transgression of boundaries. We see this in the Six and Eight characters in *Battlestar Galactica* (Chapter 3) as well as in the depiction of Seven of Nine (Chapter 2) who is 'neither written nor performed as a character whose sexuality was deliberately mobilized for power' (Palmer 2012: 87). Glau's Terminator presents a 'gamine' appearance and allure, 'in a subtler way than if she were overtly sexualized' (Bennett 2014: 13), something that further undercuts the trope of the threatening, sexual female cyborg. Offering varied depictions of cyborg embodiment allows the series to explore both 'muscular' and (in Dawn Heinecken's terms) 'female action hero' versions of embodiment, and in so doing to confuse many of the binaries associated with the image of the cyborg. In this respect, *TSCC*'s visual/physical depiction of cyborg embodiment on television offers a more flexible, and potentially more boundary-crossing model.

Cyborg Embodiment: the Muscular Cyborg and the (Female) Action Hero

The unfolding narrative of *TSCC* builds on the shifting representation of cyborgs across the *Terminator* film franchise. The Terminator of the first film (Arnold Schwarzenegger) is a monosyllabic, hypermasculine being with only superficial human-like characteristics. This cyborg can engage in simple dialogue (and make unintentional jokes) but its programming is solely focused on its mission to assassinate a named target. Its machine programming underlines its absolute difference from a human being: in the first film, Resistance fighter Kyle Reese, sent from the future to protect Sarah, explains, 'It can't be bargained with. It can't be reasoned with. It doesn't feel pity, or remorse, or fear. And it absolutely will not stop, ever, until you are dead.' With *Terminator 2* comes the possibility that a Terminator can be reprogrammed, can learn, and can develop other characteristics beside its killing function. Schwarzenegger, reprising his role, but this time as a reprogrammed model, is able to play a different kind of machine, one which develops emotional intelligence and a paternal role as a '"kinder, gentler" Terminator' (Jeffords 1993: 173). I agree that this version of the Terminator body functions in both films as 'a metaphor not of gender but of power relations' (Palmer 2012: 94), as the bulked-up, beefy Schwarzenegger contrasts with the slighter Michael Biehn as Kyle Reese and Linda Hamilton as Sarah Connor in the first, and with Edward Furlong as the young John Connor in the second.

The cyborg embodiment of Terminators alters in *Terminator 2* and *Terminator 3*, with the appearance of newer T-1000 and T-X models whose more flexible physicality contrasts with the solid T-800 (Schwarzenegger) model. Both Robert Patrick's (*Terminator 2*) and Kristanna Loken's

(*Terminator 3*) Terminators are similar in function to Schwarzenegger's original T-800: they are implacable, unstoppable killing machines and only take on superficial human attributes, mostly to do with their appearance, in order to carry out their missions. Patrick's casting gives *Terminator 2*'s T-1000 a slighter form of embodiment, departing from the image of the 'muscular cyborg'. This T-1000 cyborg can be identified as 'polygendered' (Fuchs 1995: 290): it impersonates both men and women and, especially in its liquid-metal state, has a more androgynous look. Interestingly, critics still apply criteria of the female to *Terminator 2*'s T-1000; Claudia Springer considers it an 'embodiment of feminine fluidity' (1996: 112), and Mateos-Aparicio's evaluation of how 'Schwarzenegger's solid, unchanged, ageing body competes against more flexible, multiple and adaptable representations of the cyborg' (2007: 254) similarly suggests a reading of Patrick's T-1000 as more feminine than androgynous.

In *Terminator 3*, Loken's T-X is clearly gendered female, but it is not necessarily *feminine* except in specific instances. One example, frequently noted by commentators, is the scene where the T-X alters the size of its breasts before speaking to a male police officer. This transformation is clearly signalled as a strategic response, in which the cyborg utilizes data gathered from a billboard advertisement for bras in order to create its own fantasy female body type. This cyborg 'seems to accept and adapt' for its own purpose (Mateos-Aparicio 2007: 270), using available information to masquerade as human while carrying out its mission. I see this less as a dramatization of female embodiment, and more as one transformation among many undertaken by a powerful and malleable cyborg body, a body that shifts and alters according to external demands.

Physically contrasting cyborgs, representing both the muscular and the female action hero type, appear in *TSCC*, but as I have noted, the television narrative allows for more nuanced explorations of the cyborg body. In the pilot episode, Sarah and John are threatened by Cromartie, a male-gendered Terminator who masquerades as a teacher – a figure of authority – at John's school. Cameron, programmed as John's protector, is camouflaged within the school population as just another teenage girl. Cromartie's physique matches that of Schwarzenegger's 'muscular cyborg' (the character is played by two tall actors: Owain Yeoman in the pilot episode and Garret Dillahunt in the remainder of the series). Summer Glau as the Terminator Cameron, and Shirley Manson as the liquid-metal Catherine, physically resemble the slight but flexible and malleable T-1000 and T-X cyborgs. However, these categories do not always remain stable, and we see other versions of both male and female cyborg embodiment. Season 2's cyborg John Henry, created from a combination of the Turk supercomputer and Cromartie's cyborg body, is physically imposing, but he exhibits gentle and childlike behaviour in interactions with others. By contrast, Cameron and Catherine use their slight bodies in feats of strength and physical power.

TSCC even hints that the 'muscular cyborg' model may not be the most successful, especially in counterfeiting human behaviour. In that first episode, Cromartie's attack on John is unsuccessful, while Cameron maintains her masquerade as high school girl until she decides to reveal herself to John, and she saves him from Cromartie's attack, too. Cameron's abilities with disguise may also suggest that this character's form of cyborg embodiment is a more successful model. In *TSCC*, stealth and the ability to 'pass' – for both humans and machines – is of more value than overt displays of strength, power and violence. Sarah and John adopt a series of false identities as they move from town to town, and Cameron and Catherine infiltrate and join forces with family groups. Their cyborg embodiment does not attract attention; indeed, for both these female cyborgs 'looking like a girl has real, tangible value' as they are both able to pass undetected as human (Palmer 2012: 89). In contrast Cromartie, though 'big, male, muscular' is 'just as quickly [as Schwarzenegger's T-880] *not* able to "pass" as human once his constructed outer surface begins to break down from repeated battles' (Palmer 2012: 89). So, while they retain the muscular cyborg's strength and power, the slighter, female-gendered models are more successful in terms of concealment.[2]

Further, even though the series opposes the 'bad', threatening male Terminator (Cromartie) and the 'good', protective female (Cameron), such distinctions are complicated, especially in the second season. Catherine Weaver's introduction places her character as a 'bad' Terminator simply because of her embodiment as a T-1000, which encourages the viewer to connect film franchise with television series, and therefore read Catherine as an enemy figure. Initially, Catherine's performance as a ruthless bitch-boss positions her character as an adversary before she is identified as a cyborg. Her coldly murderous actions further persuade the viewer that this cyborg is a threat to John and Sarah. Her later behaviour reveals that she is an ally for Sarah, John and the others attempting to stop the development of Skynet, and so forces the viewer to reassess her character. Conversely, while Cameron is presented more consistently as a protector and ally, significant system malfunctions mean that she has the capacity to revert to her original programming and so become an enemy figure. As Cameron's integrity in the Resistance's operations and its fight against Skynet is uncertain for much of the series, especially its second season, her character development mirrors that of various human characters, including Sarah, John and Derek, whose actions are frequently questionable, unheroic and needlessly violent.

Television Terminators and Visual Spectacle

All of the *TSCC* Terminator characters offer visual spectacle in their various embodied performances. They are more likely than the human characters to be involved in action sequences that showcase their superior strength, speed and abilities to transform their bodies. Action sequences emphasize these aspects of their cyborg embodiment, underlining the differences between their strength and the frailty of human bodies. Fighting style is another way to perform or to reveal aspects of cyborg embodiment. Where the male Terminators rely on force and bulk to overpower their opponents, the female Terminators' power is channeled through their slight embodied forms. Cameron fights with physical speed, skill and dexterity, while Catherine, as a liquid-metal model, transforms parts of her body into a range of sharp weapons. So Cameron's and Catherine's fight scenes are notable for the ways in which they use their bodies in un-human, impossible ways, and their lack of physical reaction to blows or wounds accentuates their cyborg embodiment. Cameron's fights with what appears to be a female T-X Terminator (Bonnie Morgan) is a case in point ('The Tower is Tall But the Fall is Short' 2.6). The two cyborgs fight in near-silence and with neutral facial expressions, despite receiving injuries which tear through their flesh to reveal parts of their metal skeletons. The T-X remains silent even when Cameron twists it into a mechanical pretzel; the intended effect here is to show the un-human movement of Terminator limbs, although a DVD special feature shows that Morgan, as the T-X, is able to contort her body in seemingly impossible ways, revealing that very little of this fight is created by special effects ('Cameron vs Rosie,' 2009).

Taking impossible metamorphosis even further, Catherine's set-piece action sequences focus on her abilities to use her liquid-metal form, either for purposes of disguise (since she can morph into any shape, organic or not) or for combat (her limbs can become sharp weapons such as knives or swords). Either of these purposes allow for visually arresting and narratively shocking moments when Catherine appears suddenly from an unexpected place or uses her arm or hand as a blade to dispatch an unsuspecting victim. 'The Good Wound' (2.14) features a scene in which Catherine kills the entire staff of the Desert Canyon Heat and Power warehouse with her arms morphed into sharp implements, and blows up the building for good measure, while retaining her emotionless cyborg composure and spotless white suit. Such action sequences work to frame Catherine as the sinister enemy-figure, 'passing' among humans in order to destroy them.

The series offers other ways to consider cyborg embodiment besides these feats in strength, power and fighting. Cameron, with her own developing storylines across the show's two seasons, exemplifies the flexible possibilities for cyborg embodiment. She is not solely a cyborg protector, but performs as high school student, John's sister, or Sarah's child. These embodied interactions with humans enable exploration of other facets of Cameron's physicality as a cyborg. Apparently superficial examples, such as brief shots of Cameron painting her fingernails ('Queen's Gambit' 1.5), show Cameron exploring her own embodied representation – her existence in the body of a girl. This is evident when she watches and mirrors the young female gang member 'Chola' ('Gnothi Seauton' 1.2). The way Cameron adopts Chola's slouched pose and speech patterns can be read simply as another indication of the cyborg's ability to learn from human behaviour, an important feature that makes her a successful infiltrator. However, Cameron's later interaction with the same girl, when Cameron arms her with a gun and sets her free of the gang ('What He Beheld' 1.9), suggests that Cameron has established some kind of emotional connection with Chola.

Cameron's physical representation is consistently bound up with the idea of the female cyborg as sexually – as well as technologically – threatening, but again, her representation undercuts the trope of the hypersexual female cyborg. Assertions that 'Chronicles regularly portrays Cameron as overtly sexual' (Myles 2012: 341) need to be examined in more detail, especially in the context of the character's existence as a machine. It is not possible to read Cameron straightforwardly as a sexual object or as an individual who explores her own sexuality, since such aspects are complicated by her cyborg embodiment. Cyborg characters like Cameron do not view themselves in gendered terms, even though they are embodied as female. It is the series narrative – and other characters – that gender them. So, often-cited examples of Cameron walking about in her underwear do not necessarily signify the character's (knowing, active) display of her body. There are further complications in the way that Cameron's cyborg embodiment allows *TSCC* to show her in revealing poses and situations, like the underwear scenes in the pilot episode and 'The Turk' (1.3), always covered by the excuse that hers is a cyborg body, not a human girl's. These aspects of Cameron's physical presentation are similar in many ways to Seven of Nine's in *Voyager* (see Chapter 2); both characters are frequently presented visually in ways that accentuate their female embodiment and cyborg sexuality, while at the same time their machine attributes undercut this visual representation. Further, Cameron's character appears in publicity shots that 'eroticized, even fetishized the female cyborg' with revealing poses that are never duplicated within the narrative itself (Palmer 2012: 94; Bennett 2014: 12).[3]

In other respects, Cameron's body is open to exploration and intervention because it is a cyborg body that requires maintenance and control, such as when John opens the port in her head to remove her chip ('Samson and Delilah' 2.1). Bringing together Cameron's machinic identity with her young girl's body, the notorious scene in which she instructs John in how to check her internal processors for damage presents Cameron as alluring female and as mysterious machine at the same time ('Born to Run' 2.22). While Cameron and John are apparently engaged in a task involving the maintenance of a machine component, the scene is framed as a sexual encounter, '[t]his is true not only of the action but also of the way the scene is shot […]and the dialogue, delivered in breathy whispers' (Bennett 2014: 13). Cameron gives John commands and he follows them, asking 'that's good, right?'; it is easy to see Cameron as the experienced partner instructing John, who appears tentative, especially when the script has John lying on top of Cameron on John's bed. Palmer comments on how 'most fans seemed to have found [this scene] awkward and forced' (2012: 96, note 6), but I suggest that at least some of the awkwardness identified here is connected with Cameron's cyborg embodiment. In some respects, this scene does function as a 'love scene' between John and Cameron, in which 'John accepts his role as mediator between humans and machines and between present and future worlds, as well as his love for Cameron as a machine' (Bennett 2014: 14). However, the main purpose of the encounter for Cameron is to reveal her inner technological construction, uncovering (or undressing, perhaps) her cyborg self; she first removes her shirt and bra in a dispassionate manner, and then calmly instructs John to open up her 'breastplate' with a knife she provides for the purpose. As such, this encounter underlines Cameron's cyborg embodiment, rather than downplaying it or creating any equivalence between human and cyborg embodiment. John and Cameron do not have sex, despite the framing of the scene; instead, Cameron makes John touch her cybernetic components to see 'if I'm damaged', putting him in direct contact with the parts of her that are emphatically not human.

Catherine Weaver offers another example of the female cyborg, this time in tandem with the image of the woman in power. She, like Cameron, hides in plain sight, and is perhaps the most successful of the series' three featured Terminators in her masquerade. The cyborg Catherine is counterfeiting a real human being; the narrative strongly implies that the cyborg caused the deaths of Catherine and Lachlan Weaver, so enabling it to take over Catherine's identity. That stolen identity places the cyborg as the head of tech company ZeiraCorp, and she lives her disguise among human Catherine's colleagues, friends, and especially her daughter, Savannah. Catherine 'passes' in her adoption of the human identity and in her assumption of control over the company. As cyborg, however, she has no concern with human, much less 'feminine' behaviour. Her emotionless behaviour does attract attention from the humans around her, but it can be explained in human terms – she is grief-stricken after the death of her husband, or she is adopting strategies suitable to women in power and connected with the stereotype of the 'bitch'. Her embodied representation fits her adopted role as a powerful female (and echoes Nina Sharp's, see Chapter 8) with severely styled red hair and tailored, monochrome clothing.

Occasional scenes unite different aspects of Catherine's cyborg embodiment. Catherine's identity as a Terminator is revealed in the first episode in which she appears, when she kills Mr Tuck, one of her employees ('Samson and Delilah'). This scene certainly cements her killer-cyborg identity within the television narrative, as it reveals her cyborg self in the liquid-metal form of the T-1000. However, other aspects of the scene implicitly comment on Catherine's adopted role as a woman in a corporate power structure. Following Tuck's complaints to a colleague as they pass each other in the office bathroom, he mutters, 'That bitch pisses me off', before the urinal in front of him morphs into Catherine Weaver. Fixing Tuck first with a steely, emotionless stare and then – as though she cannot be bothered to do more – with a narrow blade made out of her forefinger, as shown in Figure 10, Catherine remarks, 'Sorry I piss you off, Mr Tuck – the feeling's mutual.' In the scene, different aspects of Catherine's embodiment coalesce: the killer cyborg, the corporate female, the 'bitch-boss'. I note that Catherine is not fixed to one gender in her cyborg embodiment; she adopts male identities, for instance as Bradbury, the head of Automite Systems ('Automatic for the People' 2.2) and as a male detective ('Brothers of Nablus' 2.7). Yet, while she is clearly framed as a dangerous other – a killer cyborg – a significant number of scenes situate Catherine as a woman in

Figure 10: Catherine Weaver as the threatening liquid-metal cyborg, 'Samson and Delilah', *Terminator: The Sarah Connor Chronicles* (2.1).

a corporate environment, as someone who must assert herself continually. So, although the bathroom murder scene is obviously designed to reveal Catherine's true cyborg nature, it also appears that she kills Tuck because he insults her with a derogatory comment.[4]

Terminators, Cyborgs and Emotional Intelligence

A key theme throughout the series, especially in Season 2, focuses on the development of artificial intelligence. This is important within both series and franchise narratives, since any artificial intelligence that appears in the present-day scenes has the potential to develop into the murderous Skynet of the future. A significant thread of *TSCC*'s narrative involves the connections between advances in artificial intelligence and the ways that the major cyborg characters begin to develop their own emotional potential. Cameron, Catherine and John Henry all demonstrate increased emotional development through concentrated interactions with humans. This emotional development functions as another way of joining together human and cyborg embodiment in positive ways.

Cameron's emotional development occurs through her contact with the family group made up of Sarah, John and Derek, and is particularly evident in the storylines of Season 2. A system malfunction causes Cameron to revert to her original Terminator programming, and to attack John ('Samson and Delilah'). However, the episode's key moment is not in the set-piece fight scenes between John, Sarah and Cameron but in Cameron's verbal declaration to John that, 'I'm sorry [...] I'm fixed now [...] I love you, I love you John and you love me'. Cameron's words do not stop John from removing her chip and shutting her down, but they do encourage John to put the chip back and restore her. There is a possibility that Cameron is successfully mimicking human behaviour to save herself, and that therefore she is continuing her mission to kill John. It is also possible that Cameron is genuinely trying to communicate with John, and that therefore she is experiencing human or human-like feelings. The second possibility becomes more likely after Cameron's second system glitch in which she takes on the identity of 'Allison from Palmdale' (2.4), a human she encountered in the future; as 'Allison', she behaves as though she were fully human. This episode suggests that Cameron may have developed some of her emotional intelligence after integrating Allison's human memories and associated emotions into her own cyborg identity.

One of the strongest examples of Cameron's developing emotional intelligence is her solo dance ('The Demon Hand' 1.7). The dance scene is placed at the conclusion of the episode, as Sarah muses, in voiceover: '[machines] cannot appreciate beauty. They cannot create art. If they ever learn these things, they won't have to destroy us. They'll be us.' Sarah's voiceover slightly overlaps with shots of Derek watching Cameron dance alone in her bedroom. Chopin's C sharp major Nocturne plays as she dances, and, although it is unclear whether Cameron is dancing to this music or whether it is a non-diegetic element of the soundtrack,[5] the piano music establishes a serene and peaceful mood for the scene. Cameron's movements are smooth and beautiful, and she appears to be watching herself in the mirror as she jumps and turns.[6] Derek is clearly emotionally moved as he watches her; in an alternative version of this scene, the episode concludes with a shot of Derek in tears. Taken together with Sarah's voiceover, this scene strongly implies that Cameron *can* appreciate beauty and create art, and that therefore she is developing emotionally into a different kind of machine. This is thrown into sharper relief by Cameron's actions earlier in the episode: having protected a man and his sister, she abandons them to be killed by gangsters once she has the information she needs from them, following a logical, machine-like mode of intelligence.

Catherine, too, learns some human-like emotional behaviour, especially towards her 'daughter' Savannah. Again, taken in the context of Catherine's disguise, this can be read as another example of a cyborg simulating expected behaviour, a performance undertaken in order to 'pass' convincingly. In some respects this is exactly what Catherine is doing. She mimics emotional behaviour very literally, taking her cues from the speech and actions of particular humans. For example, she watches a piece of video footage in which the human Catherine strokes her husband's arm, and repeats the action on Savannah's arm ('The Tower is Tall'). She repeats Agent James Ellison's story about his father's death, making it seem as though she is talking about her reaction to Lachlan Weaver's death ('The Good Wound'). However, I suggest that Catherine's mimicked 'maternal' behaviour achieves some authenticity in her interactions with John Henry, who is very definitely framed as Catherine's cyborg 'son'. Her references to 'my John' bring Sarah's relationship with her son John into parallel with Catherine's connection with John Henry, placing both women as mothers. Although Catherine's 'son' is an artificial intelligence animating the former Terminator Cromartie's body, Catherine does show evidence of emotional attachment to him in gestures as well as words. After John Henry has been attacked by another AI, Catherine plugs his body back into the supercomputer mainframe, smoothing down his hair in a brief, apparently affectionate gesture as she does so ('To the Lighthouse' 2.20). Her face shows animation and pleasure when John Henry explains a game of hide-and-seek he is playing with Savannah, that involves setting and following clues. She expresses her delight at discovering the AI's logical and playful development ('Today Is the Day Part 1' 2.18).

John Henry: Cyborg as Child

John Henry complicates the cyborg embodiment of Terminators, revising many of the binary divisions that persist in the representations of muscular cyborgs and cyborg female action heroes. The entity known as John Henry begins its existence as the 'Babylon Project', a disembodied artificial intelligence that communicates by means of symbols and pictures projected onto a screen. Even though it has no embodied existence, it is still conceptualized as a child or as childlike: Catherine Weaver asks psychologist Boyd Sherman to 'help me raise' the bodiless AI, and Sherman gives it a name, symbolically baptizing it before laying the foundations for the creation of its independent identity ('The Tower is Tall'). The transfer of the artificial intelligence consciousness into the strong male machine body of the Terminator Cromartie creates a very different kind of cyborg embodiment. This cyborg body has the potential for great strength and power, which it has already demonstrated in violent examples throughout Season 1. However, the cyborg John Henry does not use physical strength, and his placid, enquiring and innocent demeanour undercuts the mature masculine appearance of his body. His character further complicates the oppositions of technophilia and technophobia in the creation and presentation of cyborg characters.

In its embodiment as John Henry, the muscular cyborg body is depicted in very different ways from its original appearance as the Terminator Cromartie. Sequences involving Cromartie in Season 1 typically involve action scenes, chases, and scenes of violence; for example, his attack on John's school ('Pilot') or on the FBI team ('What He Beheld'), in which he appears physically powerful, relentless and unstoppable. Scenes with John Henry in Season 2 show that this body remains large, tall and imposing, but it is still or static. The cyborg body is connected to its computer 'brain' by means of a thick black cable, and so is tethered or harnessed, with limited free movement. John Henry is usually shown in a series of two-shots, seated at a plain wooden table, in conversations with Ellison, Savannah or Catherine who sit facing him. Features like his tether to the computer-bank brain, and his location in a windowless interior room, place John Henry's embodiment in an entirely artificial and technological domain. The obvious cable tether emphasizes his cyborg identity and functionality and the constructed nature of his embodiment.

As an example of the cyborg as innocent child, John Henry's character reverses the trope of the threatening and deadly cyborg embodied in a mature male or female body. In fact, the bodiless Babylon Project AI is shown to be more dangerous than the embodied John Henry. Because it was never taught that its actions have consequences, the AI cannot understand that when it redirects the building's power to itself following a power outage, it interrupts the building's heating and cooling systems, and so causes Boyd Sherman to die of heatstroke ('Strange Things Happen at the One-Two Point' 2.10). The bodiless AI is dangerous because of what its programmers have left out of its development; as Ellison states, 'You taught it procedures. You taught it rules. But it has no ethics, no morals' ('Strange Things'). The AI serves as an example of out-of-control technology, but it is important to note that the gaps in its reasoning are there because of its human programmers, and not because of its own independent development. By way of contrast, Ellison's process of educating John Henry in morals and emotional intelligence shows us the cyborg learning to fill in those gaps. In this way, John Henry develops his own understanding of human behaviour, and his own connections with other individuals. His embodied presence becomes part of his development, and his cyborg body a vital part of his sense of self and individuality. Ellison's socialization of John Henry echoes John Connor's education of the T-800 in *Terminator 2*. In both storylines, cyborgs are shown to develop emotional bonds through their association with humans.

John Henry's physical presence functions additionally as a point of contrast to his developing mental and emotional state. He plays games designed to help his development, and while some of these fit with a narrative of AI development, others have more to do with emotional transformations. The chess games that John Henry and Ellison play echo other chess games between humans and machines, like the chess-playing mechanical Turk (of history, and also referencing computer programmer Andy Goode's machine in *TSCC* Season 1) and the real-world IBM computer Deep Blue that beat Garry Kasparov. In other scenes, John Henry plays with toys that appear to have been introduced deliberately in order to comment on John Henry's own cyborg identity, and on the future development of Skynet and the Terminators. In several episodes, John Henry plays with LEGO Bionicles, toys that are accompanied by a storyline describing them as part-organic, part-mechanical beings (LEGO.com, 2015). The toys reference both John Henry's cyborg embodiment and that of the Terminators more widely. John Henry draws Ellison's attention to the toys' sophisticated ball-and-socket joints that are an improvement on the joints in the human body ('The Good Wound'); we could make similar comparisons between human bodies and the Terminators' powerful metal skeletons or liquid-metal compositions.

In other respects, shots of John Henry playing with toys or singing songs offer the possibility of comic relief in an overwhelmingly dark narrative. The sequence in which John Henry sings the Scottish song 'Donald, Where's Yer Troosers?' is incongruous and so potentially humorous. Such sequences emphasize Savannah's role as a key part of John Henry's emotional development. Savannah's choice of song to teach John Henry makes connections with her emotions; this song is intimately connected to memories of her father, and so has an emotional weight, and is part of her personal history. Additionally, Savannah's intervention in John Henry's games with the Bionicles shows that she can transform his linear, logical reasoning. While John Henry initially refuses Savannah's request to have her toys join in the game, and exhibits a mechanical, computer-like (though still potentially comical) interpretation of the rules – 'I don't think there are any ducklings on the mystical island of Voya Nui' – he certainly does appear to make an emotional connection with the human girl, one that allows him to see that 'we can change the rules' ('To the Lighthouse'). And in many ways this rule-changing comes to influence the series narrative itself, as it rewrites the established framework of the film franchise.

'The answer is yes': Rethinking Them and Us

The television series storyline that follows John Henry complements and undercuts the 'canonical' film/television storyline that follows John Connor. Both storylines play on – and rely on – viewer knowledge of the film franchise narrative, in which John Connor leads the future Resistance, and the artificial intelligence Skynet develops the future killer machines. The John Henry/Catherine Weaver storyline plays with viewer expectations, since their identification as AI and as Terminator implicate them in the future development of Skynet. Catherine's ruthless and murderous actions certainly support such a reading, and she is only revealed as an ally to Sarah and John in the last moments of the series finale. That the series concludes with both Johns, John Henry and John Connor, travelling to the future creates an open-ended narrative (although this is possibly accidental, as the series' future was uncertain at the conclusion of Season 2, and it was not cancelled until after the concluding episode was broadcast)[7]. There is a strong suggestion through more than one episode that the successive time-travelling of Terminators and Resistance fighters have changed the future timeline; for example, Jesse, who travels back in time from a different future point than Derek, has no knowledge of Andy Goode, the computer programmer partly responsible for the future creation of Skynet. It is therefore quite possible that the 'John' who leads the future Resistance is John Henry instead of (or perhaps as well as) John Connor. Such examples mesh with a key principle of the film franchise, especially *Terminator 2*, in which 'there's no fate but what we make'. And these examples show a rewriting of the 'rules' that turn the narrative from one of oppositional enmity between humans and machines to one that allows the possibility of synthesis.

A key component in *TSCC*'s narrative is the way in which the human characters are shown to become more machine-like and the cyborg characters more human as the series progresses. As the cyborg characters Cameron, Catherine and John Henry are integrated into the wider cast, the television narrative allows for a more nuanced and subtle portrait of both male and female cyborg characters, blurring the distinction between cyborg and human, 'them' and 'us', that is maintained in the film franchise. The television narrative offers possibilities for humans and cyborgs to work together, with extended examples in the developing relationships between Cameron, John, Derek and Sarah, and between Catherine, Ellison, Savannah and John Henry.

In a negative view of boundaries blurred through cyborg involvement, the series shows its human characters as increasingly ruthless, and at risk of losing touch with aspects of their humanity like empathy and compassion. Sarah, John and Derek are all shown as driven and single-minded in their pursuit of any individual who might contribute to the future emergence of Skynet. Their investigations often result in the deaths of such individuals, either deliberately – as when Derek kills programmer Andy Goode ('Dungeons and Dragons' 1.6), or John kills enemy businessman Sarkissian ('Samson and Delilah') – or accidentally – as when Sarah's enquiries result in scientist Alan Park's murder ('Earthlings Welcome Here' 2.13). At times, Sarah displays emotionless behaviour that is not far removed from Catherine Weaver's; indeed, when discussing Catherine's murders and destruction at the Desert Canyon Heat and Power warehouse, Sarah admits, 'I would have done the same' ('Desert Cantos' 2.15). On the other hand, John Henry appears to feel emotion – and strong emotion, too – when he 'dies' and comes back to life ('To the Lighthouse'), and he acts to protect Savannah, something that appears to result from their kinship/friendship bond ('Adam Raised a Cain' 2.21). As Sarah becomes more emotionless, sending a message to John *not* to rescue her from jail ('Born to Run'), Catherine's behaviour becomes less stony and one-dimensional. When Catherine refers to 'my John', her use of the phrase appears to represent some genuine feeling for John Henry.

We arrive at hybridity, once more, as the means to defeat Skynet in the future. Human and cyborg characters are able to accept hybridity precisely because of their experiences in the present-day of the series. Future John Connor sends a message to the T-1000 Terminators: 'Will you join us?' ('Today Is the Day, Part 2' 2.19). In that future, the answer is no, but it seems evident from the unfolding narrative that the Terminator who refuses Future John is the same one that travels back in time to pose as Catherine Weaver. In the timeline of the series, she is working against Skynet; in the last episode of the series, she sends the same message via Ellison to Cameron. By donating her chip to John Henry and enabling him to disconnect from the mainframe and move freely, Cameron does join them, in a sense ('Born to Run'). The human message travels via the cyborg from the future to the present and from human (John) to machine (Catherine, Cameron) in a complex fashion that retraces the series' narrative complexities. Finally, in order to defeat Skynet, machines and humans must act together: John, Sarah, Cameron, Catherine, John Henry and Ellison in the present and Derek, Kyle, Allison (and possibly John Henry and John Connor working together) in the future. In this narrative, hybridity needs machines, especially cyborg bodies, as much as it needs humans.

This series strongly emphasizes the emotional development of cyborgs, their transformation towards humanity, and their engagement with aspects of human thought; as James Ellison puts it, 'ethics, morals' ('Strange Things...'). In the next two chapters, we encounter complex representations of cyborg embodiment which are closely connected to the presence or absence of ethical and moral standards. In *Dollhouse*, we find a mode of cyborg embodiment that turns personalities into simulations; in *Fringe*, several versions of cyborg embodiment complicate the boundaries between human and machine.

7

Hacking the System: *Dollhouse*

Dollhouse is not at first glance an obvious 'cyborg' narrative, but there is evidence that characters in this series are physically altered by technological components that are added to their organic bodies. The focal point of the series is the activity of the Los Angeles Dollhouse, one of several throughout the world, run by the Rossum Corporation. Naming the corporation Rossum immediately connects the series to Karel Čapek's *R.U.R* and should alert viewers to the likelihood that the inhabitants of the Dollhouse will be revealed to be a contemporary version of 'Rossum's Universal Robots'.[1] The series' premise is that a group of individuals agree, for various reasons, to have their own personalities removed and to be imprinted instead with a variety of constructed personalities. While they are imprinted with these identities, they are known as Actives; while they are in the resting state between imprints, they are known as Dolls. The agreement covers their employment as Actives for a five-year term, after which their original personalities will be restored and they will return to their own lives with a substantial payment.

This simple and possibly tempting offer nevertheless has complex ramifications which expose even the television narrative itself as potentially exploitative, situating its viewers as voyeurs complicit in its tales of exploitation (Bennett 2011; Tresca 2012; Calvert 2014b). The invention of imprinting technology is depicted as a starting point for the dangerous alteration of embodied identity, leading to a future 'thoughtpocalypse' in the two season-finale episodes ('Epitaph One' 1.13; 'Epitaph Two: Return' 2.13). These two episodes form one storyline – slightly removed from the rest of the series narrative, but building on the concerns introduced and developed there – in which the Dollhouse technology runs rampant throughout the world of 2019, erasing personalities and creating utter chaos. All the series storylines involve different Active personalities imprinted onto the same few individuals, code-named Echo (formerly known as Caroline), Victor (Tony) and Sierra (Priya). Over two seasons, viewers see these individuals as Dolls, as Actives imprinted as various personalities, and occasionally with their original personalities ('Needs' 1.8, 'Belonging' 2.4, 'Stop-Loss' 2.9).

Individuals who agree to have their own personalities removed and their bodies 'imprinted' with other, created personalities have technology embedded in their brains. This allows them to be created and recreated with a multiplicity of identities. These characters' identities are continually reset with new personalities, undermining the notion of a unified and constant identity. Instead, each character presents multiple identities which are essentially representations, imitations, or, as Jean Baudrillard argues, *simulacra*. The television narrative, which presents the same character (and actor) in different personalities from episode to episode, enables viewers to remain aware of the 'simulacra' of personality, the means by which the representation or performance of personality becomes indistinguishable from a 'core' or 'authentic' personality. Thinking about *Dollhouse* in the context of cyborg embodiment enables some questioning of Haraway's image of boundary-crossing cyborg transformation, with rather less positive inflections. The cyborgs of this series do cross boundaries and transform their embodiment; however, their identities are constantly troubled and disrupted because of their cyborg status.

Writer/director Joss Whedon and actor Eliza Dushku developed the series concept, which manages to comment on the very process of creating television fictions (Ryan 2009; Bennett 2011; Tresca 2012). The proliferation of Active identities deliberately draws attention to an actor's performance of a fictional character while it highlights the effects of the fabrication of identity within the series universe. The self-referential qualities of the series, and its focus on disturbing scenarios of sex trafficking, slavery and coercion, mean that the viewing experience can be a challenging one; there is constant tension between viewer enjoyment in watching an entertaining fiction and viewer discomfort in discovering the intended parallels between Whedon's fantasy world and our own. Indeed, Whedon's 'strategy of displacement' (Buckman 2014: xviii) antagonizes some scholars and commentators who seem unable to identify the source of the narrative's destabilizing effects, instead noting the series' 'many disappointments' which mean that its cancellation is 'hard to view as anything other than a relief' (Short 2011: 105). This kind of dismissal – in this case, a dismissal that lacks any attempt at an analysis, or even a listing, of the 'disappointments' – misses the point of the series. *Dollhouse* references 'prostitution and human trafficking' in ways that emphasize 'how morally and politically murky the sex industry is' (Mukherjea 2014: 72). As I have discussed, it is evident, too, that *Dollhouse* very intentionally provokes viewers to reconsider 'their own enjoyment of a narrative that constantly chides them for their complicity in watching objectified and exploited bodies' (2014b: 123). The series does invite us to watch, but it also invites us to question. In this respect, the intersecting storylines that reveal different aspects of cyborg embodiment trouble and confuse the expected boundaries of social behaviour, as well as those of self/other and actual/fictional identity.

In the series narrative, anyone who has volunteered to become a Doll undergoes an initial procedure – perhaps 'erasure' would be a better term – which removes the individual's own personality and fits technological 'Active architecture' into the brain. The individual is then reset with a Doll personality, described as a 'tabula rasa' or 'blank slate'. This personality is childlike and docile, able to carry out physical functions and to perform simple tasks. Between their periods as Actives, these individuals remain inside the Dollhouse in the 'tabula rasa' state, cared for by support staff who monitor their behaviour and attend to their physical needs. The 'tabula rasa' Dolls are imprinted with Active identities for particular 'engagements' with paying clients. The imprinting process, including the installation of the Active architecture and the technological creation of Active identities, turns these Doll/Active individuals into cyborgs. Their manufactured Active identities makes them simulacra – their identities replicate personality so that Actives cannot be distinguished from non-imprinted individuals. In some respects all the examples of cyborgs in this book could be described as simulacra, especially those cyborgs with technological augmentations that cannot be seen on the surface of the body (for example, the humanoid Cylons; Jaime Sommers and Sarah Corvus; the Terminators) but *Dollhouse*'s simulacra counterfeit the identity of the body, not its materiality/physicality. Both simulacra and cyborg complicate and question the concept of 'original', 'true', 'real' or 'authentic' selves and bodies.

In the case of the Doll/Active characters, their authentic or (to borrow the future-dystopian episodes' terminology) 'actual' personality is removed and stored when they are fitted with Active architecture. The Rossum Company replaces their actual personalities with synthetic, manufactured composite personalities. The Dolls after imprinting are not augmented cyborgs in the way that Seven of Nine as Borg, the bionic Jamie Sommers, or the Terminators are augmented cyborgs, with machine and organic components within their organic bodies that enable them to have superhuman abilities. Dolls on Active engagements *only* have human abilities, albeit human abilities that are enhanced through their construction and combined in optimal patterns to allow for the wishes of particular clients. However, these optimal patterns are a result of technological augmentation, and so, as I have argued, these individuals can be defined as cyborg (2010). Further, 'the body conceived of as a machinic assemblage becomes a body that is multiple' (Starr 2014: 6), enabling the cyborg to connect with a variety of simulated, technological identities. Of the different Dolls, Echo and Alpha gain what might be called superhuman abilities, because they have all of their Active imprints downloaded at once. Their simultaneous download allows them to access many different skills and abilities at the same time and to combine them into new and varied patterns. In the dystopian episodes set in the future, Victor, Kilo and other Dolls have become 'techheads' who embrace a version of Echo's and Alpha's composite imprinting, and welcome the possibility of having access to multiple imprints downloaded via their Active architecture. The possibilities of embodied transformation through technological augmentation are open to all other Doll characters, and such 'bodies that have been augmented with technology have the potential to unite oppositions of mind, body, nature, and machine' (Calvert 2010, par. 13) and to become augmented cyborg individuals.

Taking Apart the Mind and the Body

The concept of the 'tabula rasa' Dolls is itself a vision of a cybernetic future in which it is possible to separate the mind and the body. As I noted in this book's introduction, the separation of mind/brain and body envisioned by theorists and writers of fiction is entrenched in Western philosophical history: from Aristotle and Plato on the separation of soul and body, to Descartes and La Mettrie on Enlightenment ideas of body-as-machine and the disembodied mind, and on into contemporary theorists' preoccupations with technology and the future of the human body. The very idea that it would be possible to remove the mind/brain from the body and have it continue in any other physical form locates consciousness and selfhood in the mind/brain alone.

The theory of mind/body separation becomes a realistic future development from the viewpoint of some contemporary scientists, such as Hans Moravec. In the Introduction, I outlined the ways in which such a scenario is often presented: the mind exists apart from and beyond the corporeal body. The mind can be inserted into other bodies or vessels which do not suffer disintegration or disease – or if they do, the mind can be separated once again, and can continue to exist in a different body or vessel. This as-yet theoretical development is often presented as an example of empowering and liberating freedom from bodily limitations, as the self experiences a form of 'rebirth' into a bodiless posthuman future (Kroker and Kroker 1988: 31; Moravec 1988). For these theorists, the rejection of or freedom from the body is a necessary stage in the improvement of the human condition. *Dollhouse*'s narrative follows this kind of reasoning, and in several episodes suggests that the mind could be downloaded into many different bodies. This is dramatized to uncanny effect when Rossum Executive Vice Chairman Ambrose appears in the body of the Doll Victor ('Epitaph One'). He is the physical manifestation of the 'complete anatomy upgrade' the company intends to offer, 'a kind of immortality whereby a consciousness might travel from body to body, outrunning disease and overturning the boundary between life and death (Calvert 2014b: 122). In the series' dystopian future, Ambrose and fellow Rossum executive Harding use individuals whose minds have been wiped as 'suits', empty bodies that house their own consciousnesses ('Epitaph Two: Return'). Cartesian mind/body dualism surfaces during Alpha's attempt to download multiple Active imprints into Echo. Alpha uses Echo's original personality, Caroline, as a hostage of sorts. Downloading Caroline into the body of a kidnapped clothing-store assistant, he is able to threaten her – and Echo – with permanent erasure/death. When Echo demands, 'Whose body is this?' Alpha insists, 'It's just a body. They're all pretty much the same' ('Omega' 1.12). Caroline, however, asserts herself: 'I want my brain back…I want back in my brain'. She does not ask to be returned to her body but to her brain; she does not refer to the disembodied 'mind' but to the 'brain', and so her words emphasize the physical entity.[2] Divisions between mind and body feature strongly in 'The Attic' (2.10), in which enemies of the Dollhouse are imprisoned in a virtual world where they experience visions, fears, and nightmares. The mind has dominance over the body in this scenario, so 'once an individual is killed in the world of the nightmare, that person is dead in the real world' (Calvert 2010, par. 15) – a feature reminiscent of the effects of virtuality in *The Matrix*.

The series dramatizes mind/body separation with examples that show the mind possessing a continued existence in a succession of completely different bodies. It shows that the mind can be downloaded onto a data storage device: the Dolls' original personalities are stored in a vault until they have completed their five-year contract. These examples follow a theory that 'proposes that one's mind is noncorporeal and that any old body will do to hold the data. There are data suggesting that this is not possible, that a mind is more than a collection of data and that a body is necessary for its essence' (Porter and Ginn 2014: 110, note 31). Sandy Stone's declaration that 'life is lived through bodies' (Stone 1991: 113) has been argued persuasively by a succession of critics examining cyberculture and concepts of the 'posthuman' in science. Such critics question whether 'the body [will] continue to be regarded as excess baggage' or if 'versions of the posthuman [can] be found that overcome the mind/body divide' (Hayles 1997: 246). What *Dollhouse* most certainly does is *trouble* the mind/body divide, mapping versions of the 'posthuman' cyborg onto a variety of bodies and situations, often troubling the viewer in the process. That, because of imprinting, these posthuman bodies frequently perform 'overtly sexual' or violent scenarios, or are costumed in 'gratuitous' ways (Mukherjea 2014: 68, 78) adds to the troubling effects of this narrative, a point made by commentators who disliked the series (Callot 2009; meloukhia 2009).

'Hack the system': Creating a Cyborg Doll/Active

It is clear from *Dollhouse*'s series narrative that technological apparatus is required for an individual to become a Doll/Active. As well as the 'Active architecture' which enables imprints to be downloaded into a Doll's body, Dolls are fitted with additional technological devices: they can be tracked through implants in the back of the neck; their vital signs can be monitored through 'biolinks' while they are on an engagement. Those controlling the Dollhouse and its technological processes use a vocabulary of technology, especially of computing, to describe the imprinting process and the behaviour of the Dolls/Actives themselves. In 'Needs', for example, LA Dollhouse chief Adelle DeWitt, in-house physician Dr. Saunders, and technological genius Topher all refer to 'glitches' experienced in the minds or memories of the Dolls, while Dr. Saunders proposes a way of treating 'open loops' in their memories, and security officer Dominic points out that they have 'no kill switch, we can't shut them down.' At times, the Dolls need to be 'wiped' or 'scrubbed' like computer hard drives, and there are risks of erasing or switching Active personalities in the middle of an engagement, as happens to Echo in 'Gray Hour' (1.4) and to Echo and Victor in 'Belle Chose' (2.3). This vocabulary reinforces a view of the Dolls/Actives as at least partly machine-like or cyborg. Topher – who describes his work as 'programming' – insists 'our brains are natural motherboards...I just hack the system' ('Needs'), and in this explanation – as in some posthuman theory – there is a sense that everyone has cyborg potential (More 2013); everyone or anyone could be fitted with Active architecture, and programmed with new personalities. This potential is realized in the dystopian episodes that conclude each season, where even individuals with no Active architecture at all can be reprogrammed as violent 'butchers' or erased as blank 'dumbshows' with just one automated telephone call ('Epitaph One', 'Epitaph Two: Return').

One point about Active architecture, which reinforces the cyborg definition, is that once this augmentation is implanted in an individual, it cannot be removed even though the individual finishes their term of service and leaves the Dollhouse. This calls into question the idea that a Doll only becomes cyborg for a specified length of time. Since former Dolls retain the Active architecture within their brains, there is always the possibility that they could be called back into service, as with Rossum's 'Mind Whisper' project in which former Dolls are recruited as soldiers programmed with the ability to share thoughts, sound, and vision ('Stop-Loss'). Former Dolls are affected by any technology that affects Dolls in general, as is apparent with the 'remote wipe' Topher creates, which knocks out Madeleine (formerly code-named November) even though her contract as a Doll is finished and she has regained her original identity ('The Public Eye' 2.5). Furthermore, the personality restored to an individual on the completion of their contract with the Dollhouse must also be seen as an imprint, a version of the original personality, preserved from the time that individual entered the Dollhouse, was first 'wiped' and was given 'Active architecture'.

The composite personalities created in the Dollhouse make up complete personalities in themselves, containing skills or aspects of temperament that a client might request or that might be necessary for a particular engagement. Engagements take various forms, from the strategic to the euphemistically termed 'romantic'; an Active might be anything from a doula to a hostage negotiator, a singer, a soldier or a stripper. An Active might need to be able to fire a gun, do kickboxing, dance, have knowledge of medical procedures, or it might be helpful if that Active has special analytical or artistic abilities, for example. Despite these skills, however, and the appearance of a complete and unified personality for Actives, the created personalities are never 'real', but are simulations. From the outset, Topher makes it clear that any one Active imprint is a composite personality: 'I can create an amalgam of those [real] personalities, pieces from here or there, but it's not a greatest hits. It's a whole person': flaws, imperfections and all – for example, the imprint of 'Eleanor Penn', a hostage negotiator, has poor sight and requires glasses ('Ghost' 1.1). While aspects of the imprint are based on actual personalities, 'from scans of real people' ('Ghost'), the Active identity is composed in a way that is entirely artificial, and results in a *simulacrum* of identity.

Simulations, Dolls and Cyborgs

Dollhouse's cyborg identities can be usefully mapped onto Jean Baudrillard's work on simulacra and simulation. His theoretical framework gives us points of definition for the cyborg embodiment displayed in the series narrative.

Baudrillard's schematic for simulation describes four 'phases of the image' which are successively more removed from notions of reality. For the first phase, involving 'the counterfeit' or the *'imitation of nature'* (Baudrillard 1993: 50, 52, emphasis in original) and the second phase, 'production', we might think of the ways paintings or photographs represent reality. Paintings and photographs of scenes are not the same things as the scenes themselves, but paintings and photographs do have a connection to the scenes themselves, through their representation of the original concrete image. But as we move to the third and fourth phases, those connections between real-life objects and images begin to pull apart: 'any discernible distinction between images and reality begins to fall away completely' (Toffoletti 2011: 24). In the third phase, the phase of the model or 'the simulacrum', 'signs of the real' take the place of 'the real itself' (Baudrillard 1988: 166) so that 'the very notion of the real and its artificial reproduction collide and implode' (Toffoletti 2007: 44). Things go further still in the 'fourth phase' of the image, where value radiates in all directions [...] without being related to anything at all' (Baudrillard 1993: 5). With this stage of simulation, Baudrillard builds on Walter Benjamin's concept of the copy without an original (in Benjamin's essay 'The Work of Art in the Age of Mechanical Reproduction' 1955); Baudrillard describes the way in which Benjamin 'shows that reproduction absorbs the process of production, changes its goals, and alters the status of the product and producer' (Benjamin 1992; Baudrillard 1993: 55).

Baudrillard's 'simulacrum' does not 'represent' reality but instead is an image so removed from 'reality' that it 'bears no relation to any reality whatever: it is its own pure simulacrum' (Baudrillard 1988: 152). 'Reality' is equally open to question, 'not a given but rather, in a culture of simulation, images [...] perform to make the world as we know it, to generate our sense of what is real' (Toffoletti 2007: 121). This fits very well with the concept of Active personalities in *Dollhouse*. These are not actual personalities, but manufactured ones; nevertheless, anyone with such imprints behaves as though the imprint were the personality. This kind of manufactured identity 'collapses and exceeds the boundaries that once differentiated fact from fiction and illusion from reality' (Toffoletti 2007: 32). The Rossum Corporation achieves its aims by 'substituting signs of the real for the real itself' (Baudrillard 1988: 166). Part of the experience of watching

Dollhouse is never being quite sure where 'the real itself' has been exchanged for 'signs of the real', which character is an actual personality and which is a constructed Active. We see this in the opening of 'Omega' when the character we have known for the whole of the first season as Dr Saunders appears as a Doll, Whiskey, with an imprinted personality as an amoral lap dancer/murderer. Such contrasts and collisions of actual and constructed personalities create shocking moments that disrupt and challenge television conventions. Viewers see established characters and identities overturned and destroyed, and over time this creates a sense of unease; since any character could turn out to be a construct, no character identity can be regarded as secure.

An individual, once imprinted with an Active identity, behaves in accordance with that identity. She or he is not acting or role-playing, but *becomes* that identity. Adelle DeWitt explains this to a client early in Season 1: '…imagine the imprint processes […] creating a new personality, a friend, a lover, a confidant in a sea of enemies, your heart's desire made flesh…. Everything you want, everything you need, she [sic] will be honestly and completely' ('The Target' 1.2). So, an Active on an engagement *is* that person; there is no performance on their part. As we understand that an Active identity is a manufactured identity, not a duplication of a pre-existing identity, this is a process of simulation. The Active-as-simulation appears to be a real person, interacting with other real people. However, the client embarking upon an engagement with the Active knows that this person does not possess a true identity. There is an element of performance involved in the encounter between client and Active, something that itself highlights the ways in which we all perform social identities. In the engagement scenario, the client must enter fully into the imaginary world his/her wishes (and money) have created.

On occasion, an Active is given an identity which is a duplication or re-animation rather than a completely artificial construction. We see examples of imprints that are the fully-formed personalities of people who have died. Joel Mynor meets his dead wife, Rebecca, once a year, in a regular, pre-booked engagement with the Dollhouse ('Man on the Street' 1.6); Adelle de Witt's friend Margaret returns in Active disguise to investigate her own death ('Haunted' 1.10) These examples show the imprint as a re-animation of the personality (in a sense, as the return of the soul) in a new body, a means by which the dead can live again. A scenario like Rebecca Mynor's annual return from the dead is both disturbing and poignant; we might surmise that the annual contact with Rebecca softens the fact of her death by allowing Joel renewed contact with her. And in this example, it is Joel who plays/performs a role in the annual engagement; he is fully aware that Rebecca is dead and that he is experiencing a wish-fulfillment fantasy. Rebecca can only exist as a simulacrum, but Joel does not lose sight of the difference between reality and fantasy. Nolan Kinnard is equally aware of performance and of the simulated aspects of his fantasy scenario, in which the Doll Sierra, imprinted as a version of her own personality, Priya, finds Nolan completely irresistible ('Belonging'). With her *actual* personality, Priya repeatedly rejected Nolan's romantic advances. A key aspect of Nolan's fantasy scenario seems to be the fact that he can constantly and repeatedly demonstrate his power over actual-Priya. It is not important to him that Priya does not know that this is happening – she cannot know, since she is an imprinted Doll. Nolan's fantasy scenario is therefore a narcissistic revenge on a woman who rejected his advances. Still, the question remains: are these engagements so different? What is the distinction between the performance/simulacrum of Joel's imagined future with Rebecca – a future that might have been, had Rebecca not died – and the performance/simulacrum of Nolan's imaginary future with Priya – a future that might have been, had Priya not found Nolan utterly creepy and repulsive? Despite the different attitudes of Joel and Nolan to their respective fantasy scenarios, the common element is that both men are interacting with a simulacrum, and the scenarios involved are also simulacra, and bear no relation to reality. Unfortunately, the scenarios and the personalities within them become confused with reality, and have concrete effects on those caught up in them, something that is terribly apparent when, after Priya kills Nolan, she and Topher struggle with guilt and complicity.

'Tell me I know who I am': Simulated Identities and the Self

The Rebecca Mynor, Margaret and constructed-Priya personalities are temporary ones (although Nolan hopes to live out his fantasy by having

Priya imprinted with the constructed personality). Individuals that are permanently imprinted are more obviously embodied as cyborg and as simulacra. One such case, as I have noted, is the female Doll imprinted with the modified personality of the (male) Dollhouse physician, Dr Saunders, creating 'Claire Saunders' ('Omega'). Another is FBI agent Paul Ballard, who is restored to life after he is declared brain-dead by being imprinted with a version of *himself* ('A Love Supreme' 2.8). 'Claire Saunders' is, in a sense, a complete simulacrum of identity. Topher has not imprinted the Doll with the original Dr Saunders personality, but has modified it in certain key ways, making 'Claire' a distinct personality in her own right. Paul, however, becomes a *version* of himself; he is not 'Paul Ballard' but a downloaded imprint of 'Paul' captured at a particular time and with particular memories, some of them incomplete. That this is a simulated identity is reinforced when Topher reveals that he has removed some aspects of Paul's memory in order to create space to fit him with the Active architecture ('The Attic'). On regaining consciousness, Paul's 'What have you done to me?' could refer to both the imprinting process and to Topher's removal of a key aspect of Paul's original personality: his love for Echo/Caroline.

A similar process turns a real person, Daniel Perrin, into a simulacrum of himself ('The Public Eye'/'The Left Hand' 2.5–6). In contrast to Paul, Daniel is described as possessing an improved version of his own original personality. The Rossum Corporation 'needed a senator' and used Perrin's 'pedigree' – that of a long-standing and established political family – to achieve this. Thanks to the alterations of Rossum's technological apparatus, Daniel is no longer a 'party boy screw-up' or 'a spoiled, pampered, selfish child' but a committed politician, 'a man the people could trust'. Rossum has total control over the reprogrammed Daniel, and it becomes clear that their intention is to 'manufactur[e] a president' out of him. Daniel appears as an example of a successful simulacrum of an actual person, although his situation is certainly not presented as a positive outcome, and there is great irony in the point that his identity as a sincere politician is another simulation. The team at the LA Dollhouse has great difficulty in separating actual and simulated personalities once they begin to examine Daniel and his wife Cindy. At first, they believe that Cindy is a Doll, and this seems likely after Daniel comments, 'it's like they made her just for me' ('The Public Eye'). This, together with the apparently romantic exchange between Daniel and

Cindy which strongly echoes the LA Dollhouse's 'handler script' ('Did I fall asleep?' 'For a little while') alerts regular viewers, as well as the LA Dollhouse team, that something is not quite right – or authentic – here.

Daniel's struggle, on discovering that he is one of the Dolls he has pledged to help, centres on his own sense of authenticity: how much of his identity is his true self, and how far is he in control of that self? 'I know who I am,' he repeats, then appeals to Echo in desperation, 'Please tell me I know who I am' ('The Public Eye'). In the following, connected episode, however, Daniel approaches a different sort of understanding: 'They made me into something better…even if I could, I don't know if I want to be the man I was before' ('The Left Hand'). So, even before the DC Dollhouse succeeds in recapturing and reprogramming him, Daniel is already at work to reprogramme himself and to rationalize what has been done to him – in a sense, to embrace his cyborg, simulated identity and to deny his actual self.[3]

'The real deal': Sierra/Priya and the Struggle for Authenticity

The examples of Daniel and Paul have similarities with the case of Sierra/Priya, whose original personality becomes an Active simulacrum for Nolan Kinnard, a particularly nasty client. Sierra/Priya's storyline is entirely centred on questions of reality and authenticity, as well as on the demonstration of simulacra. Her complex back-story evolves over the two *Dollhouse* seasons, but is not presented as a complete narrative until the Season 2 episode 'Belonging' which uses flashbacks to explain the history of her meeting with Nolan Kinnard and his subsequent infatuation with her. Sierra/Priya is the only Doll/Active character apart from Echo/Caroline whose life and original identity before coming to the Dollhouse is shown in any such detail.[4] The flashback sequences in 'Belonging' are interwoven with a present-day plotline in which Echo helps to reveal the traumatic circumstances of Sierra's arrival at the Dollhouse and subsequent engagements as an Active.

'Belonging' acts as a pivotal point in the narrative in its overt demonstration of the horror that is constantly present in what the Dollhouse does both to those who become Dolls/Actives and to those who make use of the Dolls in those Active identities. This story uncovers the corruption and potential for corruption that is wrapped up in the way the Dollhouse counterfeits identity. The episode's key themes are authenticity/truth and deception; the whole episode dramatizes simulacra in various forms, especially the way in which Priya's own identity is turned into a simulacrum that appears to represent reality. However, as an imprinted Doll, Sierra is 'unable to give consent to the acts committed against [her body]' (Porter and Ginn 2014: 103) making clear her status as a slave, as object not subject (Sutherland and Swan 2014: 227).[5] Sierra, imprinted as a *version* of Priya, becomes an image or simulacrum that 'perform[s]...to generate [a] sense of what is real' (Toffoletti 2007: 121), in this case, to create a particular scenario to satisfy Nolan. 'Real' and 'authentic' identity is underlined in the episode dialogue. Nolan, for example, describes Priya approvingly as 'the real deal' and she is elsewhere called 'natural, unaffected';[6] there is a strong suggestion that Nolan recognizes and wants to possess that very quality of authentic individuality, Priya's 'realness'.

In a pointed and revealing flashback scene, Priya attends an art gallery for the viewing of her painting, commissioned by Nolan. For the regular viewer of *Dollhouse*, the presence of several Dolls in this scene displays its artificiality and qualities of simulation. Echo is present with an imprint designed to enthuse about Nolan, and Victor is there too, in the Active persona of Luca, introduced as 'the finest art dealer in all of Italy'. Throughout the scene, the claims about Nolan and about his supposed guests become more ridiculous and unbelievable, heightening the contrasts between authenticity and fakery. The event itself is a simulacrum: a staged event put on for Priya's benefit, in which the only individuals aware of the deception are Nolan and Rossum executive Harding (and of course, the viewer, who is made complicit in their discussions). It is impossible to say whether anything in this scene, except Priya herself, is truthful or 'real'.

Harding's solution to Nolan's problem calls on the artificial and the constructed: 'Why don't you let us build the woman you want – the perfect woman?' Nolan insists, 'I don't want a doll… I want her', and this implies that he will keep trying to attract the real Priya. Moving forward in time to the present day at the end of the episode's opening sequence, however, and we discover Nolan welcoming an Active-identity version of Priya to his apartment. In this way, Nolan does get his 'perfect woman' just as

Harding suggested – but he does not get 'her', the real Priya. Since Nolan is interacting with a Doll (authentic Priya's body with its identity removed) imprinted with an Active identity (a simulated version of Priya who *does* love him) then he is not interacting with the real Priya. Therefore, he does not possess 'the real deal'. Nolan's problem (apart from being 'a nutcase one tick shy of a murderer' according to Adelle de Witt) is that he cannot or refuses to distinguish between the Priya who is the 'real deal' and the Priya who is the simulacrum. It seems enough for him to have a *version* of Priya, a simulacrum-Priya who does and says all the things he wants, who can be controlled and manipulated. The extension of this is his demand to have Priya permanently imprinted and sent to him, and it appears that for Nolan, the permanently-imprinted version of Priya will still function as the 'real deal'.

Nolan's plan for a future with a simulated Priya disrupts the notion of an authentic, 'true' self. The true self is something that the show emphasizes time and again, with different characters insisting that it is not possible to completely erase a person, that 'who they are, at their core' will remain no matter how much Active architecture is put into a person, or how often that person is imprinted with different personalities ('Omega'). This is supported by the examples of the Dolls Victor and Sierra, who are somehow able to retain 'true' memories of each other in and (more surprisingly) out of Doll state. Towards the end of 'Belonging', Priya, with her own, authentic personality briefly reinstated, confronts Nolan and tells him she is in love, but 'it's not you, I managed to fall for someone else […] I can feel it stronger than anything, I'm crazy about him, I love him.' This suggests that Sierra's experiences as a Doll, with Victor, are at least as real as anything she has experienced in her own identity as Priya, and that these Doll experiences can somehow be retained in the memory of her Doll self. 'Victor's feelings [for Sierra, and I suggest Sierra's for him] might seem to be more authentic than other emotional or sexual connections because they are not reliant on social context or performance of social roles' (Jowett 2014: 134). We might look on such experiences and feelings as aspects of cyborg embodiment. The cyborg imprinting process allows individuals to exist outside social norms and expectations (and limits). As the cyborgs of *Dollhouse* are creatures of both mind and body, the Doll experiences that connect with a 'true' or authentic 'core self' also connect with physical, embodied experience. This may explain how Doll memories can be retained in the core self. Memory is not (or not simply) a mental activity but can be seen as something rooted in the body. In their analysis of *Dollhouse*, Tom Connelly and Shelley Rees consider 'synchronic' and 'diachronic' selves. The diachronic self is an identity constituted/formed over time 'with all those experiences, influences, and moments contributing to a multivalent, dynamic conversation'; the contrasting synchronic self is 'static', 'a constant, fixed snapshot' (2010 par. 7). As synchronic selves, the Dolls are 'disconnected from their individualities and [...] their respective histories' (2010 par. 8). Connelly and Rees do not mention that this includes disconnection from their embodied histories. As Holly Randell-Moon notes, 'identity and consciousness are dependent on embodiment in order to exist and be meaningful' (2012: 270). Memories 'leave a corporeal residue on the body' and the body itself is 'a site of somatic history' (2012: 274, 275). The body is thus absolutely key to an individual's sense of self: 'self and identity are connected with and through the body' (Calvert 2014b: 116). So alongside Sierra/Priya's cyborg embodiment, in which Active architecture is embedded in her physical self, exists the physical, embodied 'memory' of the connection she and Victor share, and that Priya is able to retain when she regains her own identity.

At the end of 'Belonging', it appears that Priya wishes to reject her somatic history. She begs Topher, 'If you wake me up again, put me back to where I was a year ago. Skip this day…I don't ever want this back, okay?' On the face of it, this is a fairly reasonable request: Priya has discovered that she has been forcibly made into a Doll, has spent a year professing her love and devotion to Nolan Kinnard, and has finally murdered him. At this point in the narrative, Topher appears to agree to Priya's request, but when Priya is again restored to her own identity ('The Attic', 'Getting Closer' 2.11) her memories of 'this day' are intact. But consideration of Priya's cyborg identity as Sierra, and of her simulacrum of identity as the Priya who loved Nolan, might help to clarify and explain Topher's decision. As Priya has asked Topher to remove parts of her original personality, she is asking to be made into a simulacrum of herself. This would be the equivalent of what Topher did to Paul, or what Rossum did to Daniel. In both those examples, although the individual has a continued embodied life, he is not the same person as he was before the Dollhouse's

Active architecture tampered with his authentic, core self. Topher's refusal to modify Priya's memory resonates with Priya's stance in 'Epitaph One' and 'Epitaph Two: Return', in which she is determined to 'set the terms for her own existence' (Mukherjea 2014: 77) and refuse the simulacrum. Significantly, since 'Epitaph One' was never broadcast in the US, it is possible that viewers continued to watch Season 2 unaware of some crucial (if future-set) plot and character developments.[7]

Return of the Imprints: Creating a Cyborg Identity

One of the theoretical functions of the cyborg image is to cross boundaries, to allow hybridity and multiplicity. While the Dolls and their Active identities can be read as simulacra and as cyborg, these often appear as partial and contingent. Any special abilities that an Active possesses are temporary, only available to access during the period of an Active engagement. Further, these 'cyborg' abilities are still human abilities. As noted above, the Dolls/Actives are not augmented by technological appendages; their abilities are bound by the limits of the human body. While the constructed-Priya imprint, and others, function as (helpless) simulacra in this narrative, other Dolls take on a more dynamic response to their constructed identities, showing the potential offered by cyborg embodiment.

Both Echo and the rogue Doll Alpha are able to access multiple Active imprints, and so combine their Active abilities in a variety of configurations. These two Dolls have abilities that could be described both as superhuman and as cyborg, and in these cases 'cyborg' suggests augmentation of the physical state through technological means. Their abilities are certainly linked to the apparatus of the imprinting technology. Adelle describes Alpha as 'an unfortunate technological anomaly' ('Omega') but it was a specific technological *malfunction* that caused the 'composite event' that simultaneously downloaded all his previous imprints via his Active architecture. Trying to repeat this process on Echo, Alpha uses a home-made imprinting chair to download all thirty-eight of her previous personalities at once ('Omega'). Unsurprisingly, Alpha struggles to control his simultaneous abilities, which manifest as psychotic behaviour. Echo, however, has already been presented in the narrative as an exceptional individual who can remember aspects of her Active imprints while in her Doll state; for example, she recalls the image of a mountain from her role as a doula ('Gray Hour') and performs the 'shoulder to the wheel' salute from her engagement with outdoor enthusiast/hunter Richard Connell ('The Target'). So, once given multiple imprints, Echo is able to learn to control them.

Echo's cyborg embodiment with multiple imprints can be read in parallel with her Doll embodiment with successive imprints. Both forms of embodiment are created through coercion and by means of technology that threatens and violates the original/actual personality or self. Alpha's home-made chair which, as Figure 11 reveals, is bristling with electric wires and stuck together with duct tape, is very clearly intended to function as 'a torture device, a site of disempowerment', and contrasts with the chair in the Dollhouse that has become 'naturalized', 'controlled, sanitized' (Connelly and Rees 2010 par. 18). The Dollhouse chair only appears in this way because, in each episode, viewers see Dolls imprinted and 'wiped' in this chair as a matter of routine. It is easy to forget that the repeated wiping and imprinting of these individuals represents a contract that allows the Dollhouse to do anything it wishes with 'the simulacrum of perpetual consent' (Nadkarni 2014: 84), so that the 'sanitized' chair is just as threatening and horrific as Alpha's makeshift one. But while Alpha's chair dramatizes the horror and pain inherent (and sometimes barely concealed) in the Dollhouse's operations, its imprinting process turns the Dollhouse's upside down. Alpha's process does not create one more in a series of Active imprints followed by a return to the Doll 'blank slate'; instead it makes it possible for Echo to 'assemble' (Starr 2014) and amalgamate her various imprints into a new, powerful cyborg self. From the moment she is multiply imprinted, Echo accepts each one of those imprints, and she is quickly able to 'slip into' identities at will, 'or rather, they slip into me' ('Omega'). With the description 'they slip into me', she identifies her embodied self as a fixed point and the imprints as alternating and shifting. Thus, 'the body is the constant through all the versions of "self" that are overlaid on it' (Calvert 2014b: 116). Echo 'chooses to embrace multivalence' (Connelly and Rees 2010 par. 19), strengthening her cyborg identity. As a cyborg with multiple identities, Echo can choose from different Active personalities those skills that are most useful for her own purpose, something she describes as 'collecting myself' ('Meet Jane Doe' 2.7). Both Echo and Alpha could be said to create their own composite super-identities once they are able to master their different imprints. Alpha appears in 'Epitaph Two' as a stable individual and an ally to those fighting the imprinting wars.

Alpha and Echo, once their composite-imprint selves are downloaded, exhibit detachment towards their authentic /original personality. Alpha literally destroys his 'true' self, in the form of the device storing his original personality: 'he took [it] and he smashed the hell out of it' ('Omega'). This is a definitive action on Alpha's part, constituting a rejection of his original serial-killer personality. Though this could perhaps be read – with extreme caution – as an affirmation of his simulated multiple identities, these multiple identities still exist in a pattern that cause him – at this point in the narrative – to be dangerous and murderous. Alpha's destruction of his original identity still constitutes a rejection of 'the real' and an embrace of the simulacrum of identity. Echo both embraces and distances herself from her original identity. At first, when she refers to the original Caroline imprint, which Alpha has used on the kidnapped store assistant Wendy, Echo says, 'she's me' ('Omega'). When Echo refers to her multiple imprints, she says, 'I'm all of them but none of them is me' ('Vows'). These

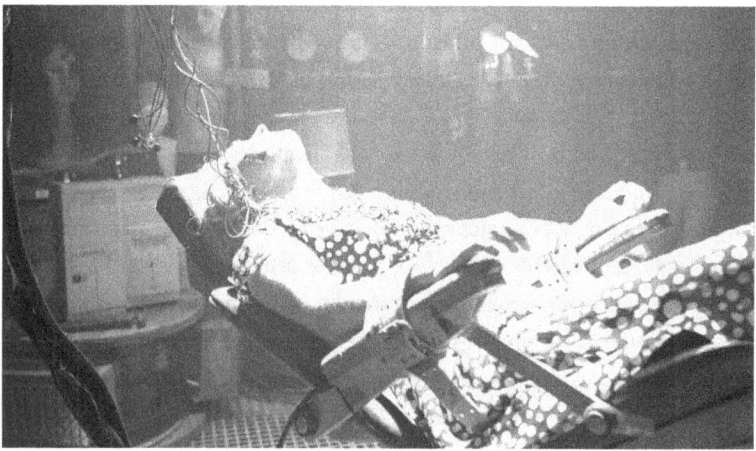

Figure 11: Wendy imprinted as Caroline in Alpha's makeshift chair, 'Omega', *Dollhouse* (1.12)

statements seem to indicate that Echo acknowledges a true, authentic, 'core' self, a 'me' distinct from any Active imprints. However, this is complicated as Season 2 progresses. It is apparent that Paul believes Caroline is 'in there', stored somewhere within Echo along with the multiple imprints. Echo, however, repeatedly insists 'I'm not her. My name is Echo…There is a me' ('Meet Jane Doe'). By this point, Echo draws a distinction between herself and Caroline as 'me' and 'her'. When she names herself towards the end of Season 2, she says 'I'm Echo' ('Getting Closer') and although other Dolls are restored to their original personalities in 'Epitaph Two', she remains 'Echo', not Caroline. Echo appears to represent a more successful version of the cyborg identity, but she, like Alpha, is still seen in a process of negotiation with her cyborg self, as she continues to struggle to balance her multiple personalities.

In the episodes set in the future we see yet another version of the cyborg. Victor, Kilo and other former Dolls become 'tech-heads' who embrace a version of Echo's and Alpha's super-imprinting. They make use of their Active architecture – which, as noted, cannot be removed from an individual once it has been fitted – and this enables them to download multiple imprints. They transform themselves into augmented cyborg individuals on the same lines as the composites Echo and Alpha. These characters are most clearly visually framed as cyborg, with punkish leather clothing, and visible USB ports in their temples. They use the ports to upload the contents of various flash drives, each containing a particular skill or attribute (we see Victor upload the English language; one of Kilo's drives is labeled 'weapons expert'). The tech-heads' continuing use of their Doll call signs links their current and former versions of cyborg embodiment. Their speech is loaded with the language of technology: Victor asks exasperatedly, 'Do I have to upload that to your brain myself?' and instead of telling him to shut up Romeo replies, 'Log off!' The tech-heads Romeo and Kilo defend their cyborg transformation, preferring 'juicy new prints' to the restoration of their original personalities, which they view as 'destroying who we are'. They have achieved cyborg embodiment through their use of the Dollhouse technology; according to Victor, 'we tweaked ourselves to fight the war' against the forced wiping and imprinting of the world's population. Having done so, however, their cyborg embodiment is compelling and addictive, and allows the tech-heads to have 'every one of those skills firing through my head […] Skip learning the hard way…just to feel the thrill of perfection.' As with the example of Paul Ballard, to be able to download multiple imprints, the tech-heads must remove parts of their personalities (Kilo, for example, has removed 'mercy', which she displays on another flash drive) and, even so, they can only download a certain number of simultaneous imprints. Kilo confirms that 'unless you're Echo' it is not possible to cope with a great number of imprints at once. So, however noble their motives, the tech-heads achieve a cyborg embodiment that is partial and damaging.

Echo is consistently portrayed as a more successful version of cyborg embodiment, with super-abilities thanks to the manipulation of her multiple imprints; this is presented as an occasionally favourable state of being. Echo's cyborg embodiment is the antithesis of the embodiment of the Dolls/Actives. Echo takes 'active control over her mental and physical states and is using her embodied augmentation [...] in an active and purposeful way' (Calvert 2010 par. 15). But of course Echo is not the only cyborg in this narrative: the Dolls, the tech-heads, Paul and Alpha can all be defined in this way. Although Echo's cyborg embodiment is often privileged in the narrative – she is a special case, she reacts differently from any other Doll thanks to specific physical characteristics – we see Sierra/Priya and Victor/Tony achieving the same control as Echo over their minds and bodies: they too are able to 'die' in the virtual world and return to a kind of cyborg rebirth in the physical world ('The Attic'). Even Alpha has more potential for cyborg embodiment: at the series end he is shown to have much more control over his multiple imprints, and he is acting as an ally in the imprinting war.

Conversely, by refusing all augmentation and insisting on her own unmediated, embodied reality, Priya embraces embodied authenticity, the 'real deal' or 'Actual' identity. Priya's stance can be viewed as problematic, as a refusal of change and as an example of technophobia that mirrors the tech-heads' 'cyberpunk technofascism' (King 2014: 172). Priya views the tech-heads' augmentation more negatively, telling Tony 'you chose to be Victor'; for Priya, the use of imprints returns individuals to a simulacrum of identity. Priya's stance is a complete refusal of cyborg potential, and a literal inscription or marking of her own authentic, physical body and embodied identity, in the form of the neck tattoo she asks Tony to give her ('Epitaph One'). Thanks to this tattoo, Priya's body will always carry her 'actual' name. As shown in Figure 12, the tattoo can be seen as a marker declares Priya's

Hacking the System: *Dollhouse*

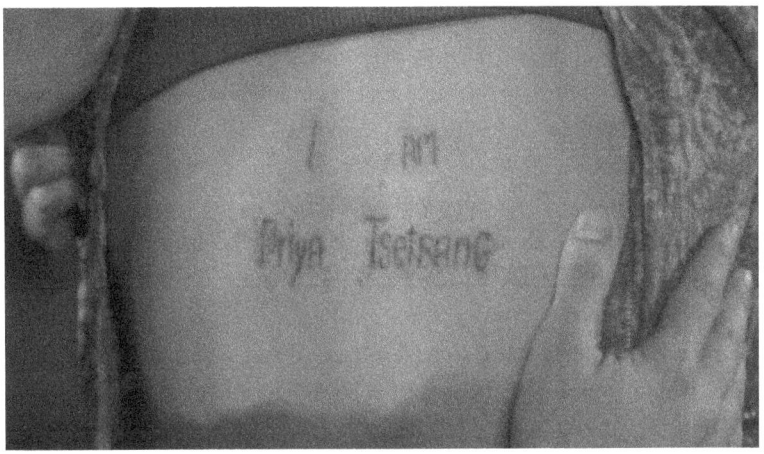

Figure 12: Priya's 'authentic' tattoo, 'Epitaph One', *Dollhouse* (1.13)

individuality. By marking her with her full name, her tattoo insists that she is not a call-sign or an interchangeable simulacrum of identity, even though her identity has been permanently compromised through her Active architecture and the manipulation of her original personality. As outlined in 'Epitaph One' and 'Epitaph Two', Priya's character embraces the embodied world. She is seen engaged in physical but arguably everyday activities like growing vegetables, or cooking; these activities might be read as a rejection of modern world, or as obsessive, survivalist self-sufficiency, but these are also things that depend on an embodied connection to, and interaction with, the concrete and physical world of heat, cold, rain and sun.

Priya's rejection of tech, her authenticating tattoo and her turn towards concrete physicality can be viewed as regression to an essentially-embodied self. In addition, Priya is a mother; her son T is one of the rare child characters to appear in the series. Of course, reading Priya – one of the few characters of colour and with a distinctive Asian identity in this narrative – *as* mother once again risks reinscribing her character as an essentially-embodied female. However, there are ways in which Priya as an example of embodied authenticity might be viewed more positively as the character who 'set[s] the terms for her own existence' (Mukherjea 2014: 77). The multiple Active identities, whether 'composite' or serially downloaded, are shown in almost every case to be negative; with Echo and (finally)

Alpha the possible exceptions, the overwhelming thematic direction of *Dollhouse*'s narrative has been to demonstrate the horror of this cyborg simulacra. So to reinstate the body, and the unmediated embodied experience, as something that has primary importance is to follow the logic of the series narrative. The Dollhouse will never produce a positive outcome because its very nature is to persuade its clients that the 'engagements' they pay for are not simulacra; in this way, it overwrites truth and disguises slavery and rape. Priya's embodied authenticity returns to 'who [you] are, at [your] core', to the notion of the true and enduring self which has been maintained throughout the series. And like Priya as mother, Tony is also reclaimed as father to T: he is drawn back into the 'body' of the family through his genetic link to the child. The end of the series retains a version of the family group at the centre of the new Dollhouse, and it appears to validate (or to wish to validate) authentic, core identity in its positive depiction of Priya and Tony, who resist any further cyborg embodiment.[8]

Paradoxically, however, the series affirms authenticity while at the same time it validates the choice to remain a cyborg. In the example of Priya, it offers a return to the authentic self and the refusal of cyborg embodiment, *and* it offers the absolute refusal of that authentic self in the examples of Echo and the tech-heads. While the Dollhouse is, finally, a space that ensures that Priya's authentic identity will be preserved, it is also a space that enables the continuation of Kilo's and Echo's cyborg identities. Kilo, who argued that she did not bargain 'for you to take our world away' with the restoration of original identities, is able to keep her cyborg being. Since she remains in the Dollhouse, in the area unaffected by Topher's electromagnetic pulse, she will retain her cyborg augmentation with the continued possibility of multiple downloaded abilities. Echo, too, remains in the Dollhouse and avoids the restoration of her actual personality. She finally asserts her separation from Caroline and preserves her own cyborg identity, going further by incorporating Paul as her last Active imprint (Starr 2014: 15), something that many commentators find most troubling of all. Alpha, however, stands in opposition to the wish to remain cyborg and to the positive depiction of the original 'authentic' personality. He leaves the safe space of the Dollhouse, an action that may indicate a wish to restore his original personality. Since that personality was a sadistic serial killer, this is a potentially reckless move, but it does suggest Alpha's refusal of his composite cyborg identity. On the other hand, we could read Alpha's actions as evidence that he has gained control as a result of his composite identity, and believes that it may even be possible to control his dangerous original personality. In that case, Alpha's cyborg self gives him at least the potential to change a damaged and dangerous authentic self into something new.

The choice to remain or to become a cyborg is a key aspect of the narrative of *Fringe*, the subject of Chapter 8. In this series, we see cyborgs represented as deadly adversaries and as agents of a dystopian future. We also find sympathetic cyborgs whose embodied augmentations reflect personal trauma, in similar ways to those experienced by Priya, Tony and Caroline in *Dollhouse*. *Fringe*'s story arcs offer ways in which an individual might adopt cyborg embodiment to empower him/herself to fight the system. Equally, it depicts a return to or reinstatement of organic modes of embodiment in order to reaffirm family bonds.

8

Complete Control: *Fringe*

Fringe's narrative is extremely complex, incorporating parallel universes, travel between parallel universes and time-travel alongside its regular investigations of strange occurrences that cannot be explained by conventional twenty-first-century science. The first season begins in a prime universe that resembles our own; over the course of that season, characters discover the existence of a parallel universe and in the second and third seasons different characters move between the two universes. Fan discussions code the prime and parallel universes 'blue' and 'red', colours that correspond to those featured in the episode title sequences. When the action is located in the prime universe in Seasons 1–3, the title sequence is coloured blue; when the action takes place in the parallel universe, the title sequence is red. The prime universe timeline is reset at the end of Season 3, and the *Fringe* storyline continues in a new 'amber' universe (again, coded by title sequence colour), in which some of the events of the previous three seasons have not happened, or have happened in different ways. In the fifth season, the characters from the amber universe are under threat from the Observers who turn out to be humans who have travelled back in time from the twenty-fifth century.

The series begins with the establishment of a team composed of FBI and civilian members, which remains in place for the entire five-season run. With FBI agent Olivia Dunham, brilliant and unpredictable scientist Walter Bishop, Walter's son Peter, and FBI research assistant Astrid, the team conducts investigations into a variety of bizarre and unexplained phenomena, sometimes with the assistance of Nina Sharp, the Chief Operating Officer of tech company Massive Dynamic. Within individual seasons, the narrative is split between more-or-less stand alone, monster- or phenomenon-of-the-week episodes, and extremely complex season story arcs that include the discovery and investigation of the parallel universe containing doubles of all the main characters, alternate timelines that reset or reinvent previous episodes or storylines, and threats from two recurring adversaries, scientists David Robert Jones and William Bell, who is Massive Dynamic's founder and Walter Bishop's former lab partner. A further ongoing plot line follows the mysterious, bald, dark-suited Observers who appear (Hitchcock-like, very fleetingly) in every episode[1] and who develop into the major adversaries of Season 5, which takes place in a near-future in which the cybernetically-enhanced 'posthuman' Observers have enslaved humanity.

Much of the action of *Fringe* episodes takes place in Walter's lab on the Harvard university campus, locating a significant part of the action within the domain of science. This chimes with the team's investigations into many cases featuring aspects of 'fringe science', which incorporate a variety of scientific/technological experimentations. These can focus on genetics or quantum physics, or on areas further removed from 'mainstream' science, such as psychic abilities or the paranormal; all of these examples feature in *Fringe*, and many are traced to Walter's scientific experimentation in the 1960s.

Like *Dollhouse*, *Fringe* is not, specifically, a show about cyborgs as are *Battlestar Galactica, Terminator: The Sarah Connor Chronicles* or *Bionic Woman*. However, the presence of cyborgs, both as adversaries and as allies, extends across all five seasons, and the cyborg, cybernetic augmentations and posthuman transformations are embedded in the show's plot and structure in a variety of ways. Cyborgs appear as enemies in such characters as the hybrid 'shapeshifters' which act as technologically enhanced body snatchers in Seasons 2 and 3, and in the Observers of Season 5. But in this complex and complicated narrative, cyborgs are not fixed as enemy-figures. *Fringe*'s Season 5 complicates the idea that cyborgs are enemies, just as it overturns, rewrites or revisits much that was established in the previous four seasons. Throughout the series, cyborg elements augment the bodies of main/recurring characters Nina and Peter and cyborgs appear in occasional stand-alone episodes. The cyborg may appear as a potential ally, or it may stand as a threatening adversary; it may figure as a commentary on dangerous scientific innovation, as a representation of hidden technological development, or as a demonstration of futuristic potential.

As these summaries suggest, the plotline of *Fringe* is extremely complex, with two or more versions of each main character and two or more versions of many events existing within the *Fringe* narrative space. For instance, Season 4 effectively overwrites the previous three seasons, creating completely new storylines in place of formerly established events; the only characters to remember events from those seasons are Peter and Olivia, while the viewers, who do remember the previous events, parallel Peter and Olivia in their double-vision of the ongoing narrative.

With its many representations of monstrous transformation and peculiar embodiment, the series is concerned with versions of estrangement. Estrangement persists in the 'fringe events', the bizarre occurrences that the team investigate, and that transform unsuspecting bodies in frightening ways. Estrangement is a standard mode of representation in science fiction, and *Fringe*'s narratives, with their constant challenges to what we might consider to be the fundamental workings of the universe, certainly work to make the everyday strange. No character is exempt; the 'monster-of-the-week' (or fringe-event-of-the-week) storylines estrange the innocent bystander or peripheral character, while the story arcs estrange established characters in the series. For example, through the introduction of their parallel universe counterparts, characters like Walter and Astrid undergo a doubling effect against their very different parallel selves Walternate and Alt-Astrid.[2] Other forms of estrangement occur through narrative investigations into regular characters' pasts; these storylines uncover events such as Olivia's childhood involvement in Walter's Cortexiphan drug trials, or Peter's birth in the parallel universe.

Cyborg embodiment offers another version of estrangement in the series narrative, and it is one that aligns with *Fringe*'s preoccupation with the disturbance 'of boundaries, norms, and bodily integrity'. Many episodes follow the aftermath of the transformation of 'unstable' bodies (Calvert 2014a: 187), allowing different explorations of the monstrous potentialities within any human (or human-like) body. Such potentialities can also position the transformed or transforming bodies as versions of the posthuman, that state in which bioscience or medical technology alters the human body (Bronson 2014: 63). We see various examples of bodies altered through posthuman modifications, such as bodies that are grown in tanks, bodies that are kept alive after death, or bodies that mutate or develop unhuman or superhuman abilities. Against such narratives, the various cyborgs that appear in this series serve as further examples of the posthuman and offer a variety of perspectives on the transformed body. The narrative includes storylines featuring cybernetic shapeshifters that duplicate human bodies, and futuristic cyborgs that enslave humanity, both of which offer nightmare visions of technological domination. However, other versions of the cyborg body include Nina and Peter, characters from the regular cast, and so help to resist technophobic interpretations of the posthuman cyborg body. These examples continue to dramatize the tensions between the organic and the cybernetic.

In this series cyborgs are more consistently gendered male (Zinder 2014: 33), and this is a point of contrast with many of the other series examined in this book, where female cyborgs, and therefore female embodiment, tend to be the focus. Male-gendered cyborgs are present most notably in the Observers, whose future posthuman embodiment appears to have eradicated the female altogether. Male bodies undergo cyborg transformations by being augmented with futuristic or future-universe technologies, as with the examples of Alistair Peck ('White Tulip' 2.18) and Peter in Season 5. Although they are often represented in male bodies, the cyborg shapeshifters are an exception since they can and do transform into male and female bodies, and into bodies of different ages and races (Bronson 2014: 68).

Any characters in this series have the potential 'to evolve beyond their current state into an advanced posthuman world not burdened by the limitations of their current bodies' (Bronson 2014: 63). We see this in Peter's affinity with the mysterious time-altering Machine, in Nina's cyborg embodiment, in Walter's experiments on his own brain, and in Olivia's Cortexiphan-fuelled telekinetic abilities. These examples suggest that post-human evolution has the potential to create improved and more powerful forms of embodiment; however, within the series storylines any such forms of embodiment are shown to be potentially problematic, sinister or threatening. Such storylines also foster uncertainty about the characters' ontological status: is Nina a cyborg or a shapeshifter? Is Peter an observer? What is Olivia? Throughout the series, posthuman/cyborg embodiment suggests further ways in which bodies may become disrupted and out of control.

'Do Shapeshifters Dream of Electric Sheep?': Cyborg Embodiment and Intertextuality

The shapeshifters of *Fringe* show no external signs of cyborg embodiment, and possess no metal shells or obvious augmentations like *Doctor Who*'s Daleks or Cybermen, *Battlestar Galactica*'s Centurions, or *Star Trek*'s Borg. The shapeshifters can move their consciousness from body to body, an ability that is reminiscent of the personality transfers of *Dollhouse*. The shapeshifters are horrific partly because their embodiment doubles and literally duplicates human bodies, so that their cyborg bodies are indistinguishable from human bodies. Further, they have the potential to duplicate any human body, making every human vulnerable to danger through interaction with a disguised shapeshifter, or to death through the duplication process. The fact that they appear as human, and give no visual clues about their cyborg nature, references other science fiction narratives like *Blade Runner* and the Philip K. Dick source novel, *Do Androids Dream of Electric Sheep?* The connection to these narratives is emphasized in the episode title 'Do Shapeshifters Dream of Electric Sheep?' (3.4). This title cues the reader to consider *Fringe*'s shapeshifters in a similar way to those in the novel and film, in which Rick Deckard's status as human is comprehensively troubled through his interactions with the artificial 'andys' and 'replicants'. A viewer of *Fringe* is offered the possibility to engage with these other narratives, and to make inferences and connections between all of them. This intertextual engagement may well dispose the viewer to be sympathetic towards the shapeshifter characters in this episode, who strive for an equal status with the humans they are supposed to hate. In early episodes, however, there are no such claims to viewer sympathy; shapeshifters are situated only as cyborg enemies.

Within the series, shapeshifters are described as 'neither and both: part machine and part organic', fitting a broad definition as cyborg ('Do Shapeshifters Dream of Electric Sheep?'). In the simplest terms, these cyborgs stand as a 'metaphor for the convergence of technology and humanity' (Stuart 2011: 93), though their representation is far more complex, and the convergence they encompass manifests itself in cyborg embodiment. As noted, the form of cyborg embodiment that the shapeshifters possess enables them to duplicate individual organic bodies (and again, this references science fiction/horror narratives like *Invasion of the Body Snatchers*). The shapeshifter absorbs the physical appearance of each individual human body in succession, and so transforms its own embodied appearance each time it engages in the duplication process. Duplication allows the shapeshifters to 'transcend their bodies', but only up to a point (Bronson 2014: 69); they never leave embodied materiality at all, but simply take on further duplicate bodies as circumstances demand.

The duplication process displays the shapeshifters' cybernetic abilities, and dramatizes a cyborg incorporation of the organic body. A form of cyborg boundary transgression is present at several points in this process. The shapeshifter brings together organic bodies and technological machinery, making even its victims into a form of cyborg through the transformation process. The shapeshifter uses a duplication device that sometimes appears entirely mechanistic, sometimes as a combination of technological and organic components: in Seasons 1 to 3, it is a box with leads ending in three-pronged plugs; in Season 4, it is a tube of organic tissue. The victim's body is violently penetrated by the duplication device, which is fitted to the roof of the mouth, making the dramatization of the process into a form of technological rape/murder.

It is evident that, even for shapeshifters, 'embodied experience changes one's identity' (Bronson 2014: 69) and may even provide them with an identity they wish to maintain. 'Do Shapeshifters Dream of Electric Sheep?' allows us to see things from the point of view of the cyborg, and follows the science fiction trope of the artificially embodied individual who masquerades as human. In this episode, we see how two shapeshifters, after spending a long period of time in one human form, are 'significantly shaped by [their] intimate, embodied experiences' (Bronson 2014: 69). It is not simply their acquisition of human embodiment that changes them, but their specific embodiment as Senator Van Horn and police officer Ray. Each shapeshifter, in taking on a specific human form, establishes his identity and develops close ties with his human family. Van Horn, in a coma and biologically dead, nevertheless responds to his wife's presence and touch, with changes in his neural activity; Ray gently soothes his son after a nightmare. Such scenes demonstrate the individual connections that these apparently monstrous cyborgs have formed. Episodes following the shapeshifter who takes over the identity of Agent Charlie Francis present further complications. Charlie is well known to regular viewers, and is a reliable, positive figure in most of the Fringe team investigations throughout its first season. It is possible that the shapeshifter-as-Charlie character could elicit more sympathy from viewers. On the other hand, revealing at the *end* of the Season 2 opening episode ('A New Day in the Old Town' 2.1) that the individual we think is Charlie is actually a shapeshifter emphasizes the shock and horror of the shapeshifters' cyborg embodiment (Calvert 2014a: 194). After all, Ray's and Van Horn's attempts to live 'human' lives are founded on the deaths of the original Ray and Van Horn, deaths that we can see are very likely to have been violent and terrible. In examples like these, *Fringe* does not simply humanize the cyborg monster-figures, but its narrative complicates the positioning of cyborg/enemy and human/hero – something that is generally consistent with *Fringe*'s depiction of enemies and heroes across all seasons.

The Sympathetic Cyborg

The second season episode 'White Tulip', like those involving named, individual shapeshifter characters, similarly complicates ideas of a cyborg enemy through a focus on its central figure, the time-travelling cyborg Alistair Peck. Peck's character begins the episode as an enemy, whose experimental time-travel causes the mysterious death of any human being in his vicinity. However, Peck develops over the course of the episode into a more sympathetic individual. His character is used as a foil for Walter, and his experimentations are contrasted with Walter's; the narrative emphasizes their mutual creativity and inventiveness, as well as their reckless risk-taking. This provides commentary, too, on the cutting-edge, dangerous work Walter has done in the past and continues under the auspices of the Fringe team.

Though Peck's body is monstrous and violently disrupted, and his time-travelling lethal and dangerous to bystanders, the episode's narrative invites sympathy with the character once the Fringe team hypothesize that he is attempting to return to the past to save his fiancée Arlette from death in a car crash. The episode narrative connects Peck's quest to travel to the past to save Arlette with Walter's rescue of Peter from certain death as a child in the parallel universe.[3] Although visually spectacular, Peck's experimentation on and transformation of his own body do not necessarily serve as examples of an individual's wish for cyborg augmentation. The mechanical/technological augmentations he carries out are solely for the purpose of achieving time-travel. Peck's character develops markedly over the brief span of the single episode. In the opening scenes he is a mysterious and threatening figure who is somehow able to draw energy from machines and from humans and is likely to kill on a large scale. By the midpoint of the episode, he develops into a more sympathetic character because of the emphasis on parallels between himself and Walter.

Still, Peck is visualized as an individual who is experiencing cyborg embodiment. Casting decisions, too, may well heighten this aspect of his character. Peck is played by Peter Weller, known for his portrayal of Alex Murphy, the police officer who becomes a very sympathetic cyborg, and a complex character, in the first two films of the *RoboCop* film franchise (1987; 1990), and once again this draws on the intertextuality of casting across cult narratives (Bussolini 2013). In an extended scene, Peck's torso is displayed as he attempts to repair and improve some of his mechanical components. Close-up shots follow him wielding surgical implements to dig into his own skin, and show Peck inserting parts reminiscent of clock components under his bloody flesh. The disturbing presentation of the body penetrated by technological/mechanical components is itself undercut by the choice of soundtrack for the scene: Peck plays Gary Numan's 'Are "Friends" Electric?' on his cassette deck, a feature that adds a twist of comedy to the scene for those viewers who recognize the musical allusion (and there is irony, too, in the outdated technology Peck uses to play it).

A possible reinforcement of Peck's sympathetic portrayal comes through the narrative's turn from spectacular representations of a disrupted cyborg body, to a more sensitive portrayal of Peck's human feelings for his fiancée. By the end of the episode, Peck's character appears to have been recuperated as a sympathetic cyborg, and this presentation is reflected in the depiction of his final journey to the past. The last disruption of Peck's body, as he travels back in time to stay with Arlette for the car crash that will – in this new timeline – now kill them both, is not shown. Instead, the camera focuses on the approaching van from the passenger seat, over Arlette's shoulder, but effects a jump cut to the exterior to show the van ploughing into the side of the car, so that the violent deaths of two bodies is displaced onto metal and machinery.

In parallel with the inclusion of the shapeshifters as enemy-adversary cyborgs, and with the stand-alone episodes featuring sympathetic posthumans like Alistair Peck, characters from the series' regular cast offer different versions of the mechanistic cyborg body. These examples develop further the notion of the sympathetic cyborg. Both Peter Bishop and Nina Sharp fall into this category. Peter's affinity with and for technology of all kinds place him in proximity to small-scale alterations that can be classified as cyborg, and continue to some major transformations in Seasons 3 and 5. Nina, with her cybernetic arm – and, in Season 5, her mechanized wheelchair – is another example of the human body augmented and changed through technology. Her complex identification encompasses her characterisation as 'cold' businesswoman in Season 1, as long-term ally to Walter as well as to Bell in Seasons 2 and 3, and finally as an essential member of the Fringe team and as a maternal/guardian figure in Seasons 4 and 5. These different identities are overlaid with visual reminders of Nina's cyborg embodiment.

In some respects, Nina's character fits the model of the woman who wields power, a characterization seen in television series of different genres. Her representation as an older woman plays with representations of authority and of ageing, as we see in her varying roles as (for instance) head of Massive Dynamic, or mother-figure. Further, Paul Zinder views Nina as 'a conservative female archetype' but not as a boundary-defying cyborg in the Haraway mode (2014: 34). Nina presents a severe, emotionless and logical façade, something that does fit the mould of the 'conservative female' type in popular culture, as do other women in power in recent US, UK and European drama series.[4] The very fact that Nina is a female at the head of a huge multinational *tech* company, Massive Dynamic, shows a different kind of representation and boundary-crossing. In that respect, Nina's severe, 'cold' demeanour is part of her identity as the Chief Operations Officer/Executive Director. Since her role is to run a science/technology company, Nina's character can be seen to challenge the binaries of 'typical' male and female behaviours presented on television (Glascock 2001: 667). She is 'a prominent woman character high in the external power structure' (Wilcox 2014: 52). Yet in many respects, Nina is no odder or colder than agent Olivia Dunham, who also presents a severe and business-like attitude to her job as a 'rational, practical' person (Stuart 2011: 14). In early seasons, both Nina and Olivia appear to conform to the stereotype of the female in power who must devote herself entirely to her job, to the detriment of her personal life and relationships.[5] Olivia is in the middle of a secret affair with fellow agent John Scott in the pilot episode, but has no further relationships until she declares her love for Peter at the end of Season 2, and it is another two seasons before they are living together as a couple. Nina has a history with Walter and with William Bell, including a love affair with Bell that is revealed some way into the series narrative. Like other women (both fictional and actual) in positions of power, Nina and Olivia face the problem of 'being simultaneously business-like enough and feminine enough' (Cassell and Walsh in Lauzen et al. 2008: 204).[6]

Nina's severe behaviour, as well as her fondness for monochrome clothing and angular hairstyles, chimes with the presentation of another fictional female executive running an innovative tech company, Catherine Weaver of *Terminator: The Sarah Connor Chronicles* (see Chapter 6). The behaviour and appearance of both characters conforms to more general aspects of the 'woman in power' stereotype, but further, their severe attitude and position of authority may also combine to encourage critics and other viewers to identify the characters as cyborg. Read in this way, these characters are severe and cold because they are cyborgs; Nina's machinic and technological augmentations, no matter how small, affect the way viewers perceive her entire character. Zinder, for example, finds that Nina's cyborg embodiment obscures other readings: 'her reticence to reveal her true nature early in the series effectually hides the positive attributes of her character behind her bionic arm' (2014: 34). Even if Nina cannot be claimed as a Haraway-mode boundary-crosser in terms of her embodiment as cyborg, her character complicates certain other boundaries, especially those dividing friend from foe. The evolving portrayal of this character makes her difficult to pin down simply as cold cyborg or as positive ally; a more nuanced reading of Nina is possible if we admit all of her identities: as cyborg, as ally, as scientist, as nurturing mother-figure and more.

Nina's 'cold' characterization alters as she and Olivia develop close bonds, and this is especially evident in the altered prime ('amber') universe early in Season 4. Again in similar ways to cyborg Catherine Weaver in *TSCC*, cold cyborg-Nina softens through a nurturing relationship; she is certainly seen to nurture and support Olivia even in early seasons, and she becomes Olivia's guardian, 'the closest thing you have to a mother' in the amber universe ('Forced Perspective' 4.10). This looks like a standard re-writing of a female character who does not conform to gendered expectations; we might compare *Fringe*'s treatment of Nina and Olivia with *Voyager*'s treatment of Janeway and Seven, with both narratives framing the relationship between older and younger woman as a mother–daughter one. However, Walter and Peter's relationship, a (possibly *the*) central relationship of the series, develops in similar ways, and this example may help to resist the return to essentialism that the Nina–Olivia relationship suggests. These father–son and mother–daughter relationships *both* begin with the individuals estranged and cold towards one another, and all characters are seen to develop emotional and nurturing bonds through successive seasons. Further, these are relationships in which the child nurtures and transforms the parent as much as the parent does the child.

Since Nina's character could well be portrayed without any form of cyborg embodiment at all, we may ask what Nina-as-cyborg offers the overall series narrative. Even before her cyborg embodiment is revealed, Nina appears to be firmly on the side of technophilic (and potentially dangerous) science through Massive Dynamic's vast intellectual and financial resources, and seeing this technology as an essential part of her body makes for a more persuasive reading of her cyborg embodiment as dangerous. She shows Olivia her bionic arm in the pilot episode, something that may well appear as 'a creepy unveiling, a warning that the science of Massive Dynamic is pervasive and mostly hidden like so many childhood monsters' (Zinder 2014: 34). The secrets, complications and confusions around Nina's arm make it an example of the way *Fringe*'s narrative constantly shows us that 'Nothing [is] As It Seems' (4.16). Nina tells Olivia that she lost her arm to cancer ('Pilot'), but Walter's flashback story shows her damaging it in the portal between the parallel worlds when she tried to stop him crossing over ('Peter' 1.16). Both stories have the potential to be rewritten when Peter disappears to create the new prime universe, and fans debate whether Nina and her parallel universe alternate retain bionic limbs. However, Season 5's Nina does have a bionic arm, and there are other opportunities in that season to read Nina as cyborg in her use of a motorized wheelchair, which makes a further link between her body and technological augmentation, especially if we read the wheelchair as a form of technological prosthesis or 'addenda' which offers 'a different form of embodiment' (Kuppers 2007: 169).[7]

Even the occasional displays of the arm's technological components can be read in different ways. The 'creepy unveiling' Zinder notes in the pilot episode is a case in point. In this scene, as Nina explains that her arm was amputated to halt the spread of cancer, she quickly strips the skin 'sleeve' from her arm to reveal the cybernetic skeleton beneath. Olivia's shocked reaction, together with the accompanying musical cue, suggests that Nina's arm is a source of unease and horror. Nina's demeanour suggests otherwise – her arm is simply a part of her; further, Olivia's shock may equally show her sympathetic response to Nina's story of the amputation. This explanation of how she became cyborg, and especially her demeanour in this scene, places Nina as the kind of person who tells a traumatic story in a restrained and unemotional way, which fits with her characterization as severe 'conservative female'. But her story also links her past together with Walter Bishop's and William Bell's, and connects her physically with the powerful company she directs. Other key examples show that Nina's is a shifting cyborg embodiment, hovering between powerful technological augmentation and helpless machine breakdown. At times, her technological components do give her advantages, for example, the Kevlar incorporated into her chest saves her from gunshots ('The Road Not Taken' 1.19). In other instances, her arm malfunctions ('Ability' 1.14), or seizes up completely ('Letters of Transit' 4.19), or it turns out to be hiding things that even Nina does not know about, like William Bell's power source ('There's More Than One of Everything' 1.20).

The mechanical appearance of Nina's arm suggests strength, control and power, but in fact it seems to have no particular additional properties, and the successive attacks and breakdowns lessen Nina's control. Again, this portrayal of the cyborg fits with *Fringe*'s overall view of the embodied self. No character in this fictional universe is whole and unaltered – all are partial, contingent, shifting, and transformed/transforming.

Technological Affinity and Cyborg Transformation

Peter Bishop is another example of a regular series character transformed through technology and brought into close proximity to a cyborg identity. Peter is shown from very early episodes as someone with the ability to build all kinds of mechanical and technological items. Early in the formation of the Fringe team, he is able to maintain complex machinery that allows Walter to carry out his experiments (and does so throughout Season 1) and to make use of technological devices in their investigations (such as the radiometer he operates in 'Midnight' 1.18). There are some ominous references in several Season 1 episodes to Peter's mysterious 'project', something that suggests that he could be misusing technology ('Unleashed' 1.16, 'Midnight'). However, this turns out to be both a red herring and a demonstration of his care for Walter: the 'project' is an audio capture machine intended to digitize Walter's damaged record collection ('The Road Not Taken'). Similarly, Peter tinkers with and mends Walter's record turntable in 'White Tulip', again showing thought and care for his father over any special desire to play with technology.

Peter's ability to build and use technology is pushed towards a cyborg-like affinity in certain episodes where he is seen to interact with technology in ways that disrupt the integrity of body and mind. Peter is persuaded to work with Walter's alarmingly improvised machinery that connects his brain to the brains of dead people ('In Which We Meet Mr Jones' 1.7; 'And Those We Left Behind' 4.6). These examples encourage viewers to identify Peter as one who 'welcomes the opportunity to become part-machine and even invites the cyborg experience', someone who '*chooses* time and time again to become part-machine to achieve the goals of the Fringe team' (Zinder 2014: 36, my emphasis). However, the series narrative maintains Peter's sceptical attitude towards many of Walter's experiments, and he constantly uses self-deprecating humour to undercut Walter's enthusiastic descriptions of the functions and properties of his dangerous creations. A case in point is his response to Walter's description of the 'Faraday cage' which fits with 'prongs either side of the wearer's spine': 'Of course it does,' says Peter ('And Those We Left Behind'). Zinder interprets this as Peter 'casually welcoming his new automated part' (Zinder 2014: 37), but the actor's style of delivery shows resignation more than 'welcome', and gives a sense that Peter's is meant to be the sane response to Walter's excited description of his apparently marvellous invention. Both Peter and Olivia interact with Walter's technology in ways that are disruptive to their own mental and physical states (Olivia does so most dramatically towards the end of Season 5, when she allows herself to be injected with Cortexiphan so that she can cross to the parallel universe, 'Liberty' 5.12) but their participation is portrayed as something done out of necessity, because the team need a clue that only Walter's 'fringe' technology can provide, more than from a specific wish to become cyborg.

    The story arc involving Peter's symbiotic and somatic connection to the mysterious Machine (Seasons 2–3) offers a more overt example of movement from organically human to cyborg embodiment. The Machine is the subject of an extended storyline in which an apparatus is constructed in both the prime (the original, 'blue') universe and the parallel ('red') one. The prime universe apparatus is made from discovered components that appear to be ancient, but are technologically extremely advanced. Once constructed, this Machine connects the two universes, and has the potential either to destroy one or both, or to mend the 'rifts' created through the different interactions of the two universes. Once again, however, Peter's engagement with the Machine is portrayed as an evolving experience which is many-layered, and encompasses unease, discomfort and fear as well as fascination and obsession. Early episodes in this arc suggest that Peter has a particular – almost mystical – connection with the Machine: its components become animated because of their proximity to him. When one component of the Machine moves independently and attaches itself to Peter's arm ('Over There Part 2' 2.22), Peter explains, 'it came alive in my hands…like it was bonded to me' ('6955 kHz' 3.6); in another dramatic moment, the entire Machine alters its configuration and moves components into place when Peter enters the room, and in response Peter has a physical reaction, a nosebleed ('Reciprocity' 3.11). Peter's potential for cyborg embodiment is made apparent through his physical interactions and reactions to these components. Peter does not incorporate the Machine into his own body, so he does not become cyborg by augmenting his physical self. Rather, in its 'reactions' and animation the Machine is incorporating *Peter* into its physical self.

Yet at this stage in the third-season narrative, as these properties of the Machine are revealed, it is evident that the bond that links Peter to the Machine does not exist because he wishes to become a cyborg. Instead, the bond exists because of Walternate's actions in the parallel universe and Peter's and Walter's actions in a future timeline of the prime universe. Walternate and the future Peter and Walter manipulate Peter's DNA in order to create an unbreakable connection with the Machine. Their actions loop into the Season 3 narrative and push Peter into working on and finally activating the Machine. Once Peter activates and physically connects with the Machine, he is either sent fifteen years into the future, or shown a vision of that possible future (it is not clear from the narrative whether he has physically time-travelled or whether he makes a mental connection with a potential, fictional future). In the timeline he witnesses, the parallel universe was destroyed in 2011 when Peter and Walter activated the Machine, and the destruction of the parallel universe has also fatally damaged the prime universe. In this version of 2026, the prime universe is falling apart. Returned to the prime universe and to his 2011, Peter understands that he must work to avoid the destruction he witnessed; instead of destroying the parallel universe, he uses the Machine to construct a bridge between the two universes, so that prime and parallel counterparts can work together ('The Day We Died' 3.22).

This story arc connects with the activities of Season 5: Peter's potential for violence and destruction, something we see in his apparently emotionless killing of shapeshifters in 'Reciprocity' (Zinder 2014: 37) and his use of the Machine in a different 2011 timeline to destroy the parallel universe ('The Day We Died'), surfaces strongly in Season 5. His physical interactions with the Machine, especially when he is figured as its component or energy source, similarly prefigure his use of the Observer technology in his own body ('An Origin Story' 5.5, 'Five-Twenty-Ten' 5.7).

In all such examples, Peter exemplifies the theory of reciprocal exchange that Walter formulates in reaction to the Season 3 storyline: 'when you touched the Machine it changed you. It weaponized you' ('Reciprocity'). In Walter's words we see the Machine (the technology) acting upon the human body; it is a reversal of the ways in which Walter and Peter have made use of the tools of technology to further their scientific experiments. The suggestion that the Machine acts upon and 'weaponizes' Peter presents a version of cyborg embodiment that is characterized by a loss of control.

As Jennifer Gonzales notes, 'historically, genetic engineering and cyborg bodies have produced similar fears about loss of human control [...] over the products of human creation' (Gonzales 1995: 274; and see also Zinder 2014: 38). The expectation for the cyborg body is that it will approach the posthuman in its abilities, that it will transform and transcend the limitations of a human body. Yet, far from adding to their corporeal capabilities, the versions of cyborg embodiment depicted in *Fringe* complicate and undermine the physical abilities of the transformed bodies. The shapeshifters' embodiment is not usually fixed in one body but operates as a series of duplications across successive bodies. Nina does not display cyborg-related strength, and in fact her cyborg augmentations tend to undermine her wholeness and her control. In Seasons 2 and 3, Peter constantly appears to be on the verge of being overcome by the Machine's technological powers. And the threat of losing control continues into Season 5 with Peter's manipulation of and experimentation with Observer technology. Peter approaches a cyborg identity in which he comes to resemble the ruthless cyborgs he attempts to fight, and in which his posthuman augmentations threaten to overwrite his free will.

'You don't even know what you don't know': Peter and Observer Technology

When the human beings of the twenty-seventh century, the Observers, appear in Seasons 1 to 4, it is not clear that they have incorporated technological devices into their bodies. This aspect of their embodiment is revealed in Season 5 ('An Origin Story'). The narrative fills in other details about these beings, revealing that they have invaded Earth in 2015 (their past, our future: Season 5 was first broadcast 28 September 2012–18 January 2013). The Observers establish themselves as controllers of the world, subdue humanity and, by the time of the events of Season 5, are preparing to create a world especially suited to their own needs, one that will be uninhabitable for twenty-first-century humans. The Season 4 episode 'Letters of Transit' leads the series cast into the Season 5 narrative, as it follows Walter, Peter, Olivia and Astrid in 2036 as they awaken after twenty-one years in suspended animation to the world altered by the Observers. A key plot point for Season 5 is Peter's and Olivia's reunion with their daughter Etta, who was lost to the Observers as a small child during the invasion of 2015; in 2036, the adult Etta is a member of the human Resistance.

The mysterious figures of the Observers – all male, and identically dressed in dark suits and hats, with white skin and bald heads – have been part of *Fringe*'s narrative since the first season, and they appear initially as quirky and puzzling characters, whose behaviour, motivation and origin remain unknown for most of the series. Their rare actions, such as the Observer known as September's intervention in Peter and Walter's history when he saves them from drowning ('Peter') seem to place them as potential allies, of no threat to the Fringe team or others, and their detachment from the events they witness likewise suggests that they are benevolent. Their appearance as very definite enemy figures towards the end of Season 4 ('Letters of Transit') and in the entirety of Season 5 once more fits with *Fringe*'s general tendency to complicate the oppositions of hero and enemy and of human and posthuman.

For all of the Observers' apparently superior abilities, they are still humans in their physicality. Their interactions with technology might give them certain abilities to manipulate the physical and the temporal; in addition to their time-travelling, they can 'read time', predicting future actions and events. Yet the apparent advantages of their cyborg embodiment are consistently questioned. The human characters describe them as 'cold fish' ('An Origin Story') and 'lizard'-like ('Anomaly XB-6783746' 5.10), images that emphasize their loss of human characteristics, especially the erasure of individuality, of emotion, of human bonds. Nina Sharp summarises everything the Observers lack in her final confrontation with Observer leader Windmark:

[The Observers'] brains have evolved over 32 million years. Yet for all their evolution, they form no bonds. Love does not exist for them. They are incapable of dreaming, of contemplating beauty, of knowing something greater than themselves. ('Anomaly XB-6783746')

As the narrative makes clear, these 'primitive' instincts and human emotions aid the all-too-human Fringe team as they work to defeat the Observers.

As examples of posthuman cyborgs, Observers figure as entities that 'literalize the transhumanist dream of a human identity located purely in the mind' (Bronson 2014: 72). They conceive of their being as governed by the mind and by mental processes; their evolutionary aims include the removal of all human emotion (recalling *Doctor Who*'s Cybermen or *Star Trek*'s Borg). But by doing so, they deny their own material existence; 'their identity is defined only by seeing themselves as disembodied beings not anchored to their materiality' (Bronson 2014: 72) and yet they remain embodied. Their manipulations have caused the world of the future to be inhospitable to them, making them look to the past for a world they can dominate and modify to suit their needs. Although these cyborgs require a very specific environment to live in – for example, they need a carbon monoxide-filled atmosphere ('Transilience Thought Unifier Model-11' 5.1) – they are still embodied and still need a *physical* environment for their bodies. Furthermore, the Observers need other bodies to achieve their aims; they use the bodies of twenty-first-century humans as soldiers and as slaves.[8] Even for Observers, 'life is lived through bodies' (Stone 1991: 113).

Peter's recombination as part-Observer is a startling and unpredictable representation of cyborg embodiment. It is possible to read Peter's apparently impulsive decision to put unknown and untested Observer technology into his own body as a form of 'cyborg-envy' (Zinder 2014: 36), but there are further contradictions and complexities in his actions. Peter does not envy the Observers' abilities, although he recognizes that through technological augmentation they have an embodied advantage over unmodified humans. By making use of their technology, he attempts to access those advantages, incorporating the Observers' special qualities into his own body. In Season 5, cybernetic augmentation becomes one possible way in which the posthuman Observers can be defeated – by making himself into a cyborg, Peter Bishop hopes to defeat cyborgs. Key to Peter's move towards cyborg embodiment is his response to a captured Observer: 'You are nothing but tech. I would be ten times what you are if I had that tech in my head' ('An Origin Story'). His interrogation of this Observer shows him that the future humans lack emotions and embodied reactions. Peter, on the other hand, is able to use 'intuition, knowledge and experience' to interact with the physical world ('An Origin Story'). He feels emotion and is strongly motivated by feelings of grief after his daughter Etta is killed by Windmark; he experiences complex impulses, reactions and motivations. It is clear that there is the potential to combine embodied human emotions with Observer tech to create a new, 'better' self. Indeed, as the season eventually makes clear, this kind of hybridity offers a positive future for Observers as well as humans. For Peter, however, incorporating Observer tech into his own embodiment puts the human part of himself at risk.

The visual representation of the Observer technology recalls the Machine components of Season 3 that appear to 'come to life' in response to Peter's physical presence. The piece of 'tech' itself is small and inert when Peter cuts it out of the Observer's body, but when he holds it near the cut he has made in his own neck, it becomes animated; it moves like an insect and, as is evident from Figure 13, burrows into his flesh. In this way it becomes, not simply a piece of technology waiting to be slotted into place, but a living part of an Observer's physical being. In relation to cyborg embodiment, Peter's extraction of the tech from the Observer, and its insertion into his own body, is portrayed in strongly physical terms: both individuals bleed, have bodily reactions, and show pain and disorientation. The mechanical 'tech' which burrows into his neck like an insect is a recognizable image of invasion or infection, something that destabilizes the corporeal self, but Peter's behaviour is equally destabilizing. As he mirrors the stiff movements and speech of the Observers, and experiences other alterations, like hair loss, Peter's body demonstrates the terrible transformation he is undergoing.

Through his cyborg augmentation, Peter is able to interact with the physical and temporal world in different ways. In response to Walter's questions about the tech's effect on Peter, Olivia replies, 'He's reading time like they do. Thinking ahead like they can. He knows what I'm going to say before I say it. It's like it's him but…it isn't' ('The Human Kind' 5.8). Peter

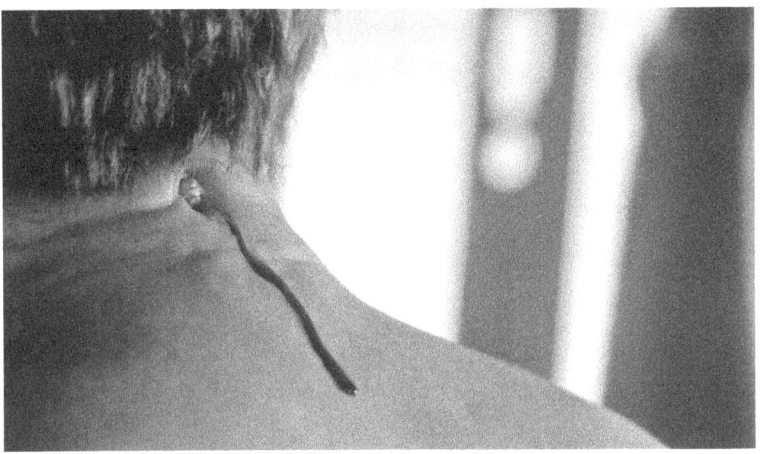

Figure 13: Observer tech burrows into Peter's neck, 'An Origin Story', *Fringe* (5.5)

is able to use the tech in order to predict future events ('Five Twenty Ten') and to manipulate time. His 'reading time' is represented through blue-washed visuals in which a glowing grid or mesh-like structure appears to be superimposed upon a scene, for example over the train compartment at the end of 'Through the Looking Glass and What Walter Found There' (5.6) as demonstrated in Figure 14. We see Peter's view of things so that we understand how he is able to point to a pile of rubble and declare that there is a doorway behind it ('Five Twenty Ten'). Peter's vision of the Observers' timelines is similarly represented visually, and colourfully, the timelines drawn and labelled in a variety of colours on a clear board as he explores and manipulates the Observer leaders' 'origin points' in his quest for revenge.

These augmentations do give him an advantage: he is able to predict some Observers' movements accurately enough to plant bombs that kill them ('Five Twenty Ten') and to physically fight Windmark ('The Human Kind'). Peter with Observer tech becomes a new individual, a cyborg, but the narrative shows that he is not a 'better' one. In many respects, Peter as cyborg reflects Rosi Braidotti's theory of the 'teratological', the monstrous interaction between self and technology in which 'the monstrous signifies the difficulty in keeping manageable margins of differentiation of the boundaries between self and other' (2000: 167). Peter turns himself into

Figure 14: Peter experiences Observer vision, 'Through the Looking Glass and What Walter Found There', *Fringe* (5.6)

a posthuman monster in order to defeat other posthuman monsters, but he begins to lose the 'margins of differentiation' in the process. His cyborg embodiment is not a triumphant but a thoroughly problematic version of boundary-crossing, and the narrative strongly stresses what Peter is losing through his transformation.

Walter's and Astrid's experiments with the Observer tech inside a pig's brain show them how the tech interacts with the brain to suppress areas of emotion ('The Human Kind'). This places Peter's loss of emotion in relation to other aspects of loss of control related to cyborg embodiment. As he loses his human emotions, he loses his human connections, too: his loving family bonds with Walter, Olivia and Etta are eroded while the tech is in his head. The tech has the effect of deadening or removing Peter's grief and pain at Etta's death, but this absence is something that Peter specifically rejects in his confrontation with the captured Observer ('An Origin Story'). In that exchange, while the Observer calls Etta's death 'irrelevant', Peter furiously insists on the continued remembrance of Etta's life and the possibility that her death has meaning. I read Peter's cyborg embodiment as a transformation that is undertaken not out of a wish to become stronger, faster or smarter, but as a wish to become those things specifically in order to avenge his daughter's death. Therefore, 'cyborg envy' alone does not give a full explanation for Peter's transformation (Zinder 2014: 36). Peter's actions following Etta's death can be seen to parallel Walter's following his son's death; both men take risks and bring themselves and others into danger because they are fuelled by emotion. And Peter's loss of emotion and of memory, especially those concerning Etta, simply underlines how far he has transformed himself into a cyborg monster following his incorporation of the Observer tech.

Humanity through Hybridity, Again

In the series finale, the Fringe team succeed in defeating the Observers and resetting the timeline, returning characters and viewers to a 2011 in which the Observers never invaded. The finale presents some problematic aspects, not least because, as Stacey Abbott notes, while 'normality is presented in the form of the restored nuclear family [...] [t]he whole notion of reassuring the audience with a return to normality undermines the thematic trajectory of *Fringe*' (Abbott 2013). This reset might appear to turn back to essentialist views of embodiment; it is possible to read the series conclusion as a privileging of the unaugmented, completely or 'purely' organic body and its experiences, and as a refusal of any advantages that an altered cyborg body could bring. Further, the conclusion places the unaugmented human within the nurturing family, potentially reinstating a world of emotion that is coded as maternal, female. But again, the narrative resists such interpretations. Through all its five seasons, *Fringe* repeatedly complicates simple binary divisions, including those of male–female, science–nature, logic–emotion and ally–enemy. Nina and Olivia, the powerful women, are logical, thoughtful, and often severe, while Walter and Peter, who occupy the scientific domain, are intuitive and impulsive, and demonstrate emotion. Midway through Season 5, Olivia persuades Peter to remove the Observer tech from his body, presenting a classic appeal to masculine intellect/reason from female emotion. However, their exchange is less stereotypical than it seems. In the episodes immediately following Etta's death, both Olivia and Peter struggle with their feelings, each unable to voice their pain to the other. Walter, the paradoxically impulsive scientist, encourages Olivia to confront and deal with her grief: 'This pain is [Etta's] legacy

[…]. You can't escape it by building walls around your heart […] or by vengeance' ('An Origin Story'). Olivia's words to Peter follow the pattern of Walter's to her:

PETER: She is dead.
OLIVIA: She's alive inside us and there's nothing Windmark can do about it because the love that we can share with her now is invulnerable to space and time – even to them. And I know that our hearts are broken and that it hurts but that's what makes us human.
PETER: Emotion is our weakness.
OLIVIA: No Peter, it's our strength because it's the one thing they don't have. We need to hold onto our connection with Etta, feeling what we felt for her, or she dies all over again. ('The Human Kind')

Olivia's speech calls on paradoxical elements – that being broken and hurting is a strength, that someone who has died can somehow still be alive – which are things that the logical cyborg Peter has rejected. Peter's short three- and four-word responses clearly demonstrate his retreat from human emotion into machine-like logic and from the ability to grasp the kind of paradox Olivia understands. He speaks a version of Windmark's phrase from their fight earlier in the episode, 'Your emotion makes you weak', which Olivia immediately transforms. Olivia calls on the same 'legacy' that Walter described, and appeals to a shared memory of time with Etta and with Peter, memories which Peter is in danger of forgetting because of the Observer tech in his body. Walter's previous involvement, his encouragement to Olivia to confront her emotions, complicates the gendered qualities in this exchange, as does Peter's retreat from technology when he removes the Observer tech. In these scenes, Peter is positioned as parent as much as Olivia: Peter is embodied and is a father just as Olivia is embodied and is a mother.[9] His bonds with Etta and with Olivia are restored in the revised 2011 in which the series concludes, so that the reinstatement of the family group becomes the end-point of their endeavours over all five seasons.

A further confusion of binaries takes place as a result of the child Michael's existence. The Fringe team first encounter the hairless, mute child in the original prime universe, in 2009; he does not appear to age, possesses unexplained abilities, and is able to make empathic connections, especially with Olivia ('Inner Child' 1.15). In the future narrative of Season 5, the Fringe team locate the child – named 'Michael' by his foster parents – and work to understand the importance of his particular abilities for their fight against the Observers ('Black Blotter' 5.9). To the Observers, Michael (or Anomaly XB-6783746) is a 'genetic defect', a 'deformity' ('Liberty', 'An Enemy of Fate' 5.13): he is a potential Observer who still retains emotional intelligence.[10] Michael is the embodiment of successful hybridity; he combines the best qualities of present- and future-human in a powerful posthuman cyborg embodiment. 'Observers do not have to sacrifice emotion for intelligence since Michael proves that both can coexist' (Bronson 2014: 73). While the Observers' defeat at the hands of the 2036 human rebellion and the 2015 Fringe team cements a rejection of their version of cyborg embodiment and its domination over the physical world, cyborg embodiment itself is not removed as a possibility. Michael's cyborg embodiment is shown to be the example that will alter the future and prevent the emotionless posthuman Observers from existing.

So, the end of the series does not bring about the total destruction of the Observers, but instead the storyline points to the possibilities for a different kind of evolution for the twenty-seventh-century humans. The humans of the revised future may still incorporate technology into their organic bodies, and transform themselves in ways that are cyborg. However, the efforts of Olivia, Peter, Astrid, Nina, Etta and Walter (representing both the family group and the chosen-family group) do suggest that twenty-seventh-century human/cyborgs will be more like the Observer child Michael, retaining emotional resonance as well as other kinds of intelligence. Once again, hybridity offers a more positive way forward for a future human body and its interactions with technology.

Conclusion: Cyborg Futures

Does the television cyborg have a future? My purpose in this book was to create an overview of television cyborgs, and to look at a variety of representations in different texts. These chapters cover examples in series that run from the 1960s to the 2010s, and we can see from these that while the image of the cyborg may shift and alter, some of the fundamental anxieties that surround this image remain more or less stable. All the series covered in this book represent cyborgs as 'others' to some extent; some of them offer threatening and monstrous technological enemies, while others show us cyborgs that strive to be more like us. We see cyborgs that are gendered male and female, and that demonstrate the tensions around the performance of specific, stereotypically gendered roles. Cyborgs on television may be alluring femmes fatales or muscular soldiers; they may be encased in steel, toweringly tall and identical; but a cyborg may also look exactly like a teenage girl. These beings remain tantalizingly difficult to pin down and define, but perhaps that is fitting for a creature 'of both imagination and material reality' that challenges us with its 'boundary breakdowns' (Haraway 1985: 66, 68).

As we move further into the twenty-first century, does the cyborg still stand as a potent image of our anxieties around technological development and its impact on our human, embodied existence? Cyborg characters still appear with some regularity in science fiction television, which suggests that the image does retain a certain fascination. Cyborgs feature in the short-running series *Almost Human* and *Intelligence*. *Intelligence* is noteworthy for its positioning of the cyborg as protagonist/hero, and for its premise: that humans are augmented with computer chips in their brains. This is very close to some of the ideas explored in classic cyberpunk fiction, such as Cadigan's 'synners' with their brain sockets, or Gibson's characters who upload new information into their minds; it also recalls *Dollhouse*'s Active architecture or *Fringe*'s Observer tech as a means to augment a human mind. *Almost Human*, too, features cyborg protagonists, and some twists on the oppositions of cyborgs and humans and on organic/technological transformations of the body. The series is set in 2048, and is based on the premise that it has become usual to pair human police officers with human-like androids known as 'synthetics'. The series' human protagonist, Kennex, loses a leg in an ambush and resumes his work in the police force with a cybernetic leg, and a new synthetic partner, an android called Dorian. In effect, Kennex is presented with two potential cyborg augmentations: his leg, and his synthetic partner. While the character Dorian is described as an android or robot rather than a cyborg, he is represented in very similar ways to the cyborg characters we have seen in other television series analysed in this book. Humans view him with suspicion, emphasizing their difference and positioning Dorian as identical to any other android. However, Dorian develops into a defined and unique character. He is represented as male and as black, and so has an embodiment that resonates with both race and gender. Further, he stresses his likeness to human beings through his emotional intelligence: 'I can't say that I was born, but I was made to feel'; he contrasts his own abilities to engage with emotions with the more up-to-date synthetic humanoids, which 'have no free will' and instead operate only on logic ('Pilot' 1.1). Dorian's technological embodiment is designed to make him 'as human as possible', while Kennex experiences an imperfect synthesis with his own cybernetic body part, and shows a tendency to reject his own cyborg embodiment.

In other respects, too, *Almost Human* resonates with contemporary anxieties about humans' interactions with all forms of technological advancement. The episode storylines show the human and synthetic police officers investigating crimes relating to such technological developments as genetic engineering, hacking, organ replacement, and cloning. These new (or newer) technologies are often diverted from their intended applications in the world – from processes that can improve the human environment, or can offer new potential for human embodiment – and instead become dangerous weapons or are manipulated for criminal purposes. Again, technology itself is viewed as inherently dangerous for humanity, despite the plot points that highlight the role of unscrupulous humans in altering the purpose of technological inventions.

The combination of cyborg characters with a police procedural setting recurs in *Continuum*, a series that runs over four seasons, and so has time for character and story development. *Continuum*'s air dates overlap with *Fringe*, and the later series shares with *Fringe* some features of plot and thematic concerns. Both series have unfolding plots that are connected to ideas of time-travel and the possibilities of rewritten timelines; in similar ways to *Fringe*'s blue, red and amber alternate universes, and varying past, present and future timelines, *Continuum*'s narrative moves between present-day (2012) and several possible future (2077) timelines, and activities in the present are seen to affect and change the events of the future. The series' central character, Keira Cameron, is a time-traveller and a cyborg, and although the time-travel features of the series tend to be foregrounded in narrative developments, Keira's cyborg embodiment is certainly a distinctive aspect of the unfolding series text.

The future world of *Continuum* (Keira's present) is represented as a dystopia, which again resonates with some of the storylines in *Fringe*. The world of 2077 is governed by corporations, and policed by City Protection Service officers or 'protectors', whose cyborg augmentations are used in the service of law and order. Keira brings several cybernetic enhancements with her when she is transported to 2012. She is a walking surveillance machine: with technology in her brain, she can record, file and store anything she sees, and recall it later on, as evidence. This echoes contemporary developments in video technologies used in policing; in *Continuum*, Keira's protector surveillance technology is as much to do with recording material that will be useful for police prosecutions as it is to do with monitoring the activities of the protectors themselves. Keira's implants give her enhanced vision and enable her to measure and analyse her surroundings in forensic detail ('A Stitch in Time' 1.1). Her standard issue Protection Service jumpsuit gives her other enhancements, such as additional strength, resistance to heat and cold, and even invisibility (which proves useful in several episodes: 'Family Time' 1.9, 'End Times' 1.10, 'Power Hour' 4.3).

Keira's cyborg embodiment is either concealed (in her suit) or invisible (in her internal technology), so that on screen she appears as a fully embodied, organic human being. This is important within the series narrative, as she must keep her true identity – and her time-travelling – a secret. However, once again technological enhancements are represented as potentially dangerous and threatening. Keira's internal technology can be hacked and altered, making her into a killing machine ('Playtime' 1.8); while her jumpsuit allows her an action hero's physical powers, it can also be used against her, to transform her embodiment in ways she does not choose. Similarly, her implants allow her to retrieve and manipulate information, but they also make her into a surveillance device, and flash-forwards show her as part of 2077's surveillance society, where everyday technology, similar to present-day activity trackers, is used to control all humans. Again this aspect of the series plays on contemporary fears around detection, surveillance, privacy and hacking.

As noted with regard to *Almost Human*, there is a drift in early twenty-first-century television series from explorations of specifically *cyborg* characters to examinations of artificial embodiment more generally. These explorations include robots, androids, and clones, but such beings still reflect the fascinations and anxieties we see with cyborg characters. The British series *Humans* (a reworking of the Swedish drama *Äkta människor* [*Real Humans*]) presents an alternative-present scenario in which synthetic humans ('synths') have become prevalent in all aspects of society. In the 'parallel present' of the series synths appear in a variety of everyday settings: handing out free newspapers at the railway station, picking up litter in the street, carrying out repetitive, boring or dangerous tasks. Synths are shown in use as housekeepers, carers, labourers, and sex workers. The possibilities and problematic aspects of this technology are explored very carefully, through interactions between human and synth characters. The series follows several complicated relationships: between the Hawkins family, especially mother Laura and daughter Mattie, and their new synth Anita; between police officer Pete Drummond, his disabled wife Jill, and his partner Karen (who in the fourth episode is revealed to be a synth disguised as a human); between George Millican, who has Alzheimer's disease, and his out-of-date synth Odi; and between the 'family' of self-aware synths, Mia, Niska, Max and Fred, created by David Elster. Elster's son Leo appears to be the human leader of the synth family, but is discovered to possess a unique form of embodiment, a combination of human and synth in one body, and so is the only character who could be described as a cyborg.

Thanks to the deliberately vague series title, the designation 'Humans' could apply equally to the synths, many of whom strive to be like human beings, or to human beings themselves, who are shown in varying stages of rejection or acceptance of their synth helpers/servants. Teenager Mattie Hawkins, a skilled hacker, recognizes the effect that synth technology will have on her own opportunities; because synths can learn to perform tasks perfectly, they will soon surpass human abilities. Antagonism towards synths is seen in the rallies of the 'We Are People' movement (1.5), and in the unease of the police officers who investigate Niska's attacks on humans (1.4). However, this narrative tends to evaluate human characters in regard to their treatment of synths. The human characters who are sympathetic towards synths, such as Millican or (eventually) Laura Hawkins, are represented positively. The series positions negatively those humans who demonstrate coldness and cruelty towards synths. This is clear in the brothel scenes, in which viewer sympathy is mobilized for Niska (1.3), or in the 'smash club', in which the fact that the club's purpose is to physically attack synths works to justify Niska's own violent reaction (1.4). *Humans*, like many of the series I have already analysed here, does appear to validate hybridity, community and family, positioning the Hawkins and Elster families – humans and synths – in an alliance of sorts by the end of the first season.

Ideas of family and community are particularly strong in my last example, the Canadian series *Orphan Black*. As with the examples above, the technological embodiment explored in this series is not a specifically *cyborg* embodiment, but it does connect with the ideas of augmented embodiment that we see in narratives that present cyborg characters. The central characters of *Orphan Black* are clones, and therefore physically and genetically identical. Their identical appearance is both accentuated and confused in their portrayal by a single actor (Tatiana Maslany, in a multi-season tour-de-force). Maslany creates distinctive physical movements, characteristics and speech patterns for each clone character, from uptight housewife Alison and free-spirit scientist Cosima to disturbed assassin Helena, and others. In interview, Maslany comments on the physicality of her preparation to play the different characters, describing her response to the written script: 'It was about physicalizing and embodying that, putting it [in] my body, walking differently depending on how I look at the world' (Ostime 2013). Even for the actor, it seems, technological embodiment is rooted in the body.

Both bodies and technology are necessary in *Orphan Black*'s production, in order to portray the clones on screen, and in this respect, we can see the bodies of actors becoming cyborg through engagement with computer-generated special-effects technology. We might consider ways in which 'the traditional sf cyborg has escaped the confines of the representational space and entered the real world of film production, where actor and computer technology are increasingly being merged into a new form of digital/human hybrid' (Abbott 2006: 91). In such examples, '[t]he increasing presence of such [CGI] cyborgs within popular cinema has gradually transformed other genres into a curious hybrid of the sf film. The bodies of actors can now be altered, extended, or made to perform in ways that defy the laws of nature, fusing the body with filmmaking technologies' (Abbott 2006: 101). This is apparent in *Orphan Black*, where the clone characters are portrayed through different forms of duplication. In scenes involving two (or more) clones, Maslany alternates roles with her body double, Kathryn Alexandre; with each actor fully costumed, the two take turns to play the clone characters (BBC America 2015a). Maslany also works on her own with motion control cameras and objects placed to mark eye-lines. Series co-creator and writer Graeme Manson describes the process in revealing terms: it is 'not conducive to organic acting' (BBC America 2015b). Technical and technological processes come together so well in *Orphan Black*, however, that it is possible to become immersed in

Figure 15: Three clones, 'Variation Under Nature', *Orphan Black* (1.3)

the story world, with its distinct visuals and musical cues that correspond to the different clones, and in Maslany's mesmerizing performances, and to forget that what is shown on the screen – for example, three clones talking together in the same frame, as in Figure 15 – is a physical impossibility (unless clones really did exist). The height of this multiplying process is the Season 2 finale set-piece, the 'clone club' dance sequence ('By Means Which Have Never Yet Been Tried' 2.10). Here, four clones, Sarah, Cosima, Helena and Alison, dance with Sarah's brother Felix and her daughter Kira; of course, this scenario requires body doubles, motion cameras, several days and three actors to create a convincing illusion (BBC America 2014).

While it may seem frivolous to suggest that a dance party is an illuminating moment for the augmented, technological body, it seems to me that a scene like this acts as a culmination of many of the themes I have explored in this book. In production terms, such a scene requires technological apparatus to create the smooth appearance of activity that occurs in the physical world (a group of people dancing together, in this case; elsewhere, in other shows, the physical depiction of a technologically enhanced body). In terms of cyborg or augmented embodiment, the scene follows the presentation of most instances of the television cyborg.

Conclusion: Cyborg Futures

In fictional terms, technology interfaces with the organic body, adds to or enhances the abilities of that body but, in visual terms, the appearance of the organic, human body is maintained. And *Orphan Black* positions technology as dangerous, out of control or apt to control human beings in ways they did not expect. This danger is present in the dance scene, where at this point in the series narrative Cosima is terminally ill as a result of scientific manipulations of her genetic makeup. Technological processes mean that the other clones are specifically identified as objects that can be owned; at the end of Season 1, Cosima discovers that they are tagged with a marker. When translated into text, it reads, 'This organism and derivative genetic material is restricted intellectual property' ('Endless Forms Most Beautiful' 1.10). By this point in the series, the regular viewer will not regard Sarah, Cosima and the others as merely 'organisms', nor see Kira as 'derivative genetic material'. By labelling the characters in this way, the series writers simply underline the ways they resist othering the clones or situating them as separate from organic humans. The clone characters, even the troubled Helena, are for the most part entirely motivated by a wish to find themselves meaningful bonds in family groups. Family most securely surrounds Alison and Sarah, but Cosima, Helena, and even the villainous Rachel Duncan strive to create or discover their own versions or variations of family. This is emphasized in season finales, which often place the clones in some kind of family gathering: the dance party of Season 2, the celebration dinner of Season 3 ('History Yet To Be Written' 3.10). So, once again, connection, community and family is revealed to be vital to augmented humans as well as to organic humans.

The examples of these more recent series suggest that, although television may represent augmented embodiment in different ways, androids, clones and cyborgs continue to have a part to play in twenty-first-century fictions. Television cyborgs still have the capacity to terrify and to be monstrous: *Doctor Who*'s Cybermen and Daleks, *Star Trek*'s Borg, the Terminators, or *Fringe*'s Observers. Yet they can also act as mirrors to ourselves, like the Cylons, the bionic women, or the Dolls/Actives; and even terrifying cyborgs can adapt, change and transform as Seven of Nine or Cameron do. The transformative, boundary-crossing cyborg of television can develop thanks to the multi-season, extended narrative of the television series, so the cyborg becomes more than a form of visual spectacle: a rounded and complex character, a part of an ongoing series cast, an individual that television's long-form narrative allows viewers to come to know over months or years. Because of this, the television cyborg can also challenge the binary oppositions of technophilia and technophobia, offering new ways to view an augmented embodiment, and showing us how technological additions might bring opportunities as well as dangers. All these themes, ideas and concerns are still circulating around the artificial bodies of television, and we will watch to discover what they have to tell us about being human.

Notes

Chapter 1: Exterminate, Upgrade: *Doctor Who*

1 The focus on artificial bodies must be seen alongside the new series' focus on the mutability of bodies more generally, something that is evident across all seasons, from the Doctor's own multi-body regenerations to Captain Jack's immortal body (which nevertheless repeatedly dies before it is reborn).
2 The technophobia of scenes like this is undercut by the fact that it is Rose's mobile phone that saves the world from the Cybermen at the end of 'Age of Steel'.
3 In this episode, the casting of Jenna Coleman as Oswin plays with viewer expectations. Coleman had already been named as the Doctor's next companion, and viewers naturally assumed that Oswin would end the episode in the TARDIS, travelling with the Doctor.
4 It is tempting to view this as a further gendering of the cyborg as stereotypically female. Oswin occupies a space (the home, especially the kitchen) and carries out tasks (like cooking) that are frequently conflated with the female and/or with femininity. However, Oswin's apparently feminine pursuits are subtly parodic – her soufflés are burnt – and in other respects her homely environment functions as a giant clue for viewers, another example of 'what we have known all along' (Charles 2011: 3). How can she keep a pot plant and a bunch of roses in her refuge? Where – as the Doctor immediately asks – do her soufflé ingredients come from? Such examples may gender Oswin's cyborg embodiment, but they also reflect the impossible, imaginary space she has constructed.
5 The strong reaction around the Brigadier-Cyberman – ranging from 'emotional' (Delgado 2014) and 'very touching' to 'absolute and utter drivel' (Lewis 2014) – may indicate that because *Doctor Who*'s writers used Danny's character in a very erratic fashion, never integrating him into the core 'team' with the Doctor and Clara, viewers did not have time to develop an emotional attachment to him, and therefore could accept his cyborg transformation. In contrast, the Brigadier has a long history with the Doctor (from 'The Web of Fear' (1968) to 'Battlefield' (1989); he also appears in *The Sarah Jane Adventures*) – and, interestingly, one that is most fully understood by adult viewers, who may also be more likely to look back on the classic series episodes with nostalgia and emotion.

6 The Doctor is often played as though he were somewhat mentally unstable, especially in the performances of Tom Baker (in the classic series) and Matt Smith (in the new series). Mental instability tends to be read differently in a male character however, and is more likely to denote the workings of a superior brain/a genius. Compare the Doctor's presentation with that of the characters Topher Brink in *Dollhouse* and Walter Bishop in *Fringe*.

Chapter 2: Resistance, Assimilation and the Collective: *Star Trek: The Next Generation* and *Voyager*

1 The actors likewise demonstrate racial diversity: Robert Beltran of Mexican heritage, biracial Roxann Dawson and African-American Tim Russ.
2 Loss of individuality is a utopian aim for the Borg, which echoes *Doctor Who*'s presentation of the Cybermen as cyborgs that will 'remove fear, [...] remove sex and class and colour and creed' ('Doomsday'). Borg lose their individual embodiment, becoming part of the Collective in embodiment and in mind. In relation to racial difference, the Borg nanoprobes appear to inhibit the production of melanin, giving all the drones uniformly 'pallid white skin', 'ghostly pallor' (Graham 2002: 145, 147).
3 The fact that, even as Borg, Seven (and other drones) retain female sexual characteristics does raise questions about Borg embodiment and the efficiencies of assimilation. None of the formerly female drones appear to be altered to conform to any neutral/neuter mode of embodiment. For example, they retain breasts, which are surely of no use to a Borg either as sexual characteristics – the Borg are asexual – or as the means to nourish children – the Borg do not reproduce and any child they encounter is put into a 'maturation chamber' ('Drone', 'Collective') until s/he reaches the required age and, presumably, physical ability.
4 I note that Janeway talks of 'your transition', here in relation to Seven's acquisition of human traits and a singular identity, but using language reminiscent of gender transition.
5 Seven's relationship with Janeway can be viewed in similar ways to Olivia Dunham's relationship with Nina Sharp in *Fringe* Season 4 (see Chapter 8). Janeway's sacrifice in the series finale is very clearly motivated by her grief at Seven's death.
6 This part of the episode has strong overtones of pro-life discourse.
7 Although I am describing the drone as 'it', the character of One is played by a male actor (J. Paul Boehmer).

Chapter 3: Toasters and Replicas: *Battlestar Galactica*

1 This feature of Cylon society immediately disturbs the boundary between 'us' and 'them', since Cylon monotheism has more in common with contemporary Western belief systems than does the Twelve Colonies' polytheistic pantheon.

2 Another is 'skinjob', a term that echoes *Blade Runner* and, through that allusion, subtly comments on the position and function of Cylons in human society. Whether they are metal-bodied or physically identical to humans, the Cylons are placed as inferior, slave-like, viewed as incapable of true personhood.
3 And despite Cavil's insistence, 'Six of One' shows Boomer dissenting from the rest of the Eights; see my discussion in this chapter.
4 I note that both Bennett and Pegues reference this representation in their article titles which allude to Puccini's opera *Madama Butterfly* and to its musical-theatre incarnation *Miss Saigon*.
5 In publicity material Tricia Helfer consistently appears as the femme fatale version of Virtual Six with tight red dress and blonde hair.
6 The presentation of the female-gendered Hybrid appears to draw on the presentation of another prescient part-human in the film *Minority Report*; Samantha Morton as pre-cog Agatha has technological apparatus attached to her bald head, and floats in a tank of 'thick, viscous, clear liquid' (Peirse 2008: 123).
7 Jones does note the presence of a male Hybrid (*Battlestar Galactica: Razor*) but comments that as he is 'presented as an elderly man' this 'renders him outside the realm of traditional masculinity' (2010: 161). I find this a puzzling observation, for much 'traditional masculinity' values and prizes older males for their experience and wisdom, something the series allows for both Adama and Tigh (and for some older females, too, for example Laura Roslin).

Chapter 4: 'Between Life and Death': Embodiment and Virtuality in *Caprica*

1 As Lorrie Palmer and Eve Bennett point out, publicity materials for *Terminator: The Sarah Connor Chronicles* visually display an actor's body (Summer Glau's) in a way that does not reflect her character's role in the drama (Palmer 2012: 94; Bennett 2014). Torresani's image is used in a very similar way in *Caprica*'s publicity visuals. Thus, the publicity imagery for both series is able to capitalize on the display of a semi-naked female body, which has nothing to do with the actual series narrative.
2 In this chapter, I concentrate on gender in respect of Zoe's and Tamara's virtual/cyborg identities; however class and race are relevant to the characterization of the two families at the centre of the drama. The white, 'Waspish' Graystones are positioned in the moneyed professional class, while the representation of the Adamas draws on markers of ethnicity that recall 'Italian, Jewish, Arab, Greek, and Latin cultures' (Thrall 2015: 172); Hispanic or Hispanic-looking actors play the Adama characters (for example, Joseph [Esai Morales], Sam [Sasha Roiz], Tamara [Genevieve Buechner], Willie [Sina Najafi]).

3 The series creators acknowledge the problems this storyline caused: if Zoe-A was in V-world the character could not interact with other characters (and therefore, actors) in the physical world; while if Zoe-A was animating the Cylon, any scenes involving her character were hugely expensive in terms of CGI special effects (Murphy 2013). Showrunner Kevin Murphy comments that, had *Caprica* gone to a second season, his first priority would have been to 'get Zoe [...] back into a skin job body so she can interact with our A-list cast'. Such examples remind us that creating virtual spaces and people on screen usually means investing in physical sets and costuming with a significant cost factor.
4 Both Clarice Willow and Graystone Industries present their proposals as virtual, digital representations. Clarice shows Apotheosis to the faithful leaders of the Soldiers of the One using holoband technology – in effect, she creates a virtual space in order to describe a virtual space. The advertisement for the Grace programme underlines artificiality when Daniel protests that the makers have computer-generated his image, to which his colleague Xander retorts, 'Then may I suggest that you reshoot it? And this time, use the actual Dr. Graystone. After all, there's no substitute for the real thing' ('False Labor'). This immediately gives the lie to the premise of the Grace programme, and potentially to the aim of Apotheosis as well. After all, no matter how well realized the 'heaven' or how convincing the avatars, the Grace replacements and the STO heaven will always remain virtual.
5 Eventually, as we know from the storyline of *Battlestar Galactica*, the integration will fail, and the Cylons' apocalyptic war with humanity will occur.
6 It is given its own title, 'The Shape of Things to Come', which further emphasizes its connections with the future we have *already* seen in *Battlestar Galactica*.

Chapter 5: The Cyborg as Action Hero: *Bionic Woman*

1 The narratives themselves are generic hybrids: *Buffy* combines horror and the supernatural with high school drama; *Alias* mixes spy storylines with melodrama (Abbott and Brown 2007); *Fringe* uses science fiction and the police procedural.
2 Again, we can see similarities in Buffy's relationship with her sister Dawn after the death of their mother, and Olivia's with her sister and niece, with Nina Sharp, and with her daughter Etta.
3 In another parallel with *Buffy*, the character Faith, another vampire slayer, is framed as a working class outsider; she lives on her own in a motel for a time, and has no close family or other relationships until the final season of the series.

Chapter 6: Us and Them: *Terminator: The Sarah Connor Chronicles*

1. Commentators question the accuracy of the dates given in *TSCC*, noting that the story should begin in 1997 to fit in with *Terminator 2's* timeline (see the series timeline, Terminator Wiki, n.d.).
2. Although humans may be baffled by the cyborgs' behaviour, they create explanations for it: Boyd Sherman believes that Cameron is on the autistic spectrum ('The Tower is Tall But the Fall is Short') while Catherine's employees believe her lack of emotional response stems from grief at the loss of her husband ('Desert Cantos').
3. This is similar to the use and undercutting of the cyborg body in publicity shots of Alessandra Torresani as Zoe in *Caprica*, see Chapter 4.
4. This is referenced at the end of 'Born to Run', when Catherine cautions Sarah against calling her a bitch, and in so doing reminds viewers of Tuck's fate.
5. Since the same music is heard in the flash-forward sequence in 'Dungeons and Dragons' in which Derek is tortured, this piece could equally be associated with Derek – perhaps playing in his head as he watches Cameron. This association brings a more ominous note to the entire dance scene.
6. Cameron's dance scene, which utilizes Summer Glau's ballet training, is quite a contrast to the cyborg dance sequence in *Caprica* (Chapter 4).
7. The final episode of Season 2 aired on 10 April, and the series' cancellation was announced on 18 May 2009 (Schneider 2009).

Chapter 7: Hacking the System: *Dollhouse*

1. The connection with Čapek's play is stated very clearly in the penultimate episode: 'Rossum is just a name, actually. From a play. Although technically you're not robots, it seemed to fit' ('Getting Closer'). As K. Dale Koontz notes, Čapek's characters are named 'robotnik' in the sense of 'peasant or serf', an appropriate connection for the imprinted individuals of the Dollhouse (2010 par. 3), and the overt comment on *R.U.R.* indicates that Whedon intends the Doll/Active characters to be artificially/technologically enhanced beings: cyborgs.
2. Caroline's personality is downloaded into a child's body in 'Epitaph One' and 'Epitaph Two: Return', creating another instance of multiple personality as child-Caroline and Echo meet. Additionally, this example presents an adult mind in a child's body, creating a disturbing 'liminality' in which the child 'both is and is not sexualized' (Nadkarni 2014: 94, note 6).
3. As a point of comparison, although Claire Saunders hacks Topher's system to reveal that she is herself a simulacrum, she does not investigate her own original

personality. When Topher asks her, 'Don't you wanna know who you really are?' she replies, firmly, 'I know who I am' ('Omega'). This appears to offer a more positive embrace of cyborg/simulated identity, but it still represents a denial of the actual personality (and is further undercut when Claire is revealed to have a 'sleeper' personality embedded in her mind, 'Getting Closer').

4 Only Caroline and Priya appear in their original identities, in flashback scenes; Caroline, Priya, Madeline and Tony briefly have their actual personalities reinstated in 'Needs'.

5 Samira Nadkarni argues that Nolan's possession of Sierra parallels other examples in which Dollhouse employees use (or abuse) Dolls: Adelle and 'Roger', Topher and his birthday 'friend', Hearn's rape of Sierra (2014: 87). Nadkarni's point is that although some of these uses are 'platonic' and could be viewed as playful, they still constitute abuse since they are performed without the Doll's consent.

6 This observation is complicated since it is made by Luca, another imprint in the body of the Doll Victor.

7 'Epitaph One' was broadcast at San Diego's ComicCon on 24 July 2009 and on the UK's Sci Fi Channel on 11 August 2009. It was included in the DVD box set in the US and internationally. 'Epitaph Two: Return' aired in the US on 29 January 2010.

8 Although, as Lorna Jowett points out, there are still problematic aspects here. We could see T as 'the culmination of a biological urge […] the imprinting of a heteronormative society, or […] the need to repopulate' after apocalypse (2014: 136).

Chapter 8: Complete Control: *Fringe*

1 Websites and wikis provide listings and screenshots of Observer appearances; see, for example, 'Observer Appearance' on FringePedia.net and 'Fringe Observer Sightings' on Fringebloggers.com.

2 Walternate, with his severe and controlled demeanour, is an obvious character contrast to Walter; Alt-Astrid has the traits of a person on the autistic spectrum.

3 This point is a complex one. Walter's stated aim in travelling from the prime universe to the parallel universe is in order to cure the alternate Peter of the disease that killed Walter's son. However, Walter does not return alternate Peter to the parallel universe, but instead brings him up as his son. Walter's actions involving alternate Peter can also be viewed as abduction or kidnapping; there is evidence that Peter knew he did not belong in the prime universe, and attempted to return to the parallel one ('Subject 13' 3.15).

4 We can see versions of the woman in power in television series from the 1980s to the present; for example, *Prime Suspect, E.R., Network, Commander in Chief, Veep, Scott and Bailey, Homeland*, and in some compelling non-English-language examples, *Engrenages* (France), *Borgen* and *Forbrydelsen* (*The Killing*) (Denmark). In the series examined in this book, we have the examples of Kathryn Janeway in *Star Trek: Voyager* and Laura Roslin in *Battlestar Galactica*.

5 Anna Torv was criticised for her 'cold' and 'wooden' portrayal of Olivia in early episodes. As producers Jeff Pinkner and J.H. Wyman point out, this portrayal followed the way the character was written (Murray 2011). As the series progressed, critics singled out Torv for praise when her performance of the parallel-universe Olivia revealed her acting abilities (Stegall 2010; Chambers 2011; Jeffery 2012).
6 In many ways, Olivia's character is more believable – and more original – as a Scully-like foil to Peter and Walter. The latter show other forms of 'gender-role-switching' (Wilcox 2014: 51), since they are more likely to display emotion and to interact as parent and child.
7 The fan confusion over whether Nina still has a bionic arm in Season 4 is just one example of the confusion viewers experience more generally, because the stories, characters and timelines of the series are rewritten over and over again; see, for example, the discussion following the review of 'Peter' on ign.com (Isler 2010).
8 In some ways, this positions the twenty-first-century humans of *Fringe* in a similar way to the Centurions of *Battlestar Galactica* and *Caprica* who provide military might and slave labour.
9 This embodiment as parent is similarly present in *Dollhouse*; see my discussion on Priya and Tony in Chapter 7.
10 The fact that the humans name Michael while the Observers give him a designation, a code, simply underlines the differences between cyborg and human in this part of the narrative.

Filmography and TV

Film

Blade Runner (Ridley Scott, USA, 1984)
Invasion of the Body Snatchers (Philip Kaufman, USA, 1978)
Matrix, The (The Wachowskis, USA, 1999)
Metropolis (Fritz Lang, USA, 1927)
Minority Report (Steven Spielberg, USA, 2002)
RoboCop (Paul Verhoeven, USA, 1987)
RoboCop 2 (Irvin Kershner, USA, 1990)
Single White Female (Barbet Schroeder, USA, 1992)
Star Trek: First Contact (Jonathan Frakes, USA, 1996)
Terminator, The (James Cameron, USA, 1984)
Terminator 2: Judgment Day (James Cameron, USA, 1991)
Terminator 3: Rise of the Machines (Jonathan Mostow, USA, 2003)

Television

Äkta människor (*Real Humans*) (Sveriges Television [SVT] 2012–)
Alias (ABC 2001–2006)
Almost Human (Fox 2013–2014)
Angel (WB 1999–2004)
Battlestar Galactica (NBC 1978–1979)
Battlestar Galactica (Sci-Fi 2004–2009)
Battlestar Galactica: Razor (Sci-Fi 2007)
Bionic Woman, The (ABC 1976–1977; NBC 1978)
Bionic Woman (NBC 2007)
Borgen (Danmarks Radio [DR1] 2010–2013)
Buffy the Vampire Slayer (WB 1997–2001; UPN 2001–2003)
Caprica (Sci-Fi 2009; Syfy 2010)
Charlie's Angels (ABC 1976–1981)
Commander in Chief (ABC 2005–2006)
Continuum (Showcase 2012–2015)

Filmography and TV

Dark Angel (Fox 2000–2002)
Doctor Who (BBC 1963–89; 2005–)
Dollhouse (Fox 2009–10)
E.R. (NBC 1994–2009)
Engrenages (Canal+ 2005–)
Forbrydelsen (The Killing) (Danmarks Radio [DR1] 2007–2012)
Fringe (Fox 2010–13)
Heroes (NBC 2006–2010)
Homeland (Showtime 2011–)
Humans (Channel 4 2015)
Intelligence (CBS 2014)
Orphan Black (BBC America 2013–)
Prime Suspect (Granada 1991)
Scott and Bailey (ITV 2011–)
Star Trek (NBC 1966–1968)
Star Trek: Deep Space Nine (Paramount 1993–1999)
Star Trek: The Next Generation (Syndicated 1987–94)
Star Trek: Voyager (UPN 1995–2001)
Terminator: The Sarah Connor Chronicles (Fox 2008–9)
Torchwood (BBC 2006–2011)
Veep (HBO 2012–)
West Wing, The (NBC 1999–2006)
Wonder Woman (ABC 1976–1977; CBS 1977–1979)
X-Files, The (FOX 1993–2002)

Bibliography

Abbott, Stacey (2006). 'Final Frontiers: Computer-Generated Imagery and the Science Fiction Film'. *Science Fiction Studies*, 33(1): 89–108.

—— (2013). 'The End of Fringe Division – or Is It?' *Critical Studies in Television* [Online] http://cstonline.tv/end-fringe (Accessed 21 March 2016).

Abbott, Stacey and Simon Brown (2007). 'Can't Live with 'Em, Can Shoot 'Em: *Alias* and the Thermonuclear Family'. In Abbott and Brown (eds) *Alias: Secrets and Spies*. London: I.B.Tauris. 87–100.

Balsamo, Anne (1988). 'Reading Cyborgs Writing Feminism'. *Communication* 10: 331–344.

—— (1995). *Technologies of the Gendered Body: Reading Cyborg Women*. Durham: Duke University Press.

Baudrillard, Jean (1988). *Selected Writings*. Trans. Paul Foss, et al. Mark Poster (ed). Cambridge: Polity Press.

—— (1993). *Symbolic Exchange and Death*. Trans. Ian Hamilton Grant. London: Sage Publications.

—— (1993). *The Transparency of Evil: Essays on Extreme Phenomena*. Trans. James Benedict. London; New York: Verso.

BBC America (2014). 'Behind The Scenes of 4 Clone Dance Party'. YouTube. [Online] https://www.youtube.com/watch?v=XE2u_N8g6cs (Accessed 18 December 2015).

BBC America. (2015a). 'A Closer Look at *Orphan Black* Season 3 – Tatiana Maslany's Clone Double'. YouTube. [Online] https://www.youtube.com/watch?v=rfC77BzANiA (Accessed 18 December 2015).

—— (2015b). '*Orphan Black* Insider: Three Clones, One Frame'. YouTube. [Online] https://www.youtube.com/watch?v=4rALHr8gV1E (Accessed 18 December 2015).

Benjamin, Walter ([1955] 1992). 'The Work of Art in the Age of Mechanical Reproduction'. In Arendt, Hannah (ed) *Illuminations*. London: Fontana.

Bennett, Eve (2011). 'Deconstructing the Dream Factory: Personal Fantasy and Corporate Manipulation in Joss Whedon's *Dollhouse*'. *Slayage: The Journal of Whedon Studies*, 9(1): n.p.

—— (2012). 'Techno-butterfly: Orientalism Old and New in *Battlestar Galactica*'. *Science Fiction Film and Television*, 5(1): 23–46.

—— (2014). 'Deus ex Machina: AI Apocalypticism in *Terminator: The Sarah Connor Chronicles*'. *The Journal of Popular Television*, 2(1): 3–19.

Bibliography

Bignell, Jonathan (2005). 'Space for "Quality": Negotiating with the Daleks'. In Jonathan Bignell and Stephen Lacey (eds) *Popular Television Drama: Critical Perspectives*. Manchester: Manchester University Press. 76–92.

Boyd, Katrina (1996). 'Cyborgs in Utopia: The Problem of Radical Difference in *Star Trek: TNG*'. In Taylor Harrison, et al. (eds) *Enterprise Zones: Critical Positions on Star Trek*. Boulder, CO: Westview. 95–113.

Braidotti, Rosi (1989). 'The Politics of Ontological Difference'. In Teresa Brennan (ed) *Between Feminism and Psychoanalysis*. London: Routledge.

—— (2000). 'Teratologies'. In Ian Buchanan and Clare Colebrook (eds) *Deleuze and Feminist Thought*. Edinburgh: Edinburgh University Press. 156–172.

Britton, Piers D. (2013). 'Making a Superior Brand of Alien Mastermind: *Doctor Who* Monsters and the Rhetoric of (Re)design'. In Matt Hills (ed) *New Dimensions of Doctor Who: Adventures in Space, Time and Television*. London: I.B.Tauris. 39–53.

Bronson, Zak (2014). '"We Were Trying to Make You More Than You Were": The Singularity, Transhumanism and Shapeshifting'. In Tanya R. Cochran, et al. (eds) *The Multiple Worlds of Fringe: Essays on the J.J. Abrams Science Fiction Series*. Jefferson, NC: McFarland. 60–76.

Brooker, Will (2013). 'Talking to the TARDIS: *Doctor Who*, Neil Gaiman and Cultural Mythology'. In Matt Hills (ed) *New Dimensions of Doctor Who: Adventures in Space, Time and Television*. London: I.B.Tauris. 71–91.

Brown, Jeffrey A. (1996). 'Gender and the Action Heroine: Hardbodies and the "Point of No Return"'. *Cinema Journal*, 35(3): 52–71.

Buckman, Alyson R. (2014). 'Fantasy Is His Business, But It Is Not His Purpose: An Introduction to Joss Whedon and His Storytelling'. In Sherry Ginn, et al. (eds) *Joss Whedon's Dollhouse: Confounding Purpose, Confusing Identity*. Lanham MD: Rowman & Littlefield. xi–xxvii.

Bukatman, Scott (1993). *Terminal Identity: The Virtual Subject in Postmodern Science Fiction*. Durham: Duke University Press Books.

Bussolini, Jeffrey (2013). 'Television Intertextuality After *Buffy*: Intertextuality of Casting and Constitutive Intertextuality'. *Slayage: The Journal of Whedon Studies*, 10(1): n.p.

Butler, Judith (1990). *Gender Trouble*. London: Routledge.

Cadigan, Pat (1991). *Synners*. London: Harpercollins.

Callot, André (2009). 'The Expired Feminism of Joss Whedon'. *Overthinking It*. 23 December. [Online] http://www.overthinkingit.com/2009/12/23/joss-whedon-feminism/ (Accessed 21 October 2015).

Calvert, Bronwen (2010). 'Mind, Body, Imprint: Cyberpunk Echoes in the Dollhouse'. *Slayage: The Journal of Whedon Studies*, 8(2–3): n.p.

—— (2012). '"The Shell I'm In": Illyria and Monstrous Embodiment'. In Mary Alice Money (ed) *Joss Whedon: The Complete Companion*. London; New York: Titan Books. 181–90.

Bibliography

—— (2014a). '"This Means Bodies": Body Horror and the Influence of David Cronenberg'. In Tanya R. Cochran, et al. (eds) *The Multiple Worlds of Fringe: Essays on the J.J. Abrams Science Fiction Series*. Jefferson, NC: McFarland. 186–200.

—— (2014b). '"Who Did They Make Me This Time?": Viewing Pleasure and Horror'. In Sherry Ginn, et al. (eds) *Joss Whedon's Dollhouse: Confounding Purpose, Confusing Identity*. Lanham MD: Rowman & Littlefield. 113–126.

'Cameron vs Rosie' (2009). *Terminator: The Sarah Connor Chronicles – The Complete First and Second Season*. Warner Home Video.

Capettini, Emily (2012). '"A Boy and His Box, Off to See the Universe": Madness, Power and Sex in "The Doctor's Wife" '. In Tara Prescott and Aaron Drucker (eds) *Feminism in the Worlds of Neil Gaiman: Essays on the Comics, Poetry and Prose*. Jefferson, NC: McFarland. 148–160.

Chambers, Becky (2011). 'Let Us Discuss How Great *Fringe's* Olivia Dunham Is'. *The Mary Sue*. [Online] http://www.themarysue.com/let-us-discuss-how-great-fringes-olivia-dunham-is/ (Accessed 17 November 2015).

Chapman, James (2013). *Inside the Tardis: The Worlds of Doctor Who: A Cultural History*. London: I.B.Tauris.

Charles, Alec (2011). 'The Crack of Doom: The Uncanny Echoes of Steven Moffat's *Doctor Who*'. *Science Fiction Film & Television*, 4(1): 1–24.

Chen, Ken (2008). 'The Lovely Smallness of *Doctor Who*'. *Film International*, 6(2): 52–59.

Coile, Charlie (2013). 'More than a Companion: "The Doctor's Wife" and Representations of Women in *Doctor Who*'. *Studies in Popular Culture*, 36(1): 83–104.

Collado-Rodriguez, Francisco (2002). 'Fear of the Flesh, Fear of the Borg: Narratives of Bodily Transgression in Contemporary U.S. Culture'. In Ramón Plo-Alastrué and María Jesús Martínez-Alfaro (eds) *Beyond Borders: Re-Defining Generic and Ontological Boundaries*. Heidelberg: Universitätsverkag C. Winter. 67–79.

Connelly, Tom and Shelley Rees (2010). 'Alienation and the Dialectics of History in Joss Whedon's *Dollhouse*'. *Slayage: The Journal of Whedon Studies*, 8(2–3): n.p.

Consalvo, Mia (2004). 'Borg Babes, Drones, and the Collective: Reading Gender and the Body in *Star Trek*'. *Women's Studies in Communication*, 27(2): 177–203.

Cook, John R. (2002). 'Adapting Telefantasy: The *Doctor Who and the Daleks* Films'. In I. Q. Hunter (ed) *British Science Fiction Cinema*. London: Routledge.

Cornea, Christine (2003). 'David Cronenberg's *Crash* and Performing Cyborgs'. *The Velvet Light Trap*, 52(1): 4–14.

—— (2007). *Science Fiction Cinema: Between Fantasy and Reality*. Edinburgh: Edinburgh University Press.

Couch, Aaron (2015). '*Star Trek*: The Story of the Most Daring Cliffhanger in *Next Generation* History'. *Hollywood Reporter* [Online] http://www.hollywoodreporter.com/heat-vision/star-trek-story-daring-cliffhanger-803642 (Accessed 2 September 2015).

Bibliography

Cranny-Francis, Anne (2000). 'The Erotics of the (Cy)borg: Authority and Gender in the Sociocultural Imaginary'. In Marleen Barr (ed) *Future Females, The Next Generation: New Voices and Velocities in Feminist Science Fiction*. Lanham MD: Rowman & Littlefield. 145–63.

—— (2009). 'Why the Cybermen Stomp: Sound in the New *Doctor Who*'. *Mosaic*, 42(2): 119–34.

—— (2013). *Technology and Touch: The Biopolitics of Emerging Technologies*. New York: Palgrave Macmillan.

Crosby, Sara (2004). 'The Cruelest Season: Female Heroes Snapped into Sacrificial Heroines'. In Sherrie A. Inness (ed) *Action Chicks: New Images of Tough Women in Popular Culture*. Basingstoke: Palgrave Macmillan. 153–78.

Cull, Nicholas J. (2001). '"Bigger on the Inside": Doctor Who as British Cultural History'. In Graham Roberts and Philip M. Taylor. (eds) *The Historian, Television and Television History: a Collection*. Luton: University of Luton Press. 95–111.

Deis, Christopher (2008). 'Erasing Difference: The Cylons as Racial Other'. In Tiffany Potter and C.W. Marshall (eds) *Cylons in America: Critical Studies in Battlestar Galactica*. London; New York: Continuum. 156–168.

Delgado, Kasia (2014). '*Doctor Who* Series Finale "Death in Heaven": The Twitter Reaction'. *Radio Times*. [Online] http://www.radiotimes.com/news/2014-11-09/doctor-who-series-finale-death-in-heaven-the-twitter-reaction (Accessed 16 October 2015).

Dell, Erin Brownlee (2013). 'Troubling Notions of Reality in *Caprica*'. In P.L. Thomas (ed) *Science Fiction and Speculative Fiction*. Rotterdam/Boston: SensePublishers. 133–144.

Dery, Mark (1996). *Escape Velocity: Cyberculture at the End of the Century*. New York: Grove Press.

Descartes, René ([1641] 1993). *Meditations on First Philosophy*. London: Routledge.

Doane, Mary Anne (1990). 'Technophilia: Technology, Representation, and the Feminine'. In Mary Jacobus, et al. (eds) *Body/Politics: Women and the Discourses of Science*. New York; London: Routledge. 163–176.

'Doctor Who Confidential: Bigger on the Inside' (2011). *Doctor Who Confidential*. BBC Three.

'Doctor Who Confidential: Cybermen' (2006). *Doctor Who Confidential*. BBC Three.

Dominguez, Diana (2005). '"It's Not Easy Being a Cast Iron Bitch": Sexual Difference and the Female Action Hero'. *Reconstruction: Studies in Contemporary Culture*, 5(4): n.p [Online]. http://reconstruction.eserver.org/Issues/054/dominguez.shtml (Accessed 15 October 2015)

Douglas, Susan (1995). *Where the Girls Are: Growing Up Female With the Mass Media*. New York: Times Books.

Dunn, Carrie (2010). 'The Alien Woman: Othering and the Oriental'. In Andrew Ireland, et al. (eds) *Illuminating Torchwood: Essays on Narrative, Character and Sexuality in the BBC Series*. Jefferson, NC: McFarland. 113–120.

Bibliography

Fleming, John (2011) 'TV writer Terry Nation talks about creating the Daleks and about his insecurities and nightmares'. *So It Goes: John Fleming's Blog* [Online] https://thejohnfleming.wordpress.com/2011/11/29/tv-writer-terry-nation-talks-about-creating-the-daleks-and-about-his-insecurities-and-nightmares/ (Accessed 12 August 2015).

Freud, Sigmund ([1919] 1961). 'The Uncanny'. In *The Standard Edition of the Complete Psychological Works of Sigmund Freud*. London: Hogarth Press. 219–256.

Fuchs, Cynthia J. (1995). '"Death is Irrelevant": Cyborgs, Reproduction, and the Future of Male Hysteria'. In Chris Hables Gray, et al. (eds) *The Cyborg Handbook*. New York: Routledge. 281–300.

Genz, Stéphanie and Benjamin Brabon (2009). *Postfeminism: Cultural Texts and Theories*. Edinburgh: Edinburgh University Press.

George, Susan A. (2008). 'Fraking Machines: Desire, Gender, and the (Post)human Condition in *Battlestar Galactica*'. In J.P. Telotte (ed.) *The Essential Science Fiction Television Reader*. Lexington: University Press of Kentucky. 159–176.

Geraghty, Lincoln (2008). 'From Balaclavas to Jumpsuits: The Multiple Histories and Identities of *Doctor Who*'s Cybermen'. *ATLANTIS: Journal of the Association of Anglo-American Studies*, 30(1): 85–100.

Giardina, Natasha (2006). 'The Face in the Mirror: Issues of Meat and Machine in *Battlestar Galactica*'. In Richard Hatch, et al. (eds) *So Say We All: An Unauthorized Collection of Thoughts and Opinions on Battlestar Galactica*. BenBella Books. 45–54.

Gibbs, Alan (2013). '"Maybe That's What Happens If You Touch the Doctor, Even for a Second": Trauma in *Doctor Who*'. *The Journal of Popular Culture*, 46(5): 950–972.

Gibson, William ([1984] 1993). *Neuromancer*. New York; London: Harper Voyager.

Gillis, Stacey (2007a). 'Cyberspace, Feminism and Technology: Of Cyborgs and Women'. In Diane Richardson and Victoria Robinson (eds) *Introducing Gender and Women's Studies*. Basingstoke: Palgrave Macmillan. 205–218.

—— (2007b). 'The (Post)Feminist Politics of Cyberpunk'. *Gothic Studies*, 9(2): 7–19.

Glascock, Jack (2001). 'Gender Roles on Prime-Time Network Television: Demographics and Behaviors'. *Journal of Broadcasting & Electronic Media*, 45(4): 656–669.

Goldman, Eric (2007). 'Guiding *The Sarah Connor Chronicles*'. *IGN.com*. [Online] http://www.ign.com/articles/2007/06/20/guiding-the-sarah-connor-chronicles (Accessed 29 September 2015).

Gonzales, Jennifer (1995). 'Envisioning Cyborg Bodies: Notes from Current Research'. In Chris Hables Gray, et al (eds) *The Cyborg Handbook*. New York: Routledge. 267–279.

Goodman, Tim (2007). 'Reviews: *Journeyman, Chuck* and *Bionic Woman*.' *SF Gate*. [Online] http://www.sfgate.com/news/article/Tim-Goodman-Reviews-Journeyman-Chuck-and-2501475.php (Accessed 24 November 2015).

Gough-Yates, Anna (2001). 'Angels in Chains? Feminism, Femininity and Consumer Culture in *Charlie's Angels*'. In Bill Osgerby and Anna Gough-Yates (eds) *Action TV: Tough-Guys, Smooth Operators and Foxy Chicks*. London; New York: Routledge. 83-99.

Graham, Elaine R. (2001). 'Cyborgs or Goddesses?: Becoming Divine in a Cyberfeminist Age'. In Alison Adam and Eileen Green (eds) *Virtual Gender: Technology, Consumption and Identity Matters*. London; New York: Routledge.

—— (2002). *Representations of the Post/Human: Monsters, Aliens and Others in Popular Culture*. Manchester: Manchester University Press.

Green, Bonnie and Chris Willmott (2013). 'The Cybermen as Human.2'. In Matt Hills (ed) *New Dimensions of Doctor Who: Adventures in Space, Time and Television*. London: I.B. Tauris. 54-70.

Green, Nicola (1997). 'Beyond Being Digital: Representation and Virtual Corporeality'. In David Holmes (ed) *Virtual Politics: Identity and Community in Cyberspace*. London; Thousand Oaks CA: Sage. 59-78.

Grosz, Elizabeth (1987). 'Notes Towards a Corporeal Feminism'. *Australian Feminist Studies*, 2(5): 1-16.

—— (1994). *Volatile Bodies: Toward a Corporeal Feminism*. Bloomington IN: Indiana University Press.

—— (1995) *Space, Time and Perversion: Essays on the Politics of Bodies*. New York: Routledge.

Gunkel, David (2000). 'We Are Borg: Cyborgs and the Subject of Communication'. *Communication Theory*, 10(3): 332-357.

Hall, Kira (1996). 'Cyberfeminism'. In Susan C. Herring (ed) *Computer-Mediated Communication: Linguistic, Social, and Cross-Cultural Perspectives*. Amsterdam; Philadelphia: John Benjamins. 147-170.

Haraway, Donna (1985). 'A Manifesto for Cyborgs: Science, Technology, and Socialist Feminism for the 1980s'. *Socialist Review*, 15(2): 65-107.

—— (1991a). 'A Cyborg Manifesto: Science, Technology, and Socialist-Feminism in the Late Twentieth Century'. In *Simians, Cyborgs and Women: The Reinvention of Nature*. New York: Routledge. 149-181.

—— (1991b). 'The Biopolitics of Postmodern Bodies: Constitutions of Self in Immune System Discourse'. In *Simians, Cyborgs and Women: The Reinvention of Nature*. London: Free Association. 203-230.

Hawk, Julie (2011). 'Objet 8 and the Cylon Remainder: Posthuman Subjectivization in *Battlestar Galactica*'. *The Journal of Popular Culture*, 44(1): 3-15.

Hayles, N. Katherine (1994). 'The Seduction of Cyberspace'. In Verena Andermatt Conley (ed) *Rethinking Technologies*. Minneapolis: University of Minnesota Press. 173-190.

—— (1996). 'Embodied Virtuality: Or How to Put Bodies Back into the Picture'. In Mary Anne Moser (ed) *Immersed in Technology: Art and Virtual Environments*. Cambridge MA: MIT Press. 1-28.

Bibliography

—— (1997). 'The Posthuman Body: Inscription and Incorporation in *Galatea 2.2* and *Snow Crash*'. *Configurations*, 5(2). 241–266.

Heinecken, Dawn (2003). *The Warrior Women of Television: A Feminist Cultural Analysis of the New Female Body in Popular Media*. New York: Peter Lang.

Heinricy, Shana (2008). 'I, Cyborg'. In Josef Steiff and Tristan D. Tamplin (eds) *Battlestar Galactica and Philosophy: Mission Accomplished or Mission Frakked Up?* Chicago: Open Court. 95–102.

Hills, Matt (2005). *The Pleasures of Horror*. New York: Bloomsbury.

—— (2010). *Triumph of a Time Lord: Regenerating Doctor Who in the Twenty-First Century*. London; New York: I.B.Tauris.

Isler, Ramsey (2010). '*Fringe*: "Peter" Review'. *IGN Boards*. [Online] http://www.ign.com/boards/threads/fringe-peter-review.190764444/ (Accessed 17 November 2015)

Jeffery, Morgan (2012). '*Fringe*: Will the Fox Sci-Fi Drama's Final Season Win an Emmy?' *Digital Spy*. [Online] http://www.digitalspy.com/tv/fringe/news/a408071/fringe-will-the-fox-sci-fi-dramas-final-season-win-an-emmy/ (Accessed 17 November 2015).

Jeffords, Susan (1993). *Hard Bodies: Hollywood Masculinity in the Reagan Era*. New Brunswick NJ: Rutgers University Press.

Jenkins, Tricia (2011). 'Nationalism and Gender: The 1970s, *The Six Million Dollar Man*, and *The Bionic Woman*'. *The Journal of Popular Culture*, 44(1): 93–113.

Johnson-Lewis, Erika (2008). 'Torture, Terrorism, and Other Aspects of Human Nature'. In Tiffany Potter and C.W. Marshall (eds) *Cylons in America: Critical Studies in Battlestar Galactica*. New York: Continuum. 27–39.

Johnson-Smith, Jan (2005). *American Science Fiction TV: Star Trek, Stargate and Beyond*. London; New York: I.B.Tauris.

Jones, Matthew (2010). 'Butch Girls, Brittle Boys and Sexy, Sexless Cylons: Some Gender Problems in *Battlestar Galactica*'. In Roz Kaveney and Jennifer Stoy (eds) *Battlestar Galactica: Investigating Flesh, Spirit and Steel*. London: I.B.Tauris. 154–161.

Jowett, Lorna (2005). 'To the Max: Embodying Intersections in *Dark Angel*'. *Reconstruction: Studies in Contemporary Culture*, 5(4): n.p [Online]. http://reconstruction.eserver.org/Issues/054/jowett.shtml (Accessed 15 October 2015).

—— (2010). 'Frak Me: Reproduction, Gender, Sexuality'. In Roz Kaveney and Jennifer Stoy (eds) *Battlestar Galactica: Investigating Flesh, Spirit and Steel*. London: I.B.Tauris. 59–80.

—— (2014). '"I Love Him…Is That Real?": Interrogating Romance through Victor and Sierra'. In Sherry Ginn, et al. (eds) *Joss Whedon's Dollhouse: Confounding Purpose, Confusing Identity*. Lanham MD: Rowman & Littlefield. 127–140.

Jowett, Lorna and Stacey Abbott (2013). *TV Horror: Investigating the Darker Side of the Small Screen*. London; New York: I.B.Tauris.

Kafer, Alison (2013). *Feminist, Queer, Crip*. Bloomington IN: Indiana University Press.

Bibliography

Kakoudaki, Despina (2000). 'Pinup and Cyborg: Exaggerated Gender and Artificial Intelligence'. In Marleen S. Barr (ed.) *Future Females, the Next Generation: New Voices and Velocities in Feminist Science Fiction Criticism*. Lanham MD: Rowman & Littlefield. 165–196.

Kapica, Steven S. (2014). '"I Don't Feel Like a Copy": Posthuman Legal Personhood and *Caprica*'. *Griffith Law Review*, 23(4): 612–633.

Kern, Louis J. (2000). 'Terminal Notions of What We May Become: Synthflesh, Cyberreality, and the Post-Human Body'. In Elisabeth Kraus and Carolin Auer (eds) *Simulacrum America: the USA and the Popular Media*. Rochester, N.Y: Camden House. 95–106.

Kind, Amy (2011). '"I'm Sharon, But I'm a Different Sharon": The Identity of Cylons'. In Jason T. Eberl (ed.) *Battlestar Galactica and Philosophy: Knowledge Here Begins Out There*. Oxford: Blackwell. 64–74.

King, Derrick (2014). '"We're Lost. We Are Not Gone": Critical Dystopia and the Politics of Radical Hope'. In Sherry Ginn, et al. (eds) *Joss Whedon's Dollhouse: Confounding Purpose, Confusing Identity*. Lanham MD: Rowman & Littlefield. 163–176.

Koistinen, Aino-Kaisa (2011). 'Passing for Human in Science Fiction: Comparing the TV Series *Battlestar Galactica* and *V*'. *NORA – Nordic Journal of Feminist and Gender Research*, 19(4): 249–263.

Koontz, K. Dale (2010). 'Czech Mate: Whedon, Čapek, and the Foundations of *Dollhouse*'. *Slayage: The Journal of Whedon Studies*, 8(2–3): n.p.

Kroker, Arthur and Marilouise Kroker (1988) 'Theses of the Disappearing Body in the Hyper-Modern Condition'. In Arthur Kroker and Marilouise Kroker (eds) *Body Invaders: Sexuality and the Postmodern Condition*. London: Macmillan. 20–34.

Kuppers, Petra (2007). 'Addenda, Phenomenology, Embodiment'. In Susan Broadhurst and Josephine Machon (eds) *Performance and Technology: Practices of Virtual Embodiment and Interactivity*. Basingstoke: Palgrave Macmillan. 169–180.

Kurzman, Steven (2001). 'Presence and Prosthesis: A Response to Nelson and Wright'. *Cultural Anthropology*, 16(3). 374–387.

La Mettrie, Julien Offray de ([1747] 1996). *Machine Man and Other Writings*. Cambridge: Cambridge University Press.

Lauzen, Martha M., et al. (2008). 'Constructing Gender Stereotypes Through Social Roles in Prime-Time Television'. *Journal of Broadcasting & Electronic Media*, 52(2): 200–214.

Leaver, Tama (2015). 'Radically Performing the Borg?: Gender Identity and Narratology in *Star Trek*'. In Douglas Brode and Shea T. Brode (eds) *The Star Trek Universe: Franchising the Final Frontier*. Lanham MD: Rowman & Littlefield. 65–74.

LEGO.com (2015) 'BIONICLE'. *LEGO Bionicle* [Online]. http://www.lego.com/en-gb/bionicle (Accessed 23 October 2015)

Bibliography

Lewis, David (2014). '*Doctor Who* Finale: A Look at the Brigadier's Last Bow in "Death in Heaven"'. *CultBox* [Online]. http://www.cultbox.co.uk/features/opinion/doctor-who-finale-a-look-at-the-brigadiers-last-bow (Accessed 16 October 2015).

Marshall, C. W. and Matthew Wheeland (2008) 'The Cylons, the Singularity, and God'. In Tiffany Potter and C.W. Marshall (eds) *Cylons in America: Critical Studies in Battlestar Galactica*. London; New York: Continuum. 91–104.

Martin, Emily (1997). 'The End of the Body?' In Roger N. Lancaster and Micaela di Leonardo (eds) *The Gender/Sexuality Reader: Culture, History, Political Economy*. New York: Routledge. 543–558.

Mateos-Aparicio, Angel (2007). 'Trespasses of Body Boundaries: The Cyborg and the Construction of a Postgendered Posthuman Identity'. In Ana M. Manzanas (ed) *Border Transits: Literature and Culture Across the Line*. Amsterdam: Rodopi. 243–276.

McNamara, Mary (2008). 'Watching TV, a Job with Regrets'. *latimes.com* [Online]. http://articles.latimes.com/2008/aug/25/entertainment/et-second25 (Accessed 24 November 2015).

Meekosha, Helen (1999). 'Superchicks, Clones, Cyborgs, and Cripples: Cinema and Messages of Bodily Transformations'. *Social Alternatives*, 18(1): 24–8.

meloukhia (2009) 'Much Ado about *Dollhouse* [Television Tuesday]'. *Deeply Problematic* [Online]. http://www.deeplyproblematic.com/2009/09/much-ado-about-dollhouse-television.html (Accessed 21 October 2015).

Mitchell, David T. and Sharon L. Snyder (2001). *Narrative Prosthesis: Disability and the Dependencies of Discourse*. Ann Arbor: The University of Michigan Press.

Moore, Robert W. (2008). '"To Be a Person": Sharon Agathon and the Social Expression of Individuality'. In Tiffany Potter and C.W. Marshall (eds) *Cylons in America: Critical Studies in Battlestar Galactica*. London; New York: Continuum. 105–117.

Moravec, Hans (1988). *Mind Children: The Future of Robot and Human Intelligence*. Cambridge MA: Harvard University Press.

More, Max (2013). 'Principles of Extropy'. *Extropy Institute* [Online]. https://web.archive.org/web/20131015142449/http://extropy.org/principles.htm (Accessed 21 October 2015).

Mukherjea, Ananya (2014). 'Somebody's Asian on TV: Sierra/Priya and the Politics of Representation'. In Sherry Ginn, et al. (eds) *Joss Whedon's Dollhouse: Confounding Purpose, Confusing Identity*. Lanham MD: Rowman & Littlefield. 65–80.

Murphy, Kevin (2013). 'The Caprica Times Exclusive Interview: Kevin Murphy'. *Caprica Times* [Online]. http://web.archive.org/web/20131101184846/http://www.capricatimes.com/the-caprica-times-exclusive-interview-kevin-murphy (Accessed 17 September 2015).

Murray, N. (2011). '*Fringe* Producers Jeff Pinkner and J.H. Wyman'. *The A.V. Club* [Online]. http://www.avclub.com/article/ifringei-producers-jeff-pinkner-and-jh-wyman-55692 (Accessed 17 November 2015).

Bibliography

Myles, Robert J. (2012). 'Terminating Samson: *The Sarah Connor Chronicles* and the Rise of New Biblical Meaning'. *Relegere: Studies in Religion and Reception*, 1(2): 329–50 [Online]. https://relegere.org/relegere/article/view/412 (Accessed 25 September 2015).

Nadkarni, Samira (2014). '"In My House and Therefore in My Care": Transgressive Mothering, Abuse and Embodiment'. In Sherry Ginn, et al. (eds) *Joss Whedon's Dollhouse: Confounding Purpose, Confusing Identity*. Lanham MD: Rowman & Littlefield. 81–95.

Oler, Tammy (2008). 'Of Woman Borg: Bionic Betties, Radical Robots, and the Evolution of the Artificial Woman'. *Bitch Magazine: Feminist Response to Pop Culture*, 9: 32–39.

Ostime, James (2013). 'Tatiana Maslany, Beside Herself'. *Interview Magazine* [Online]. http://www.interviewmagazine.com/culture/tatiana-maslany-orphan-black (Accessed 18 December 2015).

Ott, Brian L. (2008). '(Re)Framing Fear: Equipment for Living in a Post-9/11 World'. In Tiffany Potter and C.W. Marshall (eds) *Cylons in America: Critical Studies in Battlestar Galactica*. London; New York: Continuum. 13–26.

Ott, Brian L. and Eric Aoki (2015) 'Science Fiction as Social Consciousness: Race, Gender and Sexuality in *Star Trek: The Next Generation*'. In Douglas Brode and Shea T. Brode (eds) *The Star Trek Universe: Franchising the Final Frontier*. Lanham MD: Rowman & Littlefield. 53–64.

Palmer, Lorrie (2012). '"She's Just a Girl": A Cyborg Passes in *Terminator: The Sarah Connor Chronicles*'. In J.P. Telotte and Gerald Duchovnay (eds) *Science Fiction Film, Television, and Adaptation: Across the Screens*. London; New York: Routledge. 84–98.

Pegues, Juliana Hu (2008). 'Miss Cylon: Empire and Adoption in *Battlestar Galactica*'. *MELUS*, 33(4): 189–209.

Peirse, Alison (2008). 'Uncanny Cylons: Resurrection and Bodies of Horror'. In Tiffany Potter and C.W. Marshall (eds) *Cylons in America: Critical Studies in Battlestar Galactica*. London; New York: Continuum. 118–130.

Porter, Heather M. and Sherry Ginn (2014). '"I Possess The Means to Satisfy My Vagaries": What Motivates the Dollhouse Clients?' In Sherry Ginn, et al. (eds) *Joss Whedon's Dollhouse: Confounding Purpose, Confusing Identity*. Lanham MD: Rowman & Littlefield. 97–110.

Powers, Nicole (2009). 'Lena Headey: Sarah Connor Laid To Rest'. *Suicide Girls* [Online]. https://suicidegirls.com/girls/nicole_powers/blog/2680113/lena-headey-sarah-connor-laid-to-rest/ (Accessed 29 September 2015).

Quinlan, Margaret M. and Benjamin R. Bates (2008). 'Dances and Discourses of (Dis)ability: Heather Mills's Embodiment of Disability on *Dancing with the Stars*'. *Text and Performance Quarterly*, 28(1–1): 64–80.

—— (2009) 'Bionic Woman (2007): Gender, Disability and Cyborgs'. *Journal of Research in Special Educational Needs*, 9(1): 48–58.

Radio Times (2011) 'Doctor Who Writer Steven Moffat to "Rest" Daleks'. *BBC News* [Online]. http://www.bbc.co.uk/news/entertainment-arts-13594932 (Accessed 12 August 2015).

Randell, Karen (2011). '"Now the Gloves Come Off": The Problematic of "Enhanced Interrogation Techniques" in *Battlestar Galactica*'. *Cinema Journal*, 51(1): 168–173.

Randell-Moon, Holly (2012). '"I'm Nobody": The Somatechnical Construction of Bodies and Identity in Joss Whedon's *Dollhouse*'. *Feminist Media Studies*, 12(2): 265–280.

Roberts, Lynne D. and Malcolm R. Parks (2001). 'The Social Geography of Gender-Switching in Virtual Environments on the Internet'. In Alison Adam and Eileen Green (eds) *Virtual Gender: Technology, Consumption and Identity Matters*. London; New York: Routledge. 265–285.

Robins, Kevin (1995). 'Cyberspace and the World We Live In'. In Mike Featherstone and Roger Burrows (eds) *Cyberspace/Cyberbodies/Cyberpunk: Cultures of Technological Embodiment*. London; Thousand Oaks CA: Sage Publications. 135–155.

Roden, David (2008). 'Cylons in the Original Position: Limits of Posthuman Justice'. In Jason T. Eberl (ed) *Battlestar Galactica and Philosophy: Knowledge Here Begins Out There*. Malden, MA: Wiley-Blackwell. 141–151.

Rose, James (2010). 'The Suffering of the Skin: The Uncanny Nature of the Cybermen in the Russell T. Davies Era of *Doctor Who*'. In Christopher J. Hansen (ed) *Ruminations, Peregrinations, and Regenerations: A Critical Approach to Doctor Who*. Newcastle upon Tyne: Cambridge Scholars Publishing. 283–98.

Rozeman, Mark (2014). '*Doctor Who* Review: "Into the Dalek" '. *Paste Magazine* [Online]. http://www.pastemagazine.com/articles/2014/08/doctor-who-review-into-the-dalek.html (Accessed 12 August 2015).

Russell, Lynette and Nathan Wolski (2001). 'Beyond the Final Frontier: *Star Trek*, the Borg and the Post-colonial'. *Intensities: The Journal of Cult Media*, 1(Spring/Summer): n.p [Online]. https://intensitiescultmedia.com/2014/08/27/beyond-the-final-frontier/ (Accessed 17 September 2015).

Ryan, Maureen (2009). 'Sex, Secrets and *Dollhouse*: Interview with Joss Whedon'. *Chicago Tribune* [Online]. http://featuresblogs.chicagotribune.com/entertainment_tv/2009/12/dollhouse-fox-joss-whedon.html (Accessed 15 October 2015).

Schneider, Michael (2009). 'Fox Unveils Fall Schedule'. *Variety*. 18 May [Online]. http://variety.com/2009/scene/features/fox-unveils-fall-schedule-2-1118003860/ (Accessed 16 December 2015).

Scott, Joan W. (1988). 'Deconstructing Equality-Versus-Difference: Or, the Uses of Poststructuralist Theory for Feminism'. *Feminist Studies*, 14(1). 33–50.

'Seven of Nine Jeri Ryan Interview' (2013). YouTube [Online]. https://www.youtube.com/watch?v=RU7cu905CXE (Accessed 21 September 2015).

Bibliography

Shipman, Hal (2008). 'Some Cylons Are More Equal Than Others'. In Josef Steiff and Tristan D. Tamplin (eds) *Battlestar Galactica and Philosophy: Mission Accomplished or Mission Frakked Up?* Chicago: Open Court. 155–162.

Short, Sue (2011). *Cult Telefantasy Series: A Critical Analysis of The Prisoner, Twin Peaks, The X-Files, Buffy the Vampire Slayer, Lost, Heroes, Doctor Who and Star Trek*. Jefferson NC: McFarland.

Silvio, Carl (1999). 'Refiguring the Radical Cyborg in Mamoru Oshii's *Ghost in the Shell*'. *Science Fiction Studies*, 26(1): 54–72.

Smith, David (2008). '"Weedy" action heroine under fire'. *The Observer* [Online]. http://www.theguardian.com/media/2008/jan/20/television.gender (Accessed 29 September 2015).

Sofia, Zoe (1992). 'Virtual Corporeality: A Feminist View'. *Australian Feminist Studies*, 7(15). 11–24.

Soufoulis, Zoe (2003). 'Cyberquake: Haraway's Manifesto'. In Darren Tofts, et al. (eds) *Prefiguring Cyberculture: An Intellectual History*. Cambridge MA; London: MIT Press. 84–104.

Springer, Claudia (1991). 'The Pleasure of the Interface'. *Screen*, 32(3): 303–323.

—— (1996). *Electronic Eros: Bodies and Desire in the Postindustrial Age*. Austin: University of Texas Press.

Starr, Michael (2014). '"I've Watched You Build Yourself From Scratch": The Assemblage of Echo'. In Sherry Ginn, et al. (eds) *Joss Whedon's Dollhouse: Confounding Purpose, Confusing Identity*. Lanham MD: Rowman & Littlefield. 3–20.

Stegall, Sarah (2010). 'God Blinks—*Fringe*'s "Jacksonville"'. *SF Scope* [Online]. http://www.sfscope.com/2010/02/god-blinksfringes-jacksonville/ (Accessed 17 November 2015).

Stone, Allucquère Rosanne [Sandy] (1991). 'Will The Real Body Please Stand Up?: Boundary Stories About Virtual Culture'. In Michael Benedikt (ed) *Cyberspace: First Steps*. Cambridge MA: MIT Press. 81–118.

Stuart, Sarah Clarke (2011). *Into the Looking Glass: Exploring the Worlds of Fringe*. Toronto: ECW Press.

Sutherland, Sharon and Sarah Swan (2014) '"There's No Me; I'm Just a Container": Law and the Loss of Personhood in *Dollhouse*'. In Rhonda Wilcox, et al. (eds) *Reading Joss Whedon*. Syracuse NY: Syracuse University Press.

Suvin, Darko (1972). 'On the Poetics of the Science Fiction Genre'. *College English*, 34(3): 372–382.

Tasker, Yvonne (1993). *Spectacular Bodies: Gender, Genre and the Action Cinema*. London; New York: Routledge.

Terminator Wiki (no date). '*Terminator: The Sarah Connor Chronicles* Timeline'. *Terminator Wikia* [Online]. http://terminator.wikia.com/wiki/Terminator:_The_Sarah_Connor_Chronicles_timeline (Accessed 16 December 2015).

Bibliography

'Terry Nation (*Doctor Who, Blake's 7*) Interview KTEH Part 1' (2014). YouTube [Online]. https://www.youtube.com/watch?v=P7TiNuSi2HI (Accessed 21 September 2015).

Thomson, Rosemarie G. (1997). *Extraordinary Bodies: Figuring Physical Disability in American Literature and Culture*. New York: Columbia University Press.

Thrall, James H. (2015). 'What the Frak, Frankenstein!: Teenagers, Gods, and Postcolonial Monsters on *Caprica*'. *Extrapolation*, 56(2): 169–194.

Toffoletti, Kim (2007). *Cyborgs and Barbie Dolls: Feminism, Popular Culture and the Posthuman Body*. London: I.B.Tauris.

——(2011). *Baudrillard Reframed: Interpreting Key Thinkers for the Arts*. London: I.B.Tauris.

Tranter, Kieran (2007). '"Frakking Toasters" and Jurisprudences of Technology: the Exception, the Subject and Techné in *Battlestar Galactica*'. *Law and Literature*, 19(1): 45–75.

Tresca, Don (2012). '"Fantasy Is Their Business, But It Is Not Their Purpose": The Metaphor of *Dollhouse*'. In Mary Alice Money (ed) *Joss Whedon: The Complete Companion*. London: Titan Books/Popmatters. 411–425.

Turnbull, Sue (2005). 'Moments of Inspiration: Performing Spike'. *European Journal of Cultural Studies*, 8(3): 367–373.

Unruh, Wes (2013). 'Fifty Years of *Doctor Who*: Interview with Paul Booth'. *The Peabody Awards* [Online]. http://www.peabodyawards.com/stories/story/doctor-who-history (Accessed 15 December 2015).

Weintraub, Steve (2007) 'Nathan Fillion, Mary Elizabeth Winstead, Katee Sackhoff and Thomas Dekker Video Interviews'. *Collider.com* [Online]. http://collider.com/nathan-fillion-mary-elizabeth-winstead-katee-sackhoff-and-thomas-dekker-video-interviews/ (Accessed 8 December 2015).

White, Rosie (2006). 'Lipgloss Feminists: *Charlie's Angels* and *The Bionic Woman*'. *Storytelling*, 5(3): 171–183.

Wilcox, Rhonda V. (2014). 'Women With the Agency: Dana Scully, Temperance Brennan and Olivia Dunham'. In Tanya R. Cochran et al. (eds) *The Multiple Worlds of Fringe: Essays on the J.J. Abrams Science Fiction Series*. Jefferson, NC: McFarland. 43–59.

Wimmler, Jutta (2015). 'Masters of Cyber-Religion: The Female Body as God's "Interface" in the TV Series *Caprica*'. *The Journal of Religion, Media and Digital Culture*, 3(1): 120–154.

Woodward, Kathleen (1994). 'From Virtual Cyborgs to Biological Time Bombs: Technocriticism and the Material Body'. In Gretchen Bender and Timothy Druckrey (eds) *Culture on the Brink: Ideologies of Technology*. Seattle: Bay Press. 47–64.

Zinder, Paul (2014). 'Nothing but Tech: Cyborgs and the Human Question'. In Tanya R. Cochran, et al. (eds) *The Multiple Worlds of Fringe: Essays on the J.J. Abrams Science Fiction Series*. Jefferson NC: McFarland. 31–42.

Index

Abbott, Stacey 49, 203, 211, 218n1
abject 20, 25, 88
action hero, female 16, 17, 114–117, 120, 121, 123, 134, 136, 137, 140–142, 143, 152, 209
active architecture 17, 160, 161, 164–165, 169, 172, 173, 174, 177, 207
Adama, Joseph (character) 92, 103, 217n2
Adama, Tamara (character) 92, 103–107, 217n2
Alias 17, 115, 117, 120, 218n1
Almost Human 207–8
Anders, Sam (character) 88–9
androids 5, 46, 186, 207, 209, 213
androgyny 2, 7, 29, 36, 55, 62, 216n3; *see also* gender
Angel 55
assimilation 15, 44, 46, 48, 49, 50, 52, 56, 57–59, 216n3
Athena (character) 69, 72, 76, 78, 79, 80, 81–2, 83, 84, 85–86, 90, 98, 114
augmentation 11, 13, 17, 23, 26, 37, 48, 60, 115, 119, 122, 123, 125, 127, 130–134, 161, 164, 174, 178, 180, 181, 186, 189, 191, 193, 197, 200, 201, 208
Austin, Steve (character) 114, 119
authenticity 79, 91, 95, 151, 170–171, 178–180
automatons 5, 49

avatar 92–6, 98, 100, 102, 103–109, 111, 218n4; *see also* virtuality

Balsamo, Anne 6, 9, 83, 119
Baudrillard, Jean 105, 159, 165–166
Bell, William (character) 183, 191, 193
Benjamin, Walter 105, 166
Bennett, Eve 70, 80, 82, 84, 86, 138, 141, 148, 158, 159, 217n1
binary opposition 3, 5, 7, 8, 10, 71, 104, 152, 203, 214
bionic 16, 48, 114, 115, 116, 117–34, 192, 193
Bionicles 154
Bishop, Peter (character) 18, 183–186, 189, 190–205, 220n3, 221n6
Bishop, Walter (character) 183–5, 188–189, 190, 191, 192, 193, 194–197, 198, 200–201, 202, 203–4, 205, 216n6 (Ch. 2), 220n3, 221n6
body
 disability 16, 115, 130–131, 133, 134
 exploitation 99, 158, 160, 220n5
 inscription 4, 7, 9, 62, 96, 178–179
 lived experience 7, 8, 12, 30, 42, 50, 65, 80, 98, 127, 172–173, 187, 203
 self 3, 5, 11, 12, 16, 17, 32, 35, 37, 47, 49, 56, 57, 60, 64, 71, 79, 82, 93, 94, 97, 98, 101, 112, 115, 125, 129, 131, 132, 133, 148, 149, 153, 160, 162, 177, 179, 180, 181, 194, 196, 200, 201, 210
soul 14, 33, 36–39, 162, 167
threshold 7, 8, 38

Index

Boomer/Sharon Valerii (character) 69, 71, 72, 76, 80–81, 82, 83, 84, 86, 98, 112, 114, 217n3
Borg 1, 2, 3, 15, 26, 44, 45, 46, 47, 48–51, 52–67, 186, 199, 213, 216n2, 216n3; *see also* Collective
Borg Queen (character) 50, 52, 55, 65–66
boundaries 4, 8, 10, 11, 20, 38, 43, 54, 61, 68, 73, 95, 103, 121, 124, 127, 142, 159, 162, 190–192, 202, 206, 213, 216n1 (Ch. 4)
    destruction of 20, 25, 43, 51
    gender boundary 30, 96, 98, 104, 105, 141
    human/technological boundary 7–8, 13, 20, 51, 52, 57, 65, 89–90, 93, 109, 187
    transformation of 4, 6, 8, 11, 13, 14, 24, 33, 43, 57, 88–89, 96, 98, 104, 105, 106, 107–109, 111, 120, 132, 138–141, 156, 157, 159, 160, 166, 185, 192, 201
Braidotti, Rosi 3, 8, 201
Buffy the Vampire Slayer 17, 115, 117, 120, 218n1, 218n2, 218n3
Bukatman, Scott 3, 13
Bussolini, Jeffrey *see* intertextuality of casting
Butler, Judith 4, 7, 8, 12

Cadigan, Pat 13, 92, 94, 207
Cameron (character) 138–139, 141, 143–148, 150–151, 213, 219n2, 219n6
Čapek, Karel 158, 219n1
CGI 26, 98, 211, 218n3 (Ch. 5); *see also* special effects
characters of colour 26, 30, 52, 83, 120, 179; *see also* race
Charlie's Angels 115–116, 121
clones 209, 211–213

collective 35, 36, 49, 50, 58, 67
Collective 49, 51, 52, 53–54, 56–57, 58–59, 60, 66, 67, 216n2; *see also* Borg
community 16, 36, 44, 50, 57, 57, 58, 59, 70, 81, 210, 213
Connor, John (character) 137, 138, 139, 142, 143, 144, 145, 147–148, 150, 153, 155, 156, 157
Connor, Sarah (character) 137, 138, 139–141, 142, 143, 145
contamination 31, 34, 64, 85; *see also* infection
Continuum 208–209
control 1, 3, 12, 15, 23, 26, 38, 46, 48, 51, 59, 60, 87, 98, 115, 117, 121–123, 132, 147–148, 153, 169–170, 172, 174–175, 178, 181, 184, 194, 197–198, 202, 209, 213
copy 16, 78, 82, 95, 109, 111, 166; *see also* doubles
core self 37, 159, 172–174, 177, 180
corporate identity 149–150, 191
corporeality 4, 6, 11, 61, 109, 111
Corvus, Sarah (character) 16, 113, 115–131, 133, 134, 161
Cromartie (character) 17, 143–144, 152
cyberculture 6, 11, 12, 60, 92, 96, 163
Cybermen 15, 21, 22–30, 31, 36–38, 41, 43, 46, 48, 49, 73–74, 136, 186, 199, 213, 215n2, 216n2
cyberpunk 12, 60, 92, 93, 94, 178, 207
cyberspace 12
cyborg
    birth/reproduction 9, 84–85, 86, 90
    as child 17, 28, 57, 62–63, 65, 85–86, 88, 111, 144, 152–153, 160, 204–205
    cinematic 5, 9, 13, 17, 32, 74, 84, 136–137, 141
    class 47, 120, 121, 217n2 (Ch. 5), 218n3 (Ch. 6)

238

Index

death 16, 25, 28, 30, 32, 39, 43, 59–60, 66, 78–79, 80–81, 86, 90, 95, 105, 107, 108–109, 124–125, 162–163, 167–168, 185–186, 216n5
  femme fatale 55, 81, 83–84, 122–125, 134, 206, 217n5
  gender 2, 3, 4, 6–10, 12, 13, 29, 42, 47, 55–57, 61, 62, 72, 73, 83, 84, 88, 89, 96, 98, 104–105, 125, 134, 136, 139, 140, 142, 143, 144, 147, 149, 185, 192, 204, 206, 207, 215n4, 216n6; n3, 217n6, 221n6
  hard body 9, 17, 28, 30, 98
  history 2, 4–5, 69, 75, 162, 173
  hypermasculine 9–10, 140–142
  military-industrial complex 127; *see also* technology, military
  as other 4, 15–16, 20, 22–23, 50, 64, 68, 70–73, 81, 86, 88, 91, 94–95, 131, 149, 160, 201–202, 206, 213
  sexuality 70, 83, 96, 139, 141, 147
  soldier 38, 74–75, 92, 127–128, 134, 165, 206
  as sympathetic 14–15, 33, 43, 58, 95, 123, 181, 186, 188–194
Cylons
  Centurion 68, 70–71, 72, 73–76, 79, 87, 88, 90, 96–97, 98, 186, 221n8
  Final Five 69, 71, 86, 88, 90, 112
  Humanoid 15, 69, 70–72, 75, 79, 80, 81–84, 87, 88, 90, 97, 98, 161
  Hybrid 70, 72, 73, 85, 86–89, 90
  Raider 70, 71, 72, 73, 76–79, 80, 87, 90

Daleks 15, 21, 25, 25, 31–33, 37, 40, 41, 43, 46, 48, 119, 136, 186, 213
dance 100–102, 151, 165, 212–213, 219
Dark Angel 17, 115, 117, 120
Davies, Russell T. 15, 23, 27
Descartes, René 5, 6, 51, 162

difference 6, 8, 26, 30–31, 47, 50, 53, 71, 72, 81, 88, 90, 120, 142, 170, 216n2, 221n10
disease 26, 28, 162, 220n3
Do Androids Dream of Electric Sheep? (novel) 186
Dolls (characters) 158–165, 170–175, 177, 178, 213, 220n5
doubles 27, 69, 70, 79, 82, 86, 98, 119, 122, 183, 186; *see also* copy
dualism 3, 5, 6, 7, 25, 34, 51, 162–163
Dunham, Olivia (character) 120, 183–184, 185, 186, 191–193, 195, 198, 200, 202, 203–204, 205, 216n5, 218n2, 221n5, 221n6
duplication 79, 81, 167, 187, 197, 211
Dushku, Eliza 159
dystopia 161, 164, 181, 208; *see also* utopia

Eick, David 113, 114, 116, 118
emotions/emotional intelligence 23, 29, 30, 36, 37, 38, 54, 62, 64, 72, 102, 142, 146, 150–152, 153–154, 156, 157, 172, 192, 193, 198–200, 202–204, 205, 207, 215, 221n6
empowerment 13, 41, 96, 129, 139, 162, 181
estrangement 3, 184–185
ethics 153, 157
evolution 23, 31, 77, 90, 186, 199, 205

family 11, 14, 17, 30, 58, 62, 65, 82, 85, 92, 115, 117, 119–121, 136, 137, 138, 144, 150, 180, 181, 188, 202, 203, 204, 205, 210, 213, 218n3
fear 2, 4, 15, 16, 22, 24, 26, 46, 50, 51, 65, 69, 70, 71, 72, 73, 92, 97, 133, 163, 195, 197, 209, 216n2
female superhero 16, 114, 116, 117, 123
femininity 8, 9–10, 63, 81, 117, 139, 215; *see also* gender

239

femme fatale 55, 81, 83–84, 122–124, 125, 134, 206, 217n5
fight scenes 14, 90, 109, 117–118, 124, 129, 145–146, 150, 201, 204
film franchise 17, 46, 136, 137, 139, 140, 141, 142, 144, 155, 156, 189
film noir 102, 122
Frankenstein (novel) 23
fringe science 183, 185

Gaiman, Neil 39, 40, 42
gender 3, 4, 6, 7–13, 29, 42, 47, 55, 56, 57, 61, 70, 72, 73, 83, 84, 87, 88, 89, 96, 98, 104, 105, 125, 134, 136, 139, 140, 142, 143, 144, 147, 149, 185, 192, 204, 206, 207, 215, 216n3, 217n6, 221n6; *see also* androgyny; femininity; masculinity
genre hybridity 14, 207, 211, 218n1
Gibson, William 9, 12, 60, 92, 94, 207
Gillis, Stacy 10, 55
Glau, Summer 141, 143, 217n1, 219n6
Graham, Elaine R. 6, 47, 48, 56, 216n2
Graystone, Daniel (character) 92–100, 102, 107–112, 218n4
Graystone, Zoe-A (character) 16, 92–103, 105–112, 218n3
grief 64–65, 104, 148, 200, 202–203, 216n5, 219n2 (Ch. 7)
Grosz, Elizabeth 4, 6–8, 12, 25, 61

hacking 129, 164, 209, 210, 219n3 (Ch. 8)
Hamilton, Linda 139, 142
Haraway, Donna 3, 5, 6, 8, 10, 11, 12, 20, 24, 125, 159, 190, 192
 'A Manifesto for Cyborgs' 5, 6, 8, 127, 206
Hayles, N. Katherine 12, 60, 163
Headey, Lena 139–140
Heinecken, Dawn 117, 142

Helfer, Tricia 83, 217n5
heteronormativity 62, 220n8
Hills, Matt 18, 23, 31, 49
Homeland 16, 69, 220n4 (Ch. 9)
homogeneity 47, 50, 51, 56
horror 20, 25, 26, 29, 31, 49, 70, 79, 85, 88, 133, 170, 175, 180, 187, 188, 193, 218n1
Humans 209–210
hybrid/hybridity 4, 8, 10, 14, 17, 30, 68, 77, 83, 84–86, 88, 89, 115, 119, 120, 121, 125, 134, 135, 156–157, 174–183, 200, 203, 205, 210, 211

imprinting 159, 160, 161, 163, 164, 169, 172, 174–178
infection 48, 66, 200; *see also* contamination
inscription 1, 4, 7, 106, 178–179
Intelligence 207
intertextuality of casting 117, 141, 189
Invasion of the Body Snatchers 187

Janeway, Kathryn (character) 52, 53, 56–57, 58, 63, 64, 65, 66–67, 192, 216n4, 216n5, 220n4 (Ch. 9)
John Henry (character) 17, 144, 150, 151–157
Jowett, Lorna 49, 70, 72, 86, 87, 88, 120, 172, 220n8

Kroker, Arthur, and Marilouise Kroker 11, 125, 162

La Mettrie, Julien Offray de 5, 162
Leaver, Tama 53, 62, 63, 66
Locutus of Borg (character) 51, 53; *see also* Picard, Jean-Luc

machine 1, 2, 4, 5, 6, 9, 11, 25, 76, 77, 85, 98, 100, 102, 110, 119, 124, 129, 133, 142, 143, 147, 152, 161, 162, 187, 193

Index

Machine 185, 195–197, 200
Madama Butterfly (opera) 84, 217n4
madness 29, 42–43, 87
marking *see* inscription
masculinity 9, 10, 24, 29, 47, 55, 88–89, 98–99, 140–141, 142, 152, 203, 217n7; *see also* gender
Maslany, Tatiana 211–212
Matrix, The 9, 92, 105, 163
metamorphosis 5, 146
Minority Report 217n6
Miss Saigon (musical) 217n4
Moffat, Steven 15, 23, 40
monstrous/monstrosity 3, 4, 9, 20, 21, 23, 25, 31, 33, 59, 60, 81, 85, 91, 131, 184, 185, 188, 189, 201, 206, 213; *see also* teratology
monstrous female 9, 31, 85, 123
Moravec, Hans 11, 12, 28, 39, 125, 162
music/musical cues 86, 101, 118, 133, 151, 189, 193, 212, 217n4, 219n5
myth/mythology 5, 24, 39, 45, 94, 107, 136–137

narrative arc *see* story arc
Nation, Terry 21, 22
Neuromancer (novel) 9, 12, 60

Observers (characters) 183, 185, 192, 197–201, 203, 205, 213, 221n10
Orphan Black 210–213
Oswald, Clara (character) 37, 38, 39, 43, 215n5
Oswald, Oswin (character) 33–36, 37, 43, 118, 215n3, 215n4

Palmer, Lorrie 137, 139–140, 141, 142, 144, 147, 148, 217n1
parallel worlds 26, 27, 29, 91, 102, 182, 183, 189, 195, 209, 221n5
parenting 62, 63–64, 66, 67, 120, 140, 152, 179, 180, 190, 192, 204, 221n9

Peck, Alistair (character) 188–190
Pedler, Kit 22
Pegues, Juliana Hu 70, 80, 82, 84, 217n4
performance
 of character 18, 123, 141, 145, 151, 159, 211, 212, 216, 221n5
 of gender roles 3, 4, 7, 8, 12, 13, 55, 66, 84, 96, 123, 125, 140, 144, 167–168, 172, 206
performativity 4, 53, 62
personality 17, 29, 41, 79, 97, 102, 158–161, 163, 164, 165, 166–170, 172, 174–181
philosophy 5, 162
Picard, Jean-Luc (character) 1–3, 15, 46, 47, 51–2, 53, 55, 56; *see also* Locutus of Borg
posthuman 6, 11, 18, 93, 125, 162, 163, 164, 183, 185, 186, 197, 198, 199, 202, 205
postwar trauma 21, 24
power 6, 12, 14, 15, 16, 51, 81, 93, 96, 100–101, 115, 116, 117, 118, 121, 123, 142, 168, 203, 205
 technological power 20, 29, 39, 42, 43, 73, 87, 106–107, 122, 125, 131, 137, 144, 146, 152, 193, 197
 women in power 120, 148–149, 190–191, 220n4
prequel 16, 90, 92, 93, 94
programming 7, 14, 18, 27, 37, 38, 58, 61, 78, 82, 101, 106, 127, 129, 142, 143, 145, 150, 153, 164, 165, 170
prosthesis 12, 17, 48, 129–131, 193

Quinlan, Margaret M. and Benjamin R. Bates 101, 116, 130, 134

race 3, 6, 26, 47, 75, 84, 96, 120, 185, 207, 216n1, 216n2, 217n2; *see also* characters of colour

241

Randell-Moon, Holly 173
reboot 70, 74, 91, 94, 114, 116, 117, 122
religious belief 21, 70–71, 85, 93, 108–109
resurrection 16, 17, 37, 38–39, 73, 78, 79–81, 84, 85, 90, 107, 108, 124, 125
RoboCop 73, 189
R.U.R.(play) 158, 219n1 (Ch. 8)
Ryan, Jeri 55

Sackhoff, Katee 113, 117, 118, 123
Schwarzenegger, Arnold 17, 141–144
Seven of Nine (character) 10, 15, 50, 52, 53–67, 96, 118, 141, 147, 161, 192, 213, 216n5
sexuality 7, 70, 83, 96, 139, 141, 147
shapeshifters 18, 183, 185, 186–188, 190, 196, 197
Sharp, Nina (character) 18, 119, 148, 183–186, 190–194, 197, 198, 216n5, 218n2, 221n7
Short, Sue 10, 55, 160
simulacra 17–18, 159–161, 165–166, 168, 169, 170–174, 175, 176, 178, 179, 180, 219n3
simulation 95, 103, 105, 157, 161, 165, 166, 167, 168, 169–170, 171, 172, 176
Single White Female 122
slavery 16–17, 26, 48, 69, 75, 100, 160, 171, 180, 183, 185, 199, 217n2 (Ch. 4), 221n8
Sommers, Jaime (character) 114–134, 161
special effects 14, 35, 74, 133, 146, 211, 218n3 (Ch. 5); *see also* CGI
spectacle 13, 66, 115, 145–6, 189–90, 213
Springer, Claudia 5, 11, 83, 139, 143
Star Trek: Deep Space Nine 51

Star Trek: First Contact 52, 55
Starbuck (character) 69, 77 78, 85, 86, 89, 123
story arc 14, 15, 68, 69, 138, 181, 183, 184, 195, 196, 211
surveillance 3, 128, 208–209
Suvin, Darko 3
Synners (novel) 13, 92, 94, 207

TARDIS 15, 20
  as cyborg 24, 39–43
tattoos 178–179
technology, medical 21, 22, 23, 48, 72, 134, 185
technology, military 74, 97, 127, 134, 137, 221n8
technophilia 6, 28, 137, 139, 152, 192, 214
technophobia 20, 71, 137, 139, 152, 178, 185, 214, 215
teratology 2, 201; *see also* monstrosity
Terminator (characters) 17, 48, 73, 74, 137, 138, 141–146, 150, 152, 154, 155, 156, 161, 213
Terminator, The 32, 136, 137
Terminator 2: Judgment Day 137, 142, 143, 153, 155
Terminator 3: Rise of the Machines 137, 138, 143
terrorism 3, 16, 69, 109
Time Machine, The (novel) 22
time travel 20, 48, 155, 182, 188–190, 196, 198, 208, 209
title sequences 69, 118, 182
Toffoletti, Kim 93, 166, 171
Torchwood 26, 30–31, 37, 42
Torresani, Alessandra 94, 98, 99, 217n1, 219n3 (Ch. 7)
transcendence 11, 12–13, 24, 72, 93, 96, 125, 127, 134, 187

Tsetsang, Priya/Sierra (character) 159, 168, 169, 170–174, 178, 179, 180, 181, 220n4, 220n5, 221n9
Turnbull, Sue 18

uncanny, the 23, 35, 73, 79, 162
uniformity 21, 25, 26, 30, 127
utopia 26, 36, 58–59, 60, 62, 65, 67, 216n2; *see also* dystopia

violence 22, 25, 58, 102, 103, 117, 118, 122, 144, 153, 196
Virtual Six (character) 83–84, 217n5
virtuality 4, 11–12, 16, 61, 91, 93–94, 95, 97–102, 103–104, 108–111, 163; *see also* avatar
visual representation 13, 15, 29, 30, 49, 50, 55, 84, 87, 97, 98, 99, 101, 109, 114, 119, 130, 131, 141, 142, 147, 177, 189, 190, 200, 201, 213, 217n1
voyeurism 158

Walternate (character) 184, 196, 220n2
war 21, 22, 24, 32, 38, 69, 70, 71, 80, 92, 100, 127, 177, 218n5
Weaver, Catherine (character) 138, 141, 144–152, 155, 156, 191, 192
Weller, Peter 189
Whedon, Joss 159, 160, 219n1
Willow, Clarice (character) 93, 95, 103, 107–109, 111, 218n4
Wonder Woman 115
X-Files, The 12

Zinder, Paul 185, 190, 191, 193, 194, 195, 196, 197, 199, 203